THE
CALVI
AFFAIR

THE CALVI AFFAIR

Death of a Banker

Larry Gurwin

MACMILLAN LONDON

ISBN 0 333 35321 8

First published 1983 by
Macmillan London Limited
London and Basingstoke

Associated companies in Auckland, Dallas,
Delhi, Dublin, Hong Kong, Johannesburg,
Lagos, Manzini, Melbourne, Nairobi,
New York, Singapore, Tokyo, Washington
and Zaria

Typeset by Universe Typesetters Ltd.
Printed in Great Britain

Photographs by permission of Associated Press,
London; The Calvi Family Collection; Popperfoto,
London.

Contents

Those who by good fortune only rise from mere private station to the dignity of princes have but little trouble achieving that elevation, for they fly there as it were on wings; but their difficulties begin after they have been placed in that high position...[They] remain simply subject to the will and the fortune of those who bestowed greatness upon them, which are two most uncertain and variable things.

Niccolò Machiavelli
The Prince

Cast of Characters

AMBROSOLI, Giorgio. Appointed in 1974 as liquidator of Sindona's Banca Privata. Murdered in 1979.

ANDREATTA, Beniamino. Minister of the Treasury, 1980-2

ANDREOTTI, Giulio. A leading figure in the Christian Democratic Party. Served as Prime Minister five times in 1972-3, and 1976-9.

BAFFI, Paolo. Governor of the Bank of Italy, 1975-9. Falsely accused of improprieties and forced out of office.

BAGNASCO, Orazio. Businessman who became a big investor in Banco Ambrosiano in January 1982, taking the post of Deputy Chairman.

CALVI, Roberto. Born 1920. Managing Director of Banco Ambrosiano 1971-82, Chairman 1975-82. Died in 1982.

CALVI FAMILY. Clara, the banker's wife; Carlo, his son; and Anna, his daughter.

CANESI, Carlo Alessandro. A former Chairman of Banco Ambrosiano, he was one of Calvi's patrons. Died in 1981.

CASAROLI, Cardinal Agostino. The Vatican Secretary of State, roughly equivalent to the Pope's Prime Minister.

CARBONI, Flavio. Businessman from Sardinia. Lobbyist for Calvi in late 1981 and early 1982. Helped organise Calvi's trip to London.

CARLI, Guido. Governor of the Bank of Italy, 1960-75.

CIAMPI, Carlo Azeglio. Governor of the Bank of Italy since 1979.

CRAXI, Bettino. Leader of the Italian Socialist Party since 1976. Named Prime Minister in mid-1983.

DE BENEDETTI, Carlo. Chief Executive of the Olivetti company since 1978. Bought shares in Banco Ambrosiano in November 1981 and served briefly as Deputy Chairman of the bank.

GELLI, Licio. Leader of the secret P2 masonic lodge. Provided political 'protection' to Calvi.

KLEINSZIG SISTERS. Austrian girls in their twenties. Manuela Kleinszig was the mistress of Carboni, Michaela the girlfriend of Vittor. They were with Carboni and Vittor in London around the time Calvi died.

KUNZ, Hans. Swiss businessman. Helped organise Calvi's trip to London.

LEEMANS, Michel. Belgian with long experience in banking and corporate finance. Served as Managing Director of La Centrale, Ambrosiano's domestic holding company, since 1974. Dismissed in August 1982.

LEONI, Filippo. Head of the international division of Banco Ambrosiano until he was dismissed in July 1982.

MARCINKUS, Archbishop Paul. An American, became Secretary of the Istituto per le Opere di Religione (IOR), the Vatican bank, in 1967, then President in 1971.

MENNINI, Luigi. The No. 2 man at IOR, the Vatican bank.

MOZZANA, Ruggiero. A former Chairman of Banco Ambrosiano.

MUCCI, Luca. Milanese magistrate who investigated Calvi for illegal capital exports.

ORTOLANI, Umberto. With Licio Gelli, a leader of the secret P2 masonic lodge.

PAUL, Dr David. The City of London Coroner who conducted the first inquest into Calvi's death, in July 1982.

PAZIENZA, Francesco. A consultant and lobbyist for Calvi in 1981 and 1982. Boasted of strong connections with intelligence agencies and other power centres.

PELLICANI, Emilio. An aide to Carboni. Helped Calvi on the first leg of his June 1982 trip from Italy (from Rome to Trieste).

PESENTI, Carlo. The leading 'Catholic' industrialist in Italy. Holdings include cement, banking and insurance. Closely involved with the Vatican.

RIZZOLI FAMILY. Andrea Rizzoli inherited the Rizzoli publishing company, Italy's largest, from his father. Andrea's son Angelo became Chairman in 1978. The leaders of the P2 lodge obtained financing for the company from Banco Ambrosiano and acquired great influence over it. Andrea died in 1983.

ROSONE, Roberto. Deputy Chairman of Banco Ambrosiano from 1981 until he was dismissed in July 1982.

ROSSI, Guido. Chairman of CONSOB, the stock-market regulatory agency, 1981-2.

SARCINELLI, Mario. Head of banking surveillance at the Bank of Italy 1976-9. Falsely accused of improprieties and forced to resign. Later became Director General of the Treasury Ministry.

SIMPSON, Professor Keith. Considered the leading forensic pathologist in Britain. Conducted the post-mortem examination of Calvi. Gave important testimony at both inquests.

SINDONA, Michele. A powerful financier with underworld connections. A close business partner of the Vatican and Calvi. He is believed to have introduced Calvi to Gelli. In prison in the United States since 1980.

SPADOLINI, Giovanni. Prime Minister 1981-2. From the centrist Republican Party, he was the first Prime Minister not from the Christian Democratic Party since the 1940s.

VITTOR, Silvano. A petty smuggler from Trieste, he accompanied Calvi on most of the banker's trips to London. One of the last known people to see Calvi alive.

A Note on Style

Names of Companies
The official name of Calvi's bank was Banco Ambrosiano SpA. SpA stands for *società per azioni,* meaning joint-stock company. In order to avoid cluttering the text, expressions such as SpA, Inc. and Ltd have usually been dropped.

Italian Translation
Many of the quotes in the book have been translated from Italian, and are thus approximations of what the people said. In translating the titles of Ambrosiano officials, I have adopted the style found in the English-language versions of Ambrosiano brochures. Thus *presidente del consiglio d'amministrazione* is 'chairman of the board of directors' and not 'president.'

Foreign Exchange Conversion
Most amounts of money are expressed in the original currency, even though this means dealing with billions and trillions of lire. During the period when most of the events in the book took place – the early 1970s through 1982 – the lira declined from about 600 to the dollar to about 1,400. For the sake of simplicity everything is divided by 1,000 – sometimes with phrases like 'a little over' or 'a little under' added.

Financial Jargon
In American usage the terms 'stock' and 'share' are interchangeable, applying to a security representing equity in a corporation. In Britain, stock is sometimes 'loan stock' – a debt security. American style is used in this book.The distinction between loans and deposits is not always made in the text. The essential difference is that depositors take precedence over creditors when the assets of a bankrupt company are distributed. In the case of Ambrosiano (Milan), the distinction is not important, since all depositors and creditors have been paid. The depositors of Ambrosiano's foreign subsidiaries were mainly banks.

The P2 List

Many of the people on Gelli's list of about 1,000 names still insist that they were not members of the P2 Lodge. That is why it is referred to as the list of 'presumed members'. It is also not clear how many of the members were aware of the activities of Gelli and Ortolani. Some were deeply involved with the P2 leaders; others apparently knew very little.

The Ambrosiano Group

The basic structure of the Ambrosiano group was as follows: Banco Ambrosiano owned a controlling interest in La Centrale Finanziaria; La Centrale, in turn, controlled several Italian companies, the most important of which were Banca Cattolica del Veneto, Credito Varesino and Toro Assicurazioni. Outside of Italy, the bank owned the majority of the shares (just under 70 per cent) of Banco Ambrosiano Holding in Luxembourg. The principal companies controlled by BAH were Banca del Gottardo in Switzerland; Banco Ambrosiano Overseas in the Bahamas; and Banco Ambrosiano Andino in Peru. In many cases, the percentage of ownership changed over the years. The most important fact is that these companies were *controlled* by the Milan Bank.

Italian Freemasons

'Italian masonry' is often referred to in the book in connection with the P2 Lodge. It should be pointed out that there are a number of masonic groupings in Italy, and that the one with which Gelli was associated was the Grande Oriente. Armando Corona, the masonic leader lobbied by Flavio Carboni, was the grand master of the Grande Oriente.

Magistrates

In Italy the term 'magistrate' does not mean the same as it does in the Anglo-Saxon system. An investigating magistrate conducts an inquiry to see whether a crime has been committed, issues arrest warrants, and so on. He or she can be addressed as 'judge'.

Italian Politics

From the left to the right (approximately), the major political parties are the Communists (number two in size), Socialists (number three), Social Democrats, Christian Democrats (number one), Republicans, Liberals, and MSI (neo-fascist). Communist and other left-wing politicians are quoted fairly often in the book. This is because they tend to be among the most astute critics of 'the establishment'. It should also be noted that the Italian Communist Party, the second largest party and thus the principal opposition party – is more moderate than most Communist parties in the west.

Preface

When I began reporting on banking and finance, I never expected to find myself interviewing police detectives, attending coroners' inquests and reading books about terrorism and the Mafia. Research on the Calvi scandal has involved all of those things – as well as visits to Vatican City. For me, it has been an endlessly fascinating story, and I hope that this book comes close to doing justice to it.

When Calvi died, I was London correspondent for *Institutional Investor* magazine, and I asked my editors to send me to Italy to write an article on the Calvi affair. I am glad they agreed. I later joined Lafferty Publications in London, and my colleagues there, Michael Lafferty and Peter Mantle, very generously agreed to let me take the time to write this book. During the course of my research I have met a number of journalists who have provided valuable help. They include Renzo Cianfanelli, Gianfranco Modolo, Leo Sisti, Umberto Venturini and, especially, Giancarlo Bussetti. Fiammetta Rocco and my wife Angela helped me gather and translate much of the material I have used. Neil Osborn and Neil Harris read the manuscript and made a number of suggestions for improvement. Alan Samson of Macmillan has been enthusiastic and supportive throughout.

Many of the people I have interviewed – including Italian officials and bankers in Italy and other countries – requested anonymity, and so I cannot thank them by name. Of those whom I can name, I would like to single out Clara and Carlo Calvi, who made themselves available for many hours of interviews.

Finally, I want to thank my parents. Of the many things they have done for me, one is directly relevant to this book: when I told them several years ago that I wanted to study in Italy, they did not hesitate to say yes.

Larry Gurwin
London
August 1983

Introduction

At about half-past seven on the morning of Friday 18 June 1982 Anthony Huntley, a postal clerk at the *Daily Express* newspaper, was walking across Blackfriars Bridge on his way to work. The bridge, built of iron and stone eighty-three years before, spans the River Thames, connecting the City of London with the south London district of Southwark. For no particular reason Huntley happened to look down at some scaffolding put up under the bridge. What he saw made him freeze.

It was a man's head. As he looked more intently he saw a body, hanging by the neck from the scaffolding, suspended by a few feet of orange rope. Huntley rushed to his office in Fleet Street and told a friend, who phoned the Police.

'We don't get many bodies in the City,' says a detective with the City of London Police, noting that 'white collar' crimes like fraud are much more common than violent death. But this body was to prove particularly unusual. It was that of a man of about sixty, somewhat paunchy, wearing a grey suit. His eyes were partly open, his feet spread apart. The river water was just lapping his ankles. When the body was removed from the scaffolding, the police found several pieces of rock and brick stuffed into the suit, as well as nearly $15,000 worth of various currencies. The suit also contained an Italian passport in the name of Gian Roberto Calvini.

The dead man was soon identified as Roberto Calvi, chairman and managing director of Banco Ambrosiano in Milan. Calvi, the police were told, had mysteriously disappeared from his Rome apartment on 11 June.

Calvi's death in London came at the end of a strange odyssey, from Rome to Venice and then to Trieste, across the border into Austria, and after that by private plane to London. He spent the last few days of his

xv

life in a drab residential hotel in Chelsea. No one knew exactly what the banker was seeking – or escaping – when he left his own country. And it was not clear whether he had been murdered or had committed suicide. There was strong evidence to support either hypothesis. The press treated his death as a 'murder mystery' – Italian newspapers referred to it as 'Il Giallo Calvi', meaning 'The Calvi Police Thriller'.

But perhaps even more intriguing than his death was his life. Calvi's was the story of a man of modest, middle-class origins who rose to the chairmanship of one of the largest private banks in Italy. He then transformed that bank into the centrepiece of an international financial empire, represented in more than a dozen countries. At the height of his power, he was described as 'the most feared, hated and courted private banker in Italy'.

Calvi's rise to power was followed by an even more dramatic plunge. A year before his death he was embroiled in the biggest political scandal in Italy's post-war history, that of the secret 'P2' masonic lodge. The P2 was regarded as a 'state within the state', perhaps aimed at overthrowing the government through a coup d'état. Just as the P2 scandal exploded, Calvi was arrested and put on trial for illegally exporting about $20 million worth of lire, and sentenced to four years in prison. After his release pending appeal, he embarked on a desperate struggle to prevent a return to prison and to rescue his financial empire.

Calvi's death and the collapse of his bank sent shock-waves through Italy and around the world. Hundreds of banks faced huge potential losses and feared that confidence in the international banking system had been seriously undermined. Calvi was found to be a close partner of the Vatican – the Vatican bank may even have been responsible for Ambrosiano's collapse. This turned the Calvi affair into a Vatican scandal, damaging the reputation of the Holy See.

The Calvi affair, together with the other scandals with which it is intertwined, has resulted in violent deaths and financial panics. It has involved the Mafia, intelligence agencies, terrorists and arms traffickers. There have even been theories connecting it with the attempt on the life of Pope John Paul II in May 1981. The scope of the scandal can be gauged in part by the attention it has received in the international media, including cover stories in *Time* and *Newsweek* and special reports on British and American television. Archbishop Paul Marcinkus, head of the Vatican bank, has even served as the basis for fictional characters in novels. Italian tourists in London have made pilgrimages to 'Ponte Blackfriars' to see where the famous banker died, and the bridge is now singled out for particular mention in an Italian businessmen's guide to London.

Italians have found it difficult to convey the scope and impact of the scandal. Luigi Spaventa, a member of the Italian Parliament, says: 'The Ambrosiano affair has been connected with some of the worst and most mysterious things that have happened in this country.' A government official goes even further, calling it 'one of the biggest things in Italian history – because everybody's involved'.

The Calvi affair was initially regarded as a murder mystery, a banking scandal, and then a Vatican scandal. It is all of those things – and more. But it is also the story of a man's life. Who was Roberto Calvi? How did he rise so high? How did he fall so low, and with such a devastating impact?

1

The Young Calvi

In 1920, the year Roberto Calvi was born, Italy was a troubled nation. Though it had achieved political unification fifty years earlier, the country was deeply divided in many ways: the poor and feudalistic south against the relatively modern and prosperous north; the Roman Catholic Church against the largely anti-clerical government; industrialists against increasingly militant factory workers.

These strains were exacerbated in the aftermath of World War I, when millions of demobilised soldiers were thrown on the labour market during a serious economic recession. Coalition governments were unable to cope with the pressures, and one after another collapsed under the strain. Between 1918 and 1922 'five clearly distinguishable governments held office,' writes Alan Cassels in *Fascist Italy,* 'and there were constant cabinet reshuffles between major changes. None of the post-war governments disposed of sufficient authority for adequate administration.'

Into this power vacuum stepped Benito Mussolini, who had founded the Fascist Party in 1919. In August 1922 his blackshirts, known as *squadristi,* invaded Milan's city hall and expelled the Socialist administration. This was, writes Cassels, a major symbolic achievement for the Fascists, since 'Milan was Italy's richest city, the home of both Italian Socialism and Fascism, and the real capital of Italy.' Two months later, Mussolini seized the 'official capital' – Rome – and installed himself as prime minister.

Within the next few years Mussolini consolidated his power by obtaining the active or tacit support of key power groups, including industrialists, land-owners, the monarchy and the Vatican. Mussolini's courtship of the Vatican culminated in 1929, when the Vatican and the Kingdom of Italy signed the Lateran Treaty and the Concordat. In these agreements, the Vatican accepted the Italian state, while Italy recognised the new sovereign state of Vatican City. In addition, Italy granted the Church considerable privileges: Catholicism was made the state religion, religious teaching became compulsory in state schools, and the Church's word was final in marriage and divorce. Finally, the Vatican received a large financial settlement as compensation for Italy's seizure of the Papal States in 1870.

Roberto Calvi was born on 13 April 1920 in Milan. His father, Giacomo Calvi, came from Tremenico, a village in the mountains near Lake Como. His mother, Maria Rubini, was born in Venice, but her family's origins were also in Tremenico.

Giacomo Calvi was a hard-working person and had been since his youth. His parents had died when he was young and he had to support himself and a younger sister. Nonetheless, he continued his education, studying accounting. He became one of the first graduates of Milan's Bocconi University, founded around the turn of the century to specialise in business and economics. He joined the Banca Commerciale Italiana, the largest bank in Milan and the leading bank for Italy's industrial establishment. He was ambitious, and eventually rose to the middle-management post of *condirettore* (joint manager). But his career was somewhat stifled by his wife, who refused to let him accept a promotion that would have meant a posting overseas.

Roberto was the eldest of Giacomo's and Maria's four children. The second child was daughter Marina, followed by sons Leone and Lorenzo. It was a close-knit family, and they often went on outings to the Como area – where Giacomo's family still had a small home – and Roberto and his brothers would go hiking in the mountains.

Roberto Calvi's parents were very sober people, who seldom entertained guests, and lacked the quick sense of humour of many native Milanese. 'I never saw them dance or sing,' says Roberto Calvi's wife Clara. 'I never saw friends in their house.' And she believes Roberto inherited this quietness and reserve. 'This is the reason why Roberto was so closed – because of his family. He was very shy.'

The Calvi family lived in the heart of Milan, near Piazza Sant'Ambrogio, in an area that included the homes of some of the city's wealthier families. When Roberto went to secondary school, it was to Cesare Beccaria, a *liceo classico* (classical lyceum) where the children of some of the richest people in Milan studied. Roberto quickly proved to have a gift for languages. He mastered Latin and Ancient Greek well enough to be able to help some of his fellow students with their translations and also studied modern languages like German and French. But he did not feel completely comfortable at the school, not only because of his shyness, but also because he felt insecure in the company of the children of the elite. While the other teenagers dressed fashionably, Roberto's mother made him wear very simple, 'sensible' clothing. 'His mother was very conservative, very old-fashioned. So he felt different from his friends at school,' says Clara Calvi.

However, when the opportunity came, Roberto Calvi rebelled against his parents. His father was anxious to see Roberto study business at Bocconi University. Instead, he decided to join the army and in 1939 enrolled in Pinerolo, a prestigious school for training cavalry officers. His family and friends believe that he chose the cavalry for two reasons: Calvi enjoyed riding, but he also knew that the cavalry could help him later in civilian life. The mounted regiments were the typical choice of Italy's upper class and of the upwardly mobile.

According to Leo Sisti and Gianfranco Modolo, authors of the book *Il Banco Paga (The Bank Pays)*, Calvi's fellow students remember him as serious, quiet and reserved. 'He was a bit too mature for his years,' they write. 'He never spoke a word more than necessary. He was precise and serious.' When the conversation turned to politics, Calvi never became excited and never raised his voice to back his point of view. 'His friends from that time,' write Sisti and Modolo, 'still remember him . . . [with his] boots highly polished without a speck of dust, the uniform perfect, the dark hair combed back . . .' He soon began sporting the moustache which he was to wear throughout his adult life.

In June 1940 Italy joined World War II, declaring war on Britain and France. The country was grossly unprepared, the people had little desire to fight and Italy soon suffered major setbacks. Before long the country became little more than a puppet state of Nazi Germany. In June 1941 Germany invaded the Soviet Union and Mussolini offered to send Italian troops to the Russian front. In July 1941 Second Lieutenant Roberto Calvi, of the Novara Lancers, received orders to report to his command at Verona and was soon sent to the Russian front.

The Russian campaign was an ugly and bitter one for the Italian troops. The Italian Expeditionary Force suffered major casualties – particularly during the harsh winter of 1942–43. When Calvi later spoke of his war experiences the thing he remembered most was the bitter cold. He once said that to keep his hands warm he put his fingers between the feathers of a live chicken and held the chicken underneath his coat.

· A turning point in the war came in 1943. In July, the Allies landed in Sicily to prepare for the bloody fight up the Italian peninsula. The Germans occupied northern Italy, and installed Mussolini as leader of a puppet regime known as the 'Republic of Salò'. Italian troops mutinied and many of their officers deserted, provoking bloody reprisals by the Germans. According to several accounts, Lieutenant Calvi behaved honourably. He stayed with his troops, found them food and supplies and organised an orderly retreat. 'They were well organised,' says his son Carlo, 'so they didn't suffer like other parts of the Italian army.' Calvi's conduct earned him decorations from the Italians and Germans, and he was later singled out for mention in an Italian history of the cavalry's role in the Russian campaign.

Lieutenant Calvi returned to Italy in 1943. As souvenirs from the Russian campaign he had his horse's saddle and some painful injuries to his knee and to a finger. He and his troops went to the town of Medicina, near Bologna, where they then dispersed and returned to their families.

Calvi's family was no longer in Milan. They had fled because of the chaotic and dangerous war-time conditions and were living in the family home of Giacomo Calvi near Como. With northern Italy under German occupation, Roberto could be picked up by the Germans at any time and sent back to the front or to a forced labour camp. One way of avoiding those fates was to obtain a job with a state-owned company. Giacomo Calvi used his influence to obtain a job for his son at his own bank, Banca Commerciale Italiana, which had been nationalised in the 1930s.

In April 1945 Mussolini was captured by partisans as the Germans were retreating and hanged upside down with his mistress, Clara Petacci, in Milan's Piazzale Loreto – the scene of an earlier execution of partisans. The war ended throughout Europe soon after.

Roberto Calvi continued working for Banca Commerciale. He was soon posted to a branch in Lecce, in the southern Italian region of Puglia. He worked hard at the Lecce branch, but felt frustrated. He was far from his native Milan, working for a remote branch of a giant bank and, at the age of twenty-six, merely a clerk.

One afternoon his father met Francesco Bianchi, an old school friend, who was then a senior official of another Milanese bank, Banco Ambrosiano. 'They talked about their children,' says Clara Calvi, 'and my father-in-law, Giacomo, asked him if there was some possibility of Roberto improving his position. Bianchi agreed to hire Roberto, and Roberto said: "Try me out for two or three months and, if you like me, I want to become a *procuratore*"' (a slightly higher post than he had at Banca Commerciale). Bianchi agreed and, in 1946, Roberto Calvi joined Banco Ambrosiano.

4

2

'The Priests' Bank'

The contrast between the two banks reflected the split between 'lay' and 'Catholic' Italy. Banca Commerciale Italiana was the leading 'lay' bank, serving the interests of the northern Italian industrialists who dominated the Italian economy and had fought – against the wishes of the Church – for the unification of Italy. It epitomised the Italy of the Agnellis (the Fiat motor company), the Pirellis (tyres and rubber) and Orlandos (shipbuilding).

Banco Ambrosiano, on the other hand, was the product of the Catholic bourgeoisie, small artisans and traders, of northern Italy, and was closely connected with the Church. It was one of a number of 'Catholic' banks founded before the turn of the century with the help of the Church, as a counterweight to 'lay' institutions like Banca Commerciale.

Ambrosiano took its name from the patron saint of Milan, Saint Ambrose, the man who had 'Christianised' Milan in AD 313 under Emperor Constantine. Countless Milanese institutions are named after the saint. 'Always, in Milan, one comes back to Saint Ambrose,' writes H. V. Morton. 'Even members of the local Communist Party like to refer to themselves as "Ambrosiani", and you cannot read a newspaper printed in the diocese without coming across a reference to Milan as "the Ambrosian City".'

Shortly after the establishment of the bank in 1896, one of its executives wrote that the founders hoped to 'demonstrate how . . . one can exercise the function of [extending] credit without offending the great ethical principles of Christian teaching which could even be guides to regulating economic life.'

In order to prevent the bank from falling into the hands of 'lay' businessmen, the founders made several restrictions in the statutes. No individual could own more than 5 per cent of the shares, and before a shareholder could vote he needed to submit a baptismal certificate and a statement of good conduct from his parish priest to the bank's board of directors. The same attitude applied to the employees, who had to show they were 'good Catholics'. Typically, a young man would obtain a job there by presenting a letter of recommendation from his priest.

When Roberto Calvi joined Banco Ambrosiano in 1946, it retained its Catholic character. Many of its shareholders were religious institutions, and the bank managed investment portfolios for Catholic religious orders. Every year, upon closing the accounts, a call was made to Divine Providence to watch over the good financial performance of the bank. Not surprisingly, Ambrosiano was sometimes referred to as 'the priests' bank'. Banco Ambrosiano was a conservative and old-fashioned institution – 'a sleepy provincial bank,' as one Milanese banker put it. As a writer said later: 'The personnel were old and backward – not to mention ignorant.'

Calvi's superiors quickly spotted him as a young man with promise. Unlike many of the young employees he appeared ambitious, bright and relatively worldly. In the view of one banker who knew him, Calvi's drive was fuelled by his war experiences. 'He went to war and was an officer. He was cited for merit. And that completely diverted him from the idea of having a small career, of just being an employee.' He had a gift for languages, and paid attention to what was happening overseas. What is more, young Roberto Calvi was willing to put in long hours – showing little interest in such 'frivolous' persuits as going to parties or the cinema. 'He was a kind of work machine,' an associate later said. Before too long he was made a *vicedirettore* (deputy manager), a post usually reserved for much older men.

In July 1950 Roberto Calvi met the woman who was to become his wife. On the beach at Rimini he saw Clara Canetti, an attractive blonde in her twenties from Bologna, who was studying chemistry at the University of Bologna. 'I was with my brother Luciano and a girlfriend,' Clara recalls. 'I didn't pay attention to him, because I was engaged. But he spoke to me, and he had a beautiful voice. It was sweet, soft – like music.'

After she returned to Bologna, Roberto began wooing her with phone calls and letters, and she soon decided to break off her engagement. 'My parents didn't want to accept the idea that I had changed my mind,' she says. 'And his family didn't want him to get married. His father was retiring, and they were having some family problems.' For two years Roberto and Clara wrote to each other – 'every day,' she says – and were finally married on 25 June 1952. Clara's father provided them with a small flat in Milan. In July 1953 their first child, Carlo, was born.

The 1950s was a period of unprecedented economic boom for Italy; the country showed more rapid economic growth than virtually any other major country in the world. And since Milan was the undisputed business capital of Italy, this created tremendous new opportunities for Milanese banks.

During this period, Roberto Calvi developed into a formidable and respected young banker, particularly with regard to Ambrosiano's overseas business. He polished the German and French he had learned at school and begn studying English in his spare time. This linguistic ability made him one of the few members of the Ambrosiano staff who could deal easily with German, French and Swiss bankers. In 1956, Calvi was rewarded with the post of *condirettore* (joint manager) – which was the highest post his father had reached in his entire career. The same year the Calvi family moved to a larger apartment.

Calvi's rise up the ranks of Ambrosiano owed much to his personal and professional strengths. But there was another explanation: he had a patron. Italians have an expression for someone who is supported by a powerful patron. They say the person has chosen *la cordata giusta* – 'the right mountaineer's rope'. In Calvi's case it was Carlo Alessandro Canesi, one of the senior officials of the bank, later to become chairman.

Canesi was not an easy man to get along with. 'He was a very bossy and authoritarian type,' says Calvi's son Carlo. Authors Sisti and Modolo have described Canesi as fussy and pedantic: he asked to be informed of the bank's exposure to its most important clients each morning, carefully writing the information in a little pocket notebook. Yet, for some reason, Canesi took a liking to Calvi and, as Canesi rose through the ranks, Calvi followed him, receiving a series of promotions in the late 1950s.

Calvi's dedication to his work occasionally caused tensions at home. In 1958, Calvi became a personal assistant to Canesi, which involved accompanying his boss on foreign trips. Although Clara was pregnant at the time with their second child (daughter Anna, who was born in March 1959), her husband was travelling overseas with Canesi. 'I was very upset and I felt very alone,' recalls Clara. 'But I tried to understand.'

In 1960, Calvi was involved in two important ventures. Italy's 'economic miracle' had touched off a stock market boom, and Calvi found a way of helping Ambrosiano to capitalise on it. He is credited with launching Interitalia, the country's first 'mutual fund', a vehicle through which hundreds of small investors could participate in the market. It was a decade before other Italian banks followed suit. Around the same time, Ambrosiano made its first big overseas investment. It purchased controlling interest in Banca del Gottardo, a bank in the Italian-Swiss canton of Ticino. Gottardo later became one of the largest foreign-owned banks in Switzerland.

Calvi's success at the bank once again enabled him to find a larger home for his family. In September 1960 he, his wife and their two children moved into a large apartment at Via Giuseppe Frua 9, in a comfortable part of central Milan. The following year, he and Clara decided to buy a home out in the country. Since his youth Calvi had enjoyed the countryside when, during visits to his grandparents' home in Tremenico, he and his brothers hiked and rode through the mountains and countryside near Lake Como.

In the spring of 1961, Calvi and his wife drove to the village of Drezzo, near the Swiss border, where they found a seventeenth-century farm house. It was in terrible shape – no one had lived in it for years, and it had become the home of countless stray cats. But Roberto and Clara could see that, with the proper attention, it could be restored. 'It was a very big investment for us,' she recalls. They had bought the apartment in Via Giuseppe Frua the year before and the owners of the farm house wanted 8 million lire (about $13,000). The Calvis had accumulated some shares during the stock market boom of the 1950s and they sold all their shares in order to pay for the country house. A deal was finally struck: 7.5 million lire. Not long after that the stock market collapsed. 'We were very lucky,' Clara says, adding wistfully: 'For a long time, we were very lucky.'

For the next few years Calvi's life could be summarised as 'bank and family'. During the week he would put in incredibly long hours at Banco Ambrosiano and at weekends would retreat with his family to the country home in Drezzo.

By 1965 Calvi's patron, Carlo Canesi, had become *presidente* – chairman – of Banco Ambrosiano and Calvi was appointed to the post of *direttore centrale* – central manager – making him one of the top half-dozen officers of the bank.

Calvi's professional strengths and ambition – coupled with the patronage of Canesi and others – had brought him this far. But to get any higher he would need outside help. As one Italian businessman explains: 'In Italy, you can't become managing director without having political or economic support from the outside. It's like soccer: the best soccer players are the ones who can kick with both legs. In Italy, you have to be ambidextrous.'

For Calvi, this could have been a serious obstacle to his further advancement. Many northern Italian businessmen and bankers face this problem: they may be competent in business or finance, but they do not have the knack of many of their southern Italian counterparts in acquiring and cultivating contacts in the political world, of obtaining favours from politicians and bureaucrats; in short, of manipulating the levers of power in Rome. In Roberto Calvi's case the handicap was particularly pronounced. Since his youth he had been reserved and withdrawn, with few friends and associates outside his colleagues at the bank and his family. To climb further at Banco Ambrosiano he would need a new patron – someone outside the bank who had the political gifts that he lacked.

In the late 1960s, that patron appeared. Calvi was 'discovered' by one of the leading financiers in Italy: Michele Sindona. 'When I met Calvi,' Sindona says, 'he was a small manager in the foreign department of Banco Ambrosiano. [But I could see] that Calvi, of everyone in the bank, was the only one who had an international mentality . . . [and] a great brain for international operations.' According to Sindona, he then put in a good word for Calvi with Ambrosiano Chairman Carlo Canesi. Sindona concludes: 'And so began Calvi's career.'

3

The Pact

With only a little exaggeration, Michele Sindona has described the Roberto Calvi of the late 1960s as 'a small manager in the foreign office of Banco Ambrosiano'. But it is not hard to understand why Sindona had such a condescending attitude, for the Sicilian banker was one of the richest, most famous and powerful financiers in the country. While Calvi was merely an employee of his bank, Sindona was the owner of banks in Italy and Switzerland. While Calvi was shy, Sindona had a charismatic personality, and boasted of top political and banking connections on both sides of the Atlantic. But the two men had two important things in common: they both came from relatively modest origins and were extraordinarily ambitious.

Michele Sindona was born the same year as Calvi, 1920, though at the opposite end of the country, in the Sicilian town of Patti. While Calvi attended cavalry school in the late 1930s, Sindona was studying law at the University of Messina. Unlike Calvi, Sindona avoided military service in World War II, by obtaining a job in the 'vital' scurvy-reducing lemon business, according to one account. He did this, it is said, with the help of two institutions that were later to prove vitally important in the rest of his career: the Catholic Church and the Mafia.

After the Allies invaded Sicily in 1943, Sindona purchased a truck from the American forces which he used to transport lemons to the centre of the island. Sindona's biographer Luigi DiFonzo writes:

'To accomplish this task, Michele Sindona needed the protection of the Mafia because it controlled the produce industry and could supply him with the documents he needed to present to the border patrols. To this end, the bishop of Patti got in touch with Vito Genovese, a top-ranking member of the American Mafia who had helped to organize the American invasion of Sicily with the help of the Sicilian Mafia. Genovese, a major international drug smuggler and boss of the New York crime family founded by Lucky Luciano, used his influence with the Sicilian Mafia dons and members of the American invasion force to arrange for fresh produce, forged papers, and a safe route for Michele Sindona.'

After the war, Sindona opened a law practice, specialising in tax and corporation law. But he felt constrained in Sicily and decided to move to Italy's business capital. In 1948, he moved his family to Milan, bringing with him a letter of introduction from a Sicilian bishop, addressed to Giovanni Battista Montini, then a senior Vatican official and soon to become Archbishop of Milan.

Sindona flourished in Milan. He earned large fees from his legal work – often paid in the form of shares in his clients' companies – and soon branched out into the business world. He bought and sold companies and speculated in the property market, acquiring substantial wealth. In spite of Sindona's growing prominence, the financial establishment of Milan tended to look down its nose at him. It was not only his aggressiveness that put them off, but the fact that he came from the south. The typical northern Italian prejudice toward southerners is reflected in sayings like 'North of Rome is Europe, south of Rome is Africa.' But Sindona could survive the snubs and the rejection, for he had a power base that was the envy of his rivals: the Church.

The Vatican has long been a major financial power in Italy. When Mussolini signed the Lateran Treaty and Concordat in 1929 the Italian state gave the Vatican a multi-million-dollar financial settlement, which was invested through an entity known as 'APSA' – Amministrazione del Patrimonio della Sede Apostolica (Special Administration of the Patrimony of the Apostolic See). In 1942 Pope Pius XII created another institution, a bank called the Istituto per le Opere di Religione – Institute for Religious Works – popularly known as IOR or 'the Vatican bank'. During the war, IOR helped many Italians to protect their wealth from confiscation by the Germans, taking advantage of Vatican City's status as a sovereign state. This was just the beginning of IOR's role as a funnel for flight capital from Italy, a role that continued into the 1980s.

During the 1950s, as Italy's economy boomed, the Vatican expanded its holdings in industrial companies, real estate and so on. Since clergymen are seldom trained in finance, the Church relied on the advice and expertise of laymen, Catholic and non-Catholic, in managing its funds. These advisers were known as *'uomini di fiducia'* – 'men of confidence'. Sindona resolved to become a 'man of confidence'.

The attractions to a financier like Sindona were obvious. 'IOR is the best offshore bank you can think of,' notes Umberto Venturini of the business weekly *Il Mondo*. 'Instead of having the unsavoury reputation of a bank in the Caribbean, they have the moral backing of the Church. They're not answerable to any central bank governor, there's total secrecy – and no pope has ever been elected for his financial acumen.'

One of Sindona's first steps in cultivating the Vatican's money men occurred in the late 1950s, when, through a priest, he met Prince Massimo Spada, a Vatican nobleman and the senior layman at IOR. At the same time he nurtured his friendship with Giovanni Montini, who had become cardinal-archbishop of Milan in 1954. In 1959 Montini needed to raise a large sum of money for an old-people's home, and he turned to Sindona for help. Sindona reportedly raised $2 million in a single day.

In 1960, Sindona purchased a small Milanese bank called Banca Privata and, thanks to his Vatican friendships, it soon began receiving deposits from IOR. Three years later Montini was elected Pope Paul VI and Sindona's Vatican connections were unbeatable.

Sindona was not, however, the sort of man to take things for granted. When Spada retired in 1964, he offered him a post with Banca Privata. He was equally generous to Spada's successor, Luigi Mennini. Between 1967 and 1974, Mennini served on the boards of Sindona's banks. For their part, the Vatican's money men strengthened their links with Sindona's fast-growing financial empire by having IOR purchase shares in Sindona's other Italian bank, Banca Unione, and later in Sindona's Geneva bank, Banque de Financement (Finabank).

Sindona's connections went beyond the Vatican. He courted Hambros Bank, one of the oldest merchant banking houses in London; Continental Illinois National Bank in Chicago, one of the biggest banks in the United States; and Banque de Paris et des Pays Bas, a large and powerful private bank in France. During the 1960s, these and other blue-chip foreign banks purchased shares in Sindona ventures, lending him their prestige. Among Sindona's most valued contacts was David Kennedy, chairman of Continental Illinois, who introduced him into top Republican Party circles. When Richard Nixon was practising law in New York City (before his election as President in 1968) Sindona became friendly with the future president. When Nixon was elected, David Kennedy was named Secretary of the Treasury. The Sicilian financier also numbered among his friends Kennedy's successor as Secretary of the Treasury: John Connally, former Governor of Texas and multimillionaire lawyer.

The Vatican's political and financial clout in Italy was not unlimited. During the 1950s the Church-backed Christian Democratic party enjoyed almost total domination of Italian politics. But, in the 1960s, there was a shift to the left and the Vatican's wealth and privileges began to come under tough scrutiny. The Vatican had long been exempt from paying taxes on dividends from its investment portfolio, but in the 1960s there was a campaign to withdraw this privilege. The Church's investments in Italy were also the source of increasing embarrassment, as reporters began to discover that the Vatican or other Catholic entities owned shares in arms manufacturers, printing houses that produced pornographic magazines, even a pharmaceutical house named Serono that produced a popular brand of birth-control pills. In 1968, the Italian government decided to remove the tax exemption, and the Church began to diversify its investments. Instead of owning controlling stakes in banks and industrial companies, it would become a passive, 'portfolio' investor and would invest a larger portion of its funds in the United States and other countries.

When this decision was made Michele Sindona's great moment had arrived: he was named as one of the top financial advisers to the Vatican. According to several sources, the decision was made personally by the Pontiff, who initialled an agreement in the spring of 1969. Says Giuseppe D'Alema, a Communist Member of Parliament who served on a commission that later investigated Sindona: 'Paul VI considered Sindona a great genius of finance.'

During the next few years, Sindona became an intimate business partner of the Vatican bank, working closely with IOR's Paul Casimir Marcinkus, an American bishop (later archbishop), who had become secretary of IOR in 1967 and later the bank's president. Born in the Chicago suburb of Cicero in 1922, Marcinkus was the son of Lithuanian immigrants. His father washed the windows of Chicago skyscrapers. Six feet three inches tall and powerfully built, Marcinkus excelled at such sports as basketball, boxing, rugby and baseball, according to a profile of him in Nino Lo Bello's book, *The Vatican Papers*. He was ordained in 1947 and came to Rome in June 1950 to study canon law at the Pontifical Gregorian University. In 1952, Marcinkus joined the Vatican's Secretariat of State and remained in Rome except for a five-year period (1955–59) spent in Bolivia and Canada. The husky, outgoing American cleric was something of a phenomenon in Rome, so unlike the Italian stereotype of a priest. He raised eyebrows by befriending Roman children in the 1950s – visiting their homes and even teaching them baseball.

It has been said that Marcinkus eventually attracted the attention, and patronage, of the leaders of the Chicago diocese (the largest in America) and his career in the Vatican bureaucracy began to take off. His big break came in 1964 when he accompanied Pope Paul on a tour of India, impressing the Pontiff with his skills as an organiser, interpreter and bodyguard. The following year he acted as an interpreter during talks between the Pope and President Johnson of the USA. From then until the Pontiff's death in 1978, Marcinkus acted as organiser and security chief for Pope Paul's trips.

13

During a papal visit to Manila in 1970 a man leapt from the crowd with a knife, and was blocked by Marcinkus and the Pope's secretary, Monsignor Pasquale Macchi, perhaps saving the Pope's life. The following year, 1971, the Pontiff named Marcinkus as President of IOR. A few years later Marcinkus was such a well-known figure that he apparently served as the model for a character in Morris West's bestselling novel *The Salamander:* Bishop Frantisek, of the Opera Pontifica.

'He looks like a football player, talks Italian with a Brooklyn accent, has a golf handicap of five, and stands in high favour with the reigning Pontiff. He helped to reorganise the Vatican's financial arrangements and negotiate the tax settlement with the Italian Government. He's not a very good theologian. His philosophy is pure pragmatism.'

'Pragmatism', the quality attributed to the fictional Bishop Frantisek, certainly applied to Paul Marcinkus. For he apparently saw it as his job to earn as much money as possible on the Vatican's investment holdings. As he has often been quoted as saying: 'You can't run the Church on Hail Marys.'

After Sindona's appointment as a Vatican financial adviser, his business dealings with the Church increased enormously. He purchased and resold Vatican-controlled companies, made the Vatican a partner in his banks and companies, and generally took advantage of IOR's special status as 'the best offshore bank in the world'. Indeed, the affairs of Sindona and the Vatican were so intertwined that one writer later said: 'It was never altogether clear, whenever Sindona completed one of his spectacular business deals in Italy, whether the deal was Vatican business or Sindona business or both.'

In addition to his ties with leading churchmen, bankers and politicians, Sindona maintained links with more shadowy power centres. His ties with the Mafia did not end when he left Sicily in the 1940s. Indeed, his banking network proved to be a convenient vehicle for the laundering of 'dirty money' earned from heroin traffic and other mob-connected businesses. Sindona, for his part, seldom discouraged speculation about his links with organised crime – which tended to enhance his image as a powerful man. Tana de Zulueta has written in Britain's *Sunday Times* that at the height of his power 'Sindona's aura was such' that an English banker 'who returned to his Milan hotel after a day's tough talking with Sindona' was so unnerved that 'when he got to his hotel room, the banker crawled on his hands and knees to the window and closed the curtains, only then did he stand up and turn on the light.'

14

Another 'underworld' with which Sindona was linked was that of Italian freemasonry. Italian masons have long been deeply involved in politics. (Many Italian masons in the nineteenth century were active in the *Risorgimento*, the movement to unify the country. Garibaldi himself served as Grand Master of Italian freemasonry.) And Sindona's link to freemasonry was his membership in a 'covered' – that is, secret – lodge, called Propaganda 2, or 'P2'.

The leader of P2 was Licio Gelli, a businessman from Tuscany who boasted of high-level contacts in business, government, the military and intelligence agencies, in both Italy and South America. Though Gelli was virtually an unknown figure in Italy, he was, in fact, to become one of the most powerful men in the country.

Thus Michele Sindona had wealth, fame, power and contacts. And when he met Roberto Calvi and decided to help him in his career, he gave the Milanese banker the greatest gift he could: he made his contacts Calvi's contacts.

The precise dates when Calvi met Marcinkus and Gelli are in dispute, although both meetings took place some time between 1969 and 1971. According to a report in 1980 in the Italian magazine *Critica Sociale,* a meeting was held around Christmas 1969, in Rome, in the office of Gelli's P2 partner, Umberto Ortolani. Present at the meeting were Calvi, Sindona, Gelli and Ortolani. The purpose: to establish a pact to assist Calvi in his career at Banco Ambrosiano. Sindona would act as Calvi's partner in business deals, while Gelli and Ortolani would provide political protection. Marcinkus, it was said, 'blessed' the pact.

Whether that specific meeting took place or not is almost beside the point. For the fact remains that the remainder of Calvi's life – his rise and fall – seems to have been determined by his relationships with Sindona, Gelli, Ortolani and Marcinkus. With their support he climbed to the top of the financial world – and when they withdrew their support, Calvi and his empire collapsed.

4

Banque d'Affaires

Roberto Calvi's skills as a banker, together with the patronage of Carlo Canesi, had helped him to climb most of the corporate ladder at Banco Ambrosiano by the late 1960s. Soon after obtaining the help of Sindona and Sindona's friends, he climbed another rung. In February 1971 Calvi was named *direttore generale* – general manager – of the bank. There were only two important posts above that: *consigliere delegato,* the equivalent of managing director or president, and *presidente* or chairman.

In June 1971 Roberto and Clara Calvi went on holiday to St Moritz, Switzerland, with their twelve-year-old daughter Anna. Their son Carlo, eighteen that July, spent the summer in London, as a trainee at Hambros Bank, the merchant bank that worked closely with Sindona. But the vacation was soon interrupted by a phone call from Italy. There was a banking scandal – the so-called 'Marzollo scandal' – involving the Venice-based Banco San Marco which was threatening to embroil Banco Ambrosiano. Calvi rushed back to Italy, leaving his wife and daughter in St Moritz. Her husband took charge of the situation, Clara recalls, and was able to limit the damage to Ambrosiano's reputation.

In December 1971 Canesi retired and was succeeded as chairman by Ruggiero Mozzana. Roberto Calvi was promoted as well: to *consigliere delegato*. He was now number two in the bank.

In 1971 Banco Ambrosiano was not radically different from the way it had been when Calvi had joined it a quarter of a century before: conservative and provincial. 'It was,' says a former Bank of Italy official, 'a rather sleepy, small Catholic bank in Milan. Few people realised this bank could be turned into a money machine.'

Among those few were Calvi and Sindona. And they quickly set about transforming it. Their intention was to turn Banco Ambrosiano into a *'banque d'affaires'* – a bank that not only took deposits and made short-term loans, but one that operated aggressively in the stock market, bought and sold companies and generally played the role of a dynamic force in the economy. The two men wanted to push Ambrosiano far beyond the region of Lombardy, giving it national, and even international, importance. 'Their idea', says a German banker close to Ambrosiano, 'was to become a multinational merchant bank.'

There was, however, a serious obstacle in their path. As a result of a banking crisis in the 1930s, the Italian government had passed a stringent banking law in 1936 forbidding banks from owning industrial companies. But the ever-resourceful Sindona found ways around Italian laws. Since the 1950s he had been setting up companies in 'fiscal paradises' like Luxembourg and Liechtenstein – countries where taxes were low and secrecy was high. He then operated through those companies in the Italian stock market, evading Italy's banking, tax and foreign-exchange control laws. In November 1970 Ambrosiano bought one of these 'offshore' companies from Sindona, Compendium, later renamed Banco Ambrosiano Holding in Luxembourg. Calvi then used BAH to operate in the Italian market and as the vehicle through which he controlled banks and companies outside Italy. BAH became the official 'parent' of Ambrosiano's Swiss bank, Banca del Gottardo, as well as of Ultrafin International, a stockbroking firm in New York and Ultrafin AG of Zurich, a firm that participated in international loans.

In March 1971, Calvi launched a full-fledged bank, Cisalpine Overseas Bank, with headquarters in Nassau, in the Bahamas. Later this bank was renamed Banco Ambrosiano Overseas. The majority of the shares were held by BAH, Ambrosiano's Luxembourg holding company, but a minority stake was also held by the Vatican bank, with Marcinkus taking a seat on the board of directors – making him what was believed to be the only Roman Catholic bishop serving on the board of a bank. Sindona has claimed that the Bahamas bank was his idea and that he, too, held part of the shares.

Calvi's method of operating overseas through vehicles controlled by BAH, which was never one hundred per cent owned by Ambrosiano, enabled him to shield his foreign activities from the Italian banking authorities. The Bank of Italy, the country's central bank, only had the power to inspect the parent bank in Milan, and not indirectly controlled subsidiaries in foreign countries. In fact, a former Bank of Italy official recalls that when Calvi later opened a bank in South America, 'We learned about it by reading the newspapers. I can tell you that we were very upset about that.' Calvi had learned Sindona's lessons very well.

Although nothing appeared to stand in the way of Calvi's empire-building outside Italy, the Italian banking law of 1936 did appear to be an obstacle to creating a 'merchant bank' at home. In spite of that ban, however, Calvi, through a complicated series of transactions involving Sindona, Hambros Bank and other parties, bought control of an Italian holding company, La Centrale Finanziaria, in late 1971. The deal appeared to many observers to be a flagrant violation of the 1936 law. As author Gianfranco Modolo puts it: 'La Centrale had interests in marketing companies, industrial companies and so on. And the Italian banking law doesn't allow that. Since the very beginning, the "new" Ambrosiano was marked by illegality.'

Curiously, the banking authorities permitted the transaction to take place. Asked why he did not block the deal, Guido Carli, who was then Governor of the Bank of Italy, says that he approved it because La Centrale's holdings were 'preponderantly in banking and insurance'. Other observers, however, suspect that the Bank of Italy was reluctant to antagonise Sindona and Calvi, financiers who were closely linked to the Vatican – and to the ruling, and Church-backed, Christian, Democratic party. 'They knew that behind Banco Ambrosiano and Mr Calvi were the Vatican and the big Catholic party,' says Modolo. Adds Communist MP Giuseppe D'Alema: 'Carli's behaviour was very contradictory.' Perhaps, says D'Alema, Carli 'didn't feel he was strong enough politically to resist a banker with strong ties to the Christian Democrats, the Vatican and the United States.'

Carli *did* react, however, when Sindona tried to carry out his 'grand design'. By 1971 Sindona was an extraordinarily powerful figure in Italy. In spite of his wheeler-dealer reputation – and constant whispers about his underworld ties – he was hailed by many as just the sort of dynamic entrepreneur the country needed. The magazine *L'Europeo* called Sindona 'the only financier in our country who has a modern and dynamic mentality: a modern vision of business'. Calvi's son Carlo remembers that officials of Hambros Bank 'talked about Sindona as one of the greatest bankers in the world'. But Sindona was not satisfied – he wanted, in his own words, 'to form the biggest private financial group in Italy'. By any standard, his plan was extraordinary. He wanted to take over both Bastogi, one of the major industrial holding companies in Italy, and Banca Nazionale dell'Agricoltura, the largest private bank in the country, and merge them with La Centrale.

If the scheme had succeeded, Guido Carli later wrote, 'it would have been one of the major, perhaps the major, European financial corporations . . . an exorbitant concentration of power . . .' So, working with other leaders of Italy's financial establishment, Carli decided to foil Sindona's scheme. One of the many steps that Carli took was persuading several banks not to tender the Bastogi shares they controlled. Through this and other means the 'establishment' managed to crush the Sicilian parvenu.

In 1972 Sindona, his pride seriously bruised by the defeat, moved to Geneva and, some months later, to New York, leaving behind him a number of unfinished deals – including the La Centrale takeover – which were soon to be completed by Calvi. Indeed, Calvi proved to be as much of an aggressive dealmaker as his Sicilian mentor. Michel Leemans, who served for nearly a decade as managing director of La Centrale, recalls: 'Calvi had a lot of imagination [for dealmaking]. He was able to imagine financial structures – and go through complicated steps to reach the final result.' Calvi was also, says Leemans, 'a good negotiator who knew how to reach results – how to convince people the way to go about reaching some objective'.

Calvi's strategy was to dispose of the stocks in La Centrale's portfolio in non-financial companies and replace them with banks and insurance companies. 'Calvi,' says Leemans, 'said he wanted to get rid of everything that was out of our sphere of interest – everything that had nothing to do with finance or money.'

The first big banking acquisition took place in 1972, when Calvi bought Credito Varesino, a profitable bank operating in the prosperous northern Italian province of Varese. The following year, Calvi purchased a controlling interest in a Venice-based bank, Banca Cattolica del Veneto, from the Church. It was apparently from Sindona that Calvi learned that the Church might be willing to sell BCV, though Calvi said later that he had to confirm that with Marcinkus. 'I had three meetings with him [Marcinkus] regarding Banca Cattolica del Veneto,' Calvi said. 'He wanted to sell it to me. I asked him: Are you sure? Is it available to you? Is the boss [the Pope] in agreement with it? Marcinkus told me yes, he had spoken with Paul VI and had his assent. After that, the Pope received me in a private audience.'

The deal was Sindona's idea, and so – like most of his transactions – it was done through offshore companies. IOR first sold the shares to a Liechtenstein holding company controlled by Sindona and then to another company controlled by Calvi, enabling them to leave large sums of money overseas.

In 1973 Calvi also bought one of the largest insurance companies in Italy, Toro Assicurazioni. Clara Calvi remembers the negotiations vividly. Toro, she says, was controlled by the Zanon and Acutis families. 'We went to the Costa Azzura [Côte d'Azur] to the Zanons' villa because Roberto wanted to buy their shares.' But by the end of the first day of their visit, neither side had mentioned a possible deal – Calvi because he did not want to appear too eager, the Zanons because they did not want to sell out cheaply. 'They said nothing, we said nothing,' says Clara. 'But the next morning, the Zanon brothers said they wanted to sell', and the deal went ahead.

Calvi's stock-market operations soon made him a well-known figure in the Milan *Borsa,* touching off accusations that he and other operators he worked with were responsible for wild swings in the market. Calvi, and one of his then allies, a formidable businesswomen called Anna Bonomi, were known as the *golpisti,* the coup-makers, of the stock-market. But it was not simply share-dealing in its own right that interested Calvi. In connection with many of his deals, he managed, through offshore banks and companies he controlled, to smuggle millions of dollars worth of lire from Italy. The tactic (a favourite of Sindona's) was quite simple. Calvi would purchase Italian shares, and then re-sell the shares to a foreign company secretly controlled by him. He would then buy the shares back at an artificially high price. The result: several million dollars have been smuggled overseas – in violation of Italy's foreign-exchange control laws.

Given his high volume of stock-market operations, Calvi was soon paying substantial commissions to brokers. And so, in November 1971, one of his associates founded a company called Suprafin through which share-market deals were done.

Calvi's empire-building in the early 1970s certainly shook the sleepy image of Banco Ambrosiano, but the tactics he used began to attract criticism. In September 1972 a prominent Italian politician, Cesare Merzagora, wrote a letter to Guido Carli, Governor of the Bank of Italy, passing on complaints he had received from some shareholders. Merzagora wrote, in part:

'I find myself literally bombarded by Milanese telephone calls and letters, asking me to push for an intervention in the Senate . . . to ask for explanations of what's been happening . . . in certain financial and stock market circles. . . . In Milan, people are buying big Italian companies with little Luxembourg boxes. They're buying banks, holding companies and industrial companies.'

Merzagora quoted from one letter he had received: 'Today . . . acting dangerously in the dark is a bank that buys through overseas vehicles big companies and banks and creates absurd movements in the stock-market destined to make many victims.' Carli's response was that he lacked the power to stop Calvi.

Criticism also came from religious circles. Catholic depositors in Veneto complained about the sale of that region's largest bank to Calvi – but their complaints were reportedly ignored by the Church. But perhaps the most disturbing story about the new, more 'pragmatic' attitude of the Vatican's money men is of an encounter in 1973. Albino Luciani, the Patriarch of Venice – who later became Pope John Paul I, dying a month after his election – reportedly complained to Pope Paul that Banca Cattolica del Veneto was no longer paying privileged interest rates on deposits from Catholic organisations. The Pope told Cardinal Luciani to see Marcinkus, who reportedly said: 'Eminence, don't you have anything better to do?'

5

Il Crack Sindona

As Roberto Calvi was building his financial empire, that of his mentor, Michele Sindona, began to crumble. Following the defeat of his bid to take over the Bastogi company, Sindona transferred his base to the United States, after a few months in Switzerland. He felt he would be treated better in the new world than in the old. 'The Americans loved me because of my brains,' he once said. 'They did not treat me like a nigger, the way Italians treat Sicilians.' According to Sindona's biographer Luigi DiFonzo, Sindona dreamed of executing such big and impressive deals in America that the Milanese financiers who had spurned him would be forced to acknowledge his greatness. Sindona purchased a $300,000 apartment at the Pierre Hotel, rented an office on Park Avenue, and announced to Wall Street that he had money to spend.

Sindona's big splash occurred in July 1972, when he paid $40 million for controlling interest (21.6 per cent) in the Franklin National Bank, then the twentieth largest bank in the United States, with assets of more than $3.5 billion. Earlier that year, Sindona had encouraged Calvi to buy an American bank. A former Ambrosiano official recalled the conversation clearly a decade later. Calvi and Sindona were walking on a beach on Grand Bahama Island at dusk, a few colleagues trailing behind them. Sindona, according to this source, told Calvi that if he wanted to be a great international banker he had to own an American bank. And, in fact, in 1972, Ambrosiano purchased convertible bonds worth $16.4 million issued by Union Commerce Bank in Cleveland, Ohio. If the price of the stock rose to $39, Ambrosiano could convert the bonds into shares and so obtain 10 per cent of the bank. Unfortunately for Ambrosiano, Union Commerce stock traded far below that level for several years.

But that was nothing compared with the Franklin National deal, which was impressive not only because of its size but because Sindona

22

appeared to have grossly overpaid for his stock. In Italy it was common practice to pay above the market price for a stock in order to obtain a controlling interest. That was not the case in the United States and yet Sindona paid $40 a share for his Franklin stock at a time when it was trading at about $32 a share. What is more, Franklin was a far from healthy bank. In an effort to build Franklin into a giant bank, the executives had permitted lending officers to push money out to questionable clients at below-market rates, had opened costly new branches and taken on expensive staff. Just a few months before Sindona bought control of Franklin, bank examiners had classified more than $200 million of its loans as doubtful – nearly equal to the bank's capital.

Rumours about the new owner's ties to the Mafia did little to help spur confidence in Franklin, but Sindona and his associates damaged the bank in a more direct way: by engaging in enormous and reckless foreign exchange speculation and falsifying records to cover up the resulting losses.

In late 1973 the Arab oil embargo and quadrupling of oil prices sent a massive shock through the world economy and financial system. During the following months, economic growth plummeted, inflation and interest rates soared and currencies gyrated in value. Some of the most healthy banks in the world were bruised by the crisis, but Franklin National, already on the verge of collapse, was hit much harder. Several major banks refused to deal with Franklin in the foreign exchange market. In May 1974 the Federal Reserve Board (America's 'central bank') rejected an application by Franklin to acquire Talcott National, an American finance company, a ruling that further eroded confidence in the ailing bank. Big and small depositors alike withdrew funds from Franklin, creating in effect a run on the bank, so forcing the banking authorities to prop it up with loans.

Reports about Franklin's difficulties intensified worries about Sindona's Milanese banks: Banca Privata Finanziaria and Banca Unione. Depositors at those banks began to panic.

In a desperate attempt to stave off the collapse of his banking empire, Michele Sindona embarked on a frantic lobbying campaign on both sides of the Atlantic, making use of the political contacts he had cultivated over the years. In the United States he enlisted the support of David Kennedy, who, in 1973, had joined the board of Sindona's Luxembourg holding company, Fasco, through which Sindona controlled Franklin. Kennedy, as a former Treasury Secretary, had access to the right people in Washington. Sindona also retained President Nixon's former New York law firm, Mudge Rose Guthrie and Alexander. (In 1972, he had attempted to ingratiate himself with the Nixon administration by offering a secret contribution of $1 million to Nixon's re-election campaign.) Throughout the summer of 1974 – long after it should have been obvious that Franklin ought to have been taken over by a stronger bank – US banking authorities lent more than $1.7 billion to Franklin.

In Italy Sindona turned to his old friends in the Christian Democratic party, which he had been secretly helping to finance for years. In May 1974 Italians were to vote in a referendum on whether to repeal Italy's recent law permitting divorce. The Christian Democrats were desperately fighting for the divorce law to be repealed, and Sindona has confirmed reports that he 'lent' the party the equivalent of two billion lire (about $2 million) to help finance the campaign – a loan, he says, that was never repaid.

Such gestures helped Sindona to acquire the support of two of the most powerful politicians in the country: former Prime Ministers Giulio Andreotti and Amintore Fanfani. Andreotti lobbied with the Bank of Italy, various government ministries, and state-owned banks to prop up Sindona's banks. He even hailed Sindona publicly as 'the saviour of the lira'.

But perhaps the most effective lobbyist for Sindona was Licio Gelli, whose secret P2 Lodge had continued to grow in power. According to Sindona, Gelli's assistance came because Sindona had once 'helped a friend who – unknown to me – was a member of the lodge. Gelli had me visit him at the Grand Hotel in Rome, to thank me in the name of the "very dear brother" and to put himself at my disposition.' Members of Parliament who later investigated Sindona had this to say of Gelli's lobbying for Sindona:

'Gelli appears continuously, in direct or indirect ways, in all the events in this period . . . the events following Sindona's collapse . . . have a sole element that pulls together the diverse interests in the game and reinforces the relations between persons so different: the P2.'

In August 1974 the Italian authorities permitted Sindona to merge his two Italian banks to create a new institution. Soon after that, the state-owned Banco di Roma lent $100 million to the merged bank, now called Banca Privata Italiana.

Licio Gelli presumably claimed much of the credit for the Banco di Roma loan: the cabinet minister responsible for state-owned companies like Banco di Roma, Gaetano Stammati, was on the presumed membership list of Gelli's P2 Lodge.

Sindona's campaign delayed the collapse of his banks, but it did not prevent it. On 27 September 1974, Banca Privata was put into 'forced liquidation'. On 8 October Franklin National – then the twentieth largest bank in the country – was declared insolvent – making it the biggest bank failure in US history.

The collapse of Banca Privata – known in Italy as *Il Crack Sindona* – sent shockwaves through the country's financial system. The Milan stock exchange plunged, and was not to recover for several years. But the Franklin failure, coming as it did in the midst of an international economic crisis, had a world-wide impact. Already nervous depositors shifted billions of dollars from small and medium-sized banks to larger institutions, on the theory that only the biggest banks were safe from collapse. As one Arab money-manager said at the time: 'If the twentieth largest bank in the United States [Franklin] can go under, how do we know the tenth largest is safe?' So severe was the crisis of confidence at the time that Britain's giant National Westminster Bank was the subject of rumours that it had been seriously hurt by the Sindona affair, forcing NatWest to issue a denial. The international financial crisis of 1974 was the most serious in decades and one man, Michele Sindona, bore a great deal of the blame.

But before the dust had settled, Sindona himself had disappeared. In early October Licio Gelli had tipped him off that Italian magistrates were preparing warrants for his arrest. Sindona, in Switzerland at the time, fled Europe and, after a long and circuitous trip, wound up in Taiwan – from where he could not be extradited to Italy. In December he made his way back to the United States.

One victim of the Sindona affair was IOR, the Vatican bank, which had worked closely with Sindona for years. Though Archbishop Marcinkus has always denied that IOR lost any money when Sindona crashed, other sources have estimated that the Vatican lost upwards of $30 million. The Vatican had also lost its key financial adviser and partner. But it quickly found another one to take Sindona's place: Roberto Calvi.

The ties between the Vatican and Roberto Calvi were already close. IOR had long been one of the largest single shareholders of Banco Ambrosiano as well as a partner in a number of Ambrosiano-controlled companies. To mention just a few examples:

Though it had sold its controlling interest in Banca Cattolica del Veneto to Calvi, IOR still retained 5 per cent of BCV, and was represented on BCV's board by Pellegrino de Strobel, IOR's chief accountant.

IOR reportedly held 6 per cent of the stock of Calvi's Swiss bank, Banca del Gottardo, and was once again represented on the board by a

Vatican 'man of confidence'.

Banco Ambrosiano Overseas, the Bahamas-based bank Calvi had established in 1971, was part-owned by IOR.

Suprafin, the company that handled Calvi's share dealings, may have been owned, or part-owned, by IOR. In a letter to Ambrosiano in 1975, IOR officials described Suprafin as a company 'of pertinence to' IOR.

Another common link between Calvi and the Vatican bank was Carlo Pesenti, the leading 'Catholic', that is, Church-affiliated, industrialist in Italy. Pesenti, Italy's 'cement king', had purchased several banks and companies from the Vatican in the 1960s and had been a close personal friend of Pope John XXIII, whose affectionate nickname for Pesenti was 'Il Signor Carlo'. During the 1970s the Pesenti Group became a big borrower from Ambrosiano, and Pesenti himself eventually joined the boards of Ambrosiano and La Centrale.

But the relationship between Calvi and the Vatican was not exclusively financial. There were also several personal ties. Carlo Calvi recalls that Luigi Mennini, Marcinkus's deputy at the Vatican bank, was a frequent visitor to the Calvi family's country home in the late 1960s. In 1971, says Carlo, Mennini persuaded Calvi to hire his son Alessandro. Alessandro Mennini eventually became one of the top officials of Ambrosiano's international department. Other Vatican visitors were Monsignor Pasquale Macchi, Pope Paul's personal secretary, and Marcinkus himself. 'I remember the first time Marcinkus visited us in the Bahamas,' says Clara Calvi. 'He threw his arms around me and sang, "Arrivederci, Roma".'

These already close ties became closer still after the fall of Sindona. Calvi understood what Sindona had understood: the rich potential rewards of having the Church as a business partner. As Sindona has said of Archbishop Marcinkus: 'We used his name a lot in business deals. I told him clearly that I put him in because it helps me get money.' Calvi, in fact, outdid his mentor. As the magazine *Il Mondo* noted years later: 'Calvi was able to exploit his relationship with the Vatican even better than Sindona had, giving the impression of "great solidity". No one ever questioned the soundness of Ambrosiano: "The Vatican's behind it," was everybody's conclusion.'

6

Room with the Buttons

In the heart of Milan, just around the corner from La Scala opera house, is a narrow side street called Via Clerici. At Via Clerici 2 is a large, pale yellow building, facing onto a square called Piazza Paolo Ferrari: the headquarters of Banco Ambrosiano. 'It's a very closed building,' in the opinion of one frequent visitor. 'It seems like a fortress.'

Off the main banking hall is a wide, winding staircase, dominated by a huge statue of Saint Ambrose. At opposite ends of the banking hall are lifts, with buttons for the ground, first, second and third floors. In place of the fourth floor button was a keyhole. For the fourth floor was the executive suite – 'the floor considered noble', in the words of one Ambrosiano executive – and no one was allowed there without permission. 'I began working here thirty years ago,' an officer in the foreign department recalls, 'and I never went up to the fourth floor.' Ambrosiano's top executives, he explains, were much more remote and secretive than most top Italian bankers. 'The atmosphere here,' says this employee, 'was not like that of other Italian banks.'

Roberto Calvi had reached the fourth floor not long after meeting Sindona. Although he was named *direttore generale* (general manager) in 1971 and, later that year, *consigliere delegato* (managing director), he still had one more rung to climb on the corporate ladder – the chairmanship. Italians have a colourful expression for the office of a top business or political leader: they call it *'la stanza dei bottoni'* – 'the room with the buttons' – and the man who had occupied it since 1971 was Ruggiero Mozzana. Before very long, however, it was clear to everyone that the next occupant of 'the room with the buttons' would be Roberto Calvi.

In the space of a few years Calvi, through the deals he did with Sindona and the Vatican bank, had utterly transformed Banco Ambrosiano. It was no longer a 'sleepy, provincial Catholic bank' but an institution of national, and even international, importance. The

'Ambrosiano group' in Italy included three important banks (Ambrosiano, Banca Cattolica del Veneto and Credito Varesino); a leading insurance company (Toro); and the holding company La Centrale. Overseas, there was a growing network of subsidiaries and affiliates. The foreign presence was augmented in 1973 when Ambrosiano joined the Inter Alpha group, a 'club' of seven European banks that jointly operated banking subsidiaries and representative offices around the world.

Calvi's achievements generated excitement inside and outside of the bank. The employees were 'euphoric' about the changes Calvi had wrought, says one source. Gianni Bombacci, an official of a trade union representing Ambrosiano workers, says: 'The employees felt that Calvi had made this bank into a financial empire.' He adds: 'Nobody asked how he did it, though.'

The year 1974 marked what the newspaper *La Repubblica* has called Calvi's 'arrival in society'. The former bank clerk was awarded the title *'Cavaliere del Lavoro'* (Knight of Labour) by the President of the Republic. It was the rough equivalent of a British businessman being included in the Queen's honours list. As befitted his new prominence, Calvi became active in good works. He made contributions to the Ambrosian Library (connected to the Diocese of Milan) and served as an official of the Savoia Gallery. He even became a member of the board of Bocconi University, his father's alma mater, which Calvi himself had rejected in favour of the cavalry.

Around this time, the Italian press 'discovered' Calvi and wrote about him in much the same terms it had used to describe Sindona during his heyday. Calvi was 'one of the most dynamic and innovative bankers in the country' and 'the only *real* banker in Italy'. But there was one nickname that stuck until the end of his life – based on Ambrosiano's image as 'the priests' bank' – and that was 'God's Banker'.

On 19 November 1975 Ruggiero Mozzana retired, and Roberto Calvi was elected *presidente* – chairman. In a special tribute from the board, Calvi was allowed to retain the position of managing director of the bank.

Presidente Calvi was not a remarkable person in physical appearance. He was of average height, a little overweight and largely bald. The only distinguishing features of his face were the moustache he wore all his adult life and a pair of penetrating eyes. Appropriately for a banker, he wore dark, conservative suits and subdued shirts and ties. Perhaps his only concession to vanity was that he dyed his hair back to its original black after it began to turn grey.

Calvi's most notable characteristic was his extraordinary reserve or, as many regarded it, coldness. In conversation, he seldom looked the other person in the eye. Instead, he would stare at his shoes or let his eyes dart around the room. He seldom smiled, or, indeed, showed any emotions at all. Michel Leemans, for several years head of La Centrale, recalls a time when Calvi tried to sit down on a non-existent chair, not realising that it had been moved from where it was supposed to be, and fell to the ground. When he emerged from behind the table, after what must have been a painful experience, Calvi showed absolutely no reaction on his face. Calvi soon acquired another nickname in the Italian press besides 'God's Banker': *'l'uomo dagli occhi di ghiaccio'* – the man with the eyes of ice.

Calvi had few friends and almost no social life. A Milanese banker who served on a board of directors with him for several years says: 'I have never met a man who was so reserved. Very few people knew Calvi beyond the relationship they had with him because of business.' After board meetings, says this man, 'I might say to someone, "Let's go and have a coffee." But Calvi was not the sort of person I would ask. He did not mix socially.' Leemans, one of Calvi's closest colleagues for a decade, says that 'he never invited me to his home – and I never expected to be invited.'

Calvi's reserve meant that, in spite of his growing prominence in the financial world, he was not well-known on a personal level by top bankers in New York or London – or even in his native Milan. Says a former Bank of Italy official: 'Mr Calvi was almost an unknown figure. If you went to Banca Commerciale and asked senior directors about Calvi, very often they would tell you: "I have never met him." He was almost a stranger to the banking community in Milan. In a sense, he was the lone banker.'

His only real relaxation was with his family, with whom he spent weekends at the country home in Drezzo. Over the years the property was enlarged from four to ten hectares and Calvi enjoyed playing the part of the gentleman farmer. He and Clara raised chickens, turkeys, cows and pigs, and would summon a butcher from time to time to prepare meat, which would be stored in freezers. He also enjoyed making repairs and improvements on the property, either by himself, or by calling in craftsmen from the village. 'He was always working on some new project,' recalls Carlo Calvi. 'He was always building something new.' Holidays were often spent in the Bahamas, where the family owned a small house at Lyford Cay. Since Ambrosiano had a subsidiary in Nassau, Calvi was able to combine business with pleasure.

Another characteristic of Calvi's – not as obvious as his coldness, but nonetheless apparent to his family and close associates – was a strong sense of insecurity. He had long felt ill at ease with people from wealthy backgrounds – even after he became a senior executive of Ambrosiano. Calvi had a weakness for people with aristocratic titles. 'If counts or barons went to him, he was immediately impressed,' Sindona once said. And, in fact, under Calvi's chairmanship, Ambrosiano continued its tradition of giving directorships to titled Italians, including three counts and a marquis.

Michel Leemans cites one example of the banker's insecurity. Calvi, he says, was very anxious to give the impression of being a sophisticated international traveller and, on a visit to New York in 1973, suggested: 'Let's stay at the Pierre, because when I'm in New York, I always stay at the Pierre.' But when they arrived at the hotel, Calvi walked through the wrong door. And at the registration desk, no one recognised him. When the rooms were allocated, there was an embarrassing mix-up, with Calvi walking into Leemans's room by mistake. 'If he had really been there three or four times before,' says Leemans, 'that wouldn't have happened. Calvi liked to give an impression of himself which was very different from reality – as a person who is very used to moving in a certain world. Calvi,' he concludes, 'was not *sicuro di sè* – self-assured.'

These characteristics – the coldness, the insecurity, the isolation – intensified after Calvi became chairman of the bank. 'I think he changed around 1974 to 1975,' says Leemans. 'He became much more difficult to talk to, even more unfriendly than before.' Calvi's family agree. 'Most people, when they reach a position of power, put up some sort of mask,' says Carlo. Calvi's brother Leone adds: 'He changed after he became *presidente*. It's obvious that after you become *presidente* you become isolated.'

One reason for this change was that Calvi had reached what was almost a unique position in the Italian economy. Most major banks and companies in the private sector were headed by members of the founding families – the Agnellis, Pirellis and Pesentis – who had been groomed for their whole lives to wield power and behave as public figures. The major public-sector companies were generally run by people with strong political connections in Rome, who enjoyed political patronage. Calvi, with neither a wealthy background nor a knack for cultivating politicians, felt in some ways unprepared for his new role. 'He was a very good banker,' says Clara Calvi, 'but he didn't understand how to be a public person, how to be accepted by the establishment,' Adds Carlo: 'He didn't have the training to deal with politicians.'

With the insecurity came an almost obsessive secretiveness and suspiciousness. Calvi used to speak in an ambiguous, almost oblique way – as if afraid that something he said would get him into trouble. He was reluctant to put things in writing. He carried sensitive documents in a briefcase everywhere he went, so they would not fall into 'the wrong hands'. The fourth floor executive suite, already remote from the rest of the bank, became even more so. Heavy doors with bullet-proof glass were installed beside the lifts and discreetly armed male 'receptionists' checked the identity of visitors. Calvi installed an array of security devices in his office: bullet-proof glass; an electronic field to prevent 'bugs' from transmitting out of the room; a 'scrambler' telephone to prevent eavesdroppers from understanding his telephone conversations.

Equally elaborate security arrangements operated at Calvi's apartments in Milan and Rome and at the country home in Drezzo. The country property was surrounded by a large fence and protected by security men and guard dogs. 'Coming in was like arriving at a military camp,' says a businessman who visited Calvi there. The tightened security at Drezzo eventually provoked a rift between the Calvi family and the townspeople because the property contained a tiny chapel, the Church of the Assumption, which Calvi's security men prevented people from visiting. Eventually, an agreement was worked out with the parish priest, permitting access once a year for the Feast of the Assumption. After the dispute, Calvi seldom ventured to Drezzo as he had done before.

Because of these security arrangements, Calvi's life became 'a continuous passage from one bunker to the other,' according to the newspaper *Il Giornale Nuovo*. 'A bunker apartment in Via Frua in Milan, a bunker apartment in Via Capranica in Rome, a bunker on the fourth floor of Ambrosiano, in Via Clerici.' When moving between these various 'bunkers', Calvi used armoured cars, and bodyguards were responsible for his security and that of his family. One can only conclude that Calvi, in spite of his successful career, was a man haunted by fears: fear of showing his emotions, fear of appearing unworldly, fear of divulging his secrets, fear for his physical safety.

But there was another fear that seems to have dominated all others: the fear that the financial empire he had constructed so laboriously might be taken away from him. He had spent nearly thirty years climbing to the top of Ambrosiano and transforming it into a financial empire. 'Ambrosiano was something he identified with,' says a banker in the Inter Alpha group. 'It was an incarnation. When he talked about his group, I had the feeling that he saw himself as its architect and he wanted to have control.' The potential threats to Calvi's control came from two directions: his shareholders and the government. The first threat was that a powerful financial group could collect enough stock to oust Calvi at an annual meeting. And, in fact, there were constant rumours of plans to take over the bank. The second threat was that the political parties could make life difficult for Calvi – perhaps, he felt, even nationalise the bank.

At a certain point, Calvi resolved to take steps to protect himself from both threats. He conceived and carried out the boldest, and potentially the most dangerous, financial operation of his career: a secret plan to seize control of Banco Ambrosiano.

7

Dangerous Plan

The founders of Banco Ambrosiano had made it possible for Calvi to carry out his secret plan because they had restricted the percentage of shares any individual could hold. The result was that there was no 'control group' – in fact, no single shareholder held more than a few per cent of the stock. So for Calvi to achieve effective control of the bank he would only need about 15 to 20 per cent of the stock. Calvi was also helped by the fact that Ambrosiano's shares were not traded on the Milan stock exchange, but on the so-called 'restricted market'. What this meant was that all shares were bought and sold *through Ambrosiano branches,* with bank employees controlling the transfers.

The first step in the plan began before Calvi became chairman and consisted of placing shares in 'friendly' hands. Ambrosiano stock was sold to Italian and foreign companies controlled by Ambrosiano, such as Toro insurance. After Ambrosiano joined the Inter Alpha group of banks, shares were sold to some of the member banks, including Crédit Commercial de France and Berliner Handels-und Frankfurter Bank. Ambrosiano, in turn, bought shares in the French bank. An Inter Alpha source explains that Ambrosiano and CCF officials believed that owning each other's shares could help block nationalisation in the future: 'They felt that if there were international shareholders, their banks would not be nationalised, due to all the political implications.' (The French bank was mistaken; President François Mitterand showed no hesitation in nationalising CCF and other private banks in 1981.) Another Inter Alpha partner, Kredietbank of Brussels, was also an Ambrosiano shareholder, but it had been since the 1960s.

So far Calvi had done nothing untoward. But he soon moved on to phase two of his plan: Ambrosiano would, in effect, own itself. In this scheme, he was aided by the Sindona crash of 1974, which so shook the Italian stock market that Calvi could buy Ambrosiano stock at bargain prices. Working through Suprafin Calvi collected thousands of shares in

Ambrosiano, 'parking' them with other companies he controlled in Italy and abroad. As a 'front man' for some of the shares, he chose Andrea Rizzoli, head of the giant Rizzoli publishing group. When Rizzoli joined the Ambrosiano board in March 1976, it raised some eyebrows in Catholic circles, since Signor Rizzoli was often the escort of young starlets and fashion models. Calvi, however, explained that Rizzoli was entitled to the seat since he owned 6 per cent of Ambrosiano. (It was not until early in 1982 that Rizzoli's son Angelo revealed that his father never saw any of the shares he supposedly owned.)

In 1977 Calvi made more permanent arrangements for the Ambrosiano shares he had collected. He created a network of about a dozen 'ghost companies' in 'fiscal paradises', such as Panama and Liechtenstein, with exotic names like Marbella, Rekofinanz and Cascadilla. The shares were then purchased by these 'ghost companies'. The fact that Calvi was involved with these companies can be deduced from the fact that several of the ghost companies' directors were Ambrosiano employees – including the switchboard operator of Calvi's Bahamas bank.

How the ghost companies paid for the shares was quite simple. Ambrosiano's foreign subsidiaries borrowed the money from international banks and then re-lent it to the ghost companies. The international banks that lent the money to Calvi asked few questions, since banks, unlike corporate borrowers, were seldom asked tough questions about how they intended to use the money they raised in the international market. It was enough for Ambrosiano officials to say that they were 'financing Italian exports' – without, of course, saying that the 'exports' in question were Ambrosiano shares.

Calvi used a variety of ploys to conceal his ghost company scheme. He shifted shares and money among the companies and he kept the domestic and international operations of Ambrosiano separate. Only a few officials in the international department were involved in raising loans and deposits and sending telexes with instructions about where to move the money. Some of these officials may have had only a partial idea of what was going on. The international department was headed by Filippo Leoni – a man who was afraid of flying. 'Have you ever heard of a bank where the international chief doesn't fly?' one Ambrosiano official asks incredulously. 'Leoni never even visited [the foreign subsidiaries] he was in charge of!'

Within a few years, the ghost company scheme enabled Calvi to become the *de facto* owner of Banco Ambrosiano. He was able to walk into each annual meeting with 15 to 20 per cent of the votes in his

34

pocket – representing the shares in 'friendly' hands and the ones he had sold to the 'ghost companies'. Although no one could prove that Calvi controlled the ghost companies, it was widely suspected, further enhancing his power within the bank. He alone decided who would sit on the board, which clients would receive big loans, which executives would be promoted and which would be sacked. Board meetings, in the words of a former director, 'were only rituals. Calvi would quickly read the minutes, list the credits given…and ask for approval. And then he would conclude: "If you'd like to read the documents, they're down there" – a pile of papers on a table two meters from where we were all sitting.' Calvi was not only chairman and managing director, he was the *padrone* – the owner.

But as strong as Calvi was inside the bank, he still felt vulnerable to the politicians in Rome and felt he needed political protection. Sindona had sought protection in the 1960s and early 1970s by making secret payments to the Christian Democratic party. But the political climate had changed since then, with the second and third biggest parties – the Communists and Socialists – growing in power. So Calvi spread his largesse more broadly – financing 'lay' parties as well. An Ambrosiano official revealed years later that the bank provided lines of credit to nearly every major party – the Christian Democrats, Socialists, Communists, Social Democrats and Republicans. Of those only the Republican Party, said this official, did not use its line to borrow from the bank.

Secret loans and payments to political parties were routine in Italy, but Calvi went a step further. He felt the need for a link with the world of *potere occulto* – 'hidden power' – which he defined as 'the real power'. The concept of *potere occulto* is not easy to explain. Essentially, it is the idea that powerful groups and individuals manipulate the government and other institutions from behind the scenes. The widespread belief among Italians in *potere occulto* is a product of the country's history. For centuries most of the country was occupied and ruled by foreign powers, breeding a deep distrust in 'official' government. As a result, Italians developed alternatives to government – relying on their family and friends, forming guilds and secret organisations and so on. The best-known examples are the Sicilian Mafia and the Neapolitan Camorra. But even in the north hidden organisations thrived, such as the freemasons and the Carbonari in the nineteenth century.

The unification of Italy in the nineteenth century did not wipe out people's distrust of 'official' power. Instead, what could be called the 'Mafia mentality' permeated the new Italian state, with politicians dispensing favours in exchange for votes and cash. As the writer Leonardo Sciascia has put it, peninsular Italy was *'Sicilianizzata'* – Sicilianised.

To a certain extent all Italians are aware of the existence, and importance, of hidden power, the *sottogoverno* (undergovernment) – whatever it is called. But to Roberto Calvi, a particularly insecure and personally isolated human being, it became something of an obsession. He was convinced, says one banker, that 'in the world, only a few obscure persons command and decide, and that it's important to have connections and friendships with those circles.' Carlo Calvi has said that his father 'was fascinated by secret societies'.

One indication of Calvi's belief in 'hidden power' was that he regarded Mario Puzo's Mafia novel *The Godfather* as a masterpiece, a key to understanding how the world works. One financier recalls that Calvi earnestly recommended the book to him. 'Do you know *The Godfather*?' Calvi asked him one day. 'It's a masterpiece, because everything is in it.' This man recalls with amazement: 'He spoke of it as if he were talking about Dante or Shakespeare.'

Not only did Calvi attach great importance to *potere occulto,* he was very quick to believe tales of mystery, conspiracy and intrigue. 'Someone could show him a picture of people sitting around a table and tell him that these are the men who would decide the wars that will be fought in the world and who would profit by selling them arms – and he would believe it,' says Leemans. One of his lawyers once said that Calvi thought 'the world is run by conspiracies'.

These beliefs made Calvi terribly vulnerable to fixers and middlemen who claimed to be connected with powerful secret societies, intelligence agencies and the like. 'My father,' says Carlo, 'was basically naive. People would sometimes recommend a person to him and say: "He's a spy" or "He's a very powerful person," and my father would believe it.' So it is not surprising that when Licio Gelli, leader of the secret P2 masonic lodge, invited Calvi to join, the banker accepted. According to Gelli's records, the initiation took place in Geneva, on 23 August 1975 – three months before Calvi became chairman of Ambrosiano.

Calvi, in other words, appeared to be protected on all fronts. He was chairman, managing director and *de facto* owner of Ambrosiano, he had influence with political parties because of the money he had lavished on them and, through Licio Gelli and P2, he was connected to the world of 'hidden power'.

He must have felt that there was no way he could be toppled.

8

Vendetta

Roberto Calvi had miscalculated. Although his fortifications appeared to be strong, they were to be badly shaken by an assault from Michele Sindona.

Sindona had fled Europe in October 1974, after Gelli warned him that warrants for his arrest were to be issued. After a brief stay in Taiwan, he soon decided to return to New York and fight against his legal troubles from there. The legal threats against Sindona centred on allegations that he had plundered both Banca Privata and Franklin National and thus bore much of the blame for their failure. In Italy the crime is known as 'fraudulent bankruptcy'.

Sindona campaigned to have the charges against him dropped, or at least reduced, and he fought on several fronts. In the USA he carried out a high-powered public relations campaign, aimed at portraying himself as a respectable, pro-American financier who was the victim of a 'Communist plot'. With the help of a New York public relations man, Sindona arranged a lecture tour of American business schools, delivering talks on such weighty themes as 'The Effects of Foreign Investments on the Balance of Payments' and even 'International Liquidity and Special Drawing Rights'. Licio Gelli collected affidavits testifying to Sindona's 'good character' from prominent figures in Italy and other countries. One affidavit, from John McCaffrey, Hambros Bank's former representative in Italy, went so far as to say that Sindona had been involved in plotting a right-wing, 'pro-American' *coup d'état* in Italy – in the apparent belief that this would win Sindona favour with the Republican administration then in power in Washington, which would rule on any request that might be made to extradite Sindona to Italy.

Sindona spared little effort in backing up his claims of a 'Communist plot'. He retained the services of Luigi Cavallo, a sort of professional *agent provocateur,* who had worked for both the extreme right and the extreme left during his checkered past. In 1976, according to Luigi DiFonzo: 'Cavallo hired leftist students to paint *"Morte a Sindona"* on public buildings and to march in the streets of Rome and Milan chanting and carrying signs with the same message.' Cavallo then photographed the demonstrations and posters and forwarded them to Sindona to be used as 'proof' of the leftist plot.

But the Sicilian banker went beyond lobbying, speech-making and staging left-wing protests. He was not averse to using even cruder tactics. Throughout his campaign, a long list of Sindona enemies received 'requests' and 'warnings' – the classic Mafia style of threatening one's enemies.

Of all the people who could assist Sindona, the bankrupt financier regarded Roberto Calvi as perhaps the man who was most obliged to help. Calvi, Sindona claimed, had only been able to climb to a position of power, and build Ambrosiano into what it was, because of Sindona's assistance. As Luigi Cavallo later told a prosecutor:

'Sindona gave me...some documents relative to Roberto Calvi telling me that he had been his *de facto* partner and that he [Calvi] had successively usurped his position. In particular, Sindona told me that Calvi had taken over in this way various banks (Cattolica del Veneto, Credito Varesino) or corporations (like Toro), and he was particularly bothered by the fact that Calvi had used his techniques...to climb to power at Banco Ambrosiano. Sindona argued that Calvi had been able to effect this rise to power on the basis of advice and directives...from Sindona.'

In spite of repeated appeals that he received from Sindona for help, Calvi was either unable, or unwilling, to do so. And so began Sindona's vendetta.

The first salvo was fired in February 1977, when Luigi Cavallo published a damaging report on Calvi's banking deals in a news bulletin he published called *Agenzia A*. The report was on the founding of Calvi's Bahamas bank, Banco Ambrosiano Overseas, and Sindona's reputed role in it. Calvi still refused to help and Licio Gelli appeared as a mediator, trying to make peace between the two – to no avail. In the summer another blow was struck. One morning in July, Ambrosiano employees coming to work saw that walls near the bank were covered with posters attacking Calvi for alleged financial misdeeds. This was followed in October with another article in *Agenzia A*, entitled 'Inquiry into Roberto Calvi'. In November, there was another poster campaign. On walls in the centre of Milan, white, blue and yellow posters appeared, bearing a long diatribe against Calvi. Entitled 'Roberto Calvi in Prison', they said in part:

'The chairman and managing director of Banco Ambrosiano, Roberto Calvi, is guilty of fraud, falsification of accounts, embezzlement, exportation of capital and tax fraud. In relation to the sale of share blocks of Bastogi, Centrale, Credito Varesino, Finabank, Zitropo (Pacchetti), etc., Roberto Calvi has transferred tens of millions of dollars into the following Swiss accounts belonging to him...

In mid-November, copies of *Agenzia A*, containing information similar to that in the wall posters, were distributed around Milan to newspapers, magazines and press agencies.

On 24 November 1977 Cavallo delivered the *coup de grâce*: a long, detailed letter addressed to the Governor of the Bank of Italy, Paolo Baffi, listing Calvi's alleged financial misdeeds. At the end of the letter, Cavallo delivered a threat: if Baffi did not investigate these allegations, Cavallo said, he would make sure that Baffi was prosecuted for criminal dereliction of duty.

How had Calvi held up under this campaign? Sindona's lawyer, Rodolfo Guzzi, visited Calvi in December to find out. According to Guzzi, Calvi described the press campaign as a 'purely extortionary initiative' of Sindona and refused to budge. In notes of the conversation later discovered in Guzzi's office, the lawyer wrote in part: 'Calvi has been forced to speak of the scandalous operation to the board of the bank, but he found full support...'

Calvi may have appeared unperturbed, but his family and closest collaborators noticed changes in him after the Sindona vendetta began. Calvi knew of Sindona's links with the underworld, and his fears for his physical safety intensified. 'After the attacks by Cavallo,' says Leemans, 'Calvi began running around with even more bodyguards.' Clara Calvi has confirmed that her husband was afraid of Sindona, because of Sindona's underworld ties. 'I can tell you that after his last meeting with Sindona, Roberto trembled,' she says. 'I can't tell you what Sindona told him, because here we're entering dangerous terrain.'

9

The Inspection

In many capital cities, one of the most imposing buildings is the headquarters of the central bank, an edifice designed to give the impression of strength and stability. And that is because the central banker sees himself as the defender of his country's currency against the ravages of inflation and as the protector of the banking system from panics and crises. Central bankers themselves strive for an aura of dignity and sobriety – which often makes them appear arrogant and pompous. They often emphasise that they are *not* politicians – politicians are the people who *cause* inflation – and certainly not lowly civil servants.

On Via Nazionale in the centre of Rome is the headquarters of the Bank of Italy: a massive grey palazzo, built in neo-classical style just before the turn of the century. It is an excellent example of 'central bank architecture'. But more important than the outward appearance is the way it has functioned. Almost alone among public institutions in Italy, the country's central bank was regarded as a model of efficiency, integrity and independence from political pressure.

Of course, no central bank is *completely* free from political interference – not even Germany's Bundesbank or America's Federal Reserve System, which enjoy high degrees of legal independence. That the Bank of Italy was relatively autonomous in the 1960s and early 1970s was a testimony to the political acumen of the Governor, Guido Carli. He knew how far he could push without provoking a backlash. In August 1975 Carli retired and was succeeded by Paolo Baffi, a man of undisputed integrity and technical competence, but not as politically perceptive as Carli.

Baffi did not need a threatening letter from a Sindona henchman to spur him into investigating Banco Ambrosiano. When Luigi Cavallo's letter arrived in November 1977, Baffi had been Governor for two years, and he had shown no reluctance to probe into the affairs of banks

– no matter how 'well connected' they were with politicians. In 1977, the Bank of Italy's tough new head of banking surveillance, Mario Sarcinelli, had ordered a probe of Italcasse, an institution that acts as a clearing house for Italy's savings banks. When inspectors discovered that the savings banks had made a huge volume of improper loans to companies connected with political parties, the findings were submitted to the magistrates and some fifty savings bank chairmen were arrested. Baffi and Sarcinelli also turned a deaf ear to appeals from politicians to bail out Sindona, in spite of the potential dangers that this attitude could provoke.

Early in 1978, it was the turn of Ambrosiano to be examined. On 17 April a team of Bank of Italy inspectors, led by Giulio Padalino, arrived at Via Clerici to begin a massive investigation of the Milanese bank – the first full-scale inspection since Calvi had become chairman. For months Padalino and his men pored over documents and questioned Ambrosiano officials. Calvi himself was asked to explain some of his more obscure financial operations and did not make a very good impression. Sarcinelli recalls that 'Calvi tried to portray Banco Ambrosiano as a very discreet, very law-abiding, bank. But he was always surrounded by lawyers – which made me suspect that he was operating just on the edge of the law.' Another Bank of Italy official says that Calvi seemed incapable of giving clear, direct explanations of what he was up to: 'He used a circle of words.'

On 17 November 1978, precisely seven months after the inspection had begun, Padalino and his colleagues withdrew from Via Clerici, taking with them massive amounts of documents, which served as the basis of a 500-page report.

The 'Padalino Report', as it has become known, is written in the dry, bureaucratic language typical of such documents, yet the portrait it gives of Ambrosiano is a fascinating one. The inspectors found an institution that appeared to be dominated by one man, Roberto Calvi, and one that appeared to be controlled by a network of mysterious offshore companies. What is more, the inspectors discovered that the bank had been engaged in a long series of complicated financial operations – the purposes of which were often hard to fathom. Among the findings of the reports were that:

Power was heavily concentrated in Calvi's hands.

'The chairman and managing director, Mr Roberto Calvi, is invested with all powers for ordinary and extraordinary administration of the corporation, except for those that the law says cannot be delegated.'

Calvi, the inspectors wrote, appeared to make all the key decisions.

> 'In essence, the administration of the bank hinges on the chairman and managing director, Mr Roberto Calvi, who, assisted by the extremely loyal members of the "directorate", has become practically the arbiter in the bosom of the corporation of every important initiative, and in doing that is favoured by his particular competence in banking business and by the supine acquiescence of the other members of the collegial organs.'

The board of directors, the report implied, was little more than a rubber stamp for decisions already taken by Calvi.

> 'The board meets monthly...and interests itself in the management of the bank in a rather formal manner. In fact it limits itself to examining the periodic reports by the managing director [Calvi], in many cases ratifying events and decisions already taken and not always overseeing the general progress of the company.'

The bank was controlled by a group of shadowy foreign companies
The shareholding structure of the bank had changed dramatically since earlier inspections, the report said, with large blocks of shares having been bought by Italian subsidiaries of the Ambrosiano group, 'and, above all, by foreign corporations in Panama and Liechtenstein...' The report went on to cite evidence that these ghost companies could be a screen to conceal control by Calvi or by IOR, the Vatican bank.

In the words of the report:

> '...it cannot be excluded that the above mentioned purchasers could be part of the "Ambrosiano group", given the wide and uncontrollable possibilities for manoeuvre by banks and foreign financial affiliates, or of IOR'.

Calvi and his colleagues, the report noted, did not explain who owned the ghost companies. They have not, the report said, 'furnished evidence that can be used to put light on the real owners of the foreign corporations mentioned'.

The Vatican bank was involved in countless questionable deals with Ambrosiano.
More than twenty-five pages of the inspectors' report were devoted to relations between Ambrosiano and IOR, including descriptions of complicated financial dealings. 'Apart from its position of shareholder,' the report noted:

'IOR is linked to the "Ambrosiano group" by close relationships of interest, as is demonstrated by its constant presence in some of the most significant and delicate operations... about the nature of which the fullest reserve is expressed.'

Billions of lire were exported – perhaps illegally – from Italy.

But the most damaging finding of all was that Calvi appeared to have flagrantly violated Italy's exchange control laws, by exporting some 25 billion lire from Italy (more than $20 million), by selling Italian shares overseas at artificially low prices, then buying them back at inflated prices.

On 14 December 1978 Padalino submitted his findings to his Bank of Italy superiors, to the Treasury Ministry, to the head of the Italian Foreign Exchange Office and to the Italian magistracy. The case was given to one of the most respected investigating magistrates in Milan, Emilio Alessandrini. If he found that exchange control laws had been violated, Calvi and his colleagues could find themselves behind bars.

Sindona's vendetta may have helped to undermine Calvi, but his own legal problems continued – and so did his pressures on Calvi and others. During the early part of 1978, Luigi Cavallo continued to publish attacks on Calvi in *Agenzia A*. Half the January-February issue was devoted to Calvi, under the headline 'Justice?' The newsletter included photocopies of documents backing up the charges against Calvi. Sindona's lawyer, Rodolfo Guzzi, phoned Calvi at least three times during March, evidently to find out whether the press campaign was producing the desired effect.

Sindona's position took a serious turn for the worse in May, when the Italian government requested that the United States extradite him to Italy. This prompted Sindona to draft a plan for the Bank of Italy to bail out Banca Privata. In July, the plan was shown to Prime Minister Giulio Andreotti, who arranged for it to be passed on to Gaetano Stammati, Minister of Public Works. Stammati, in turn, showed the plan to Francesco Cingano, managing director of Banca Commerciale Italiana, who judged it unworkable. In September it was shown to Mario Sarcinelli, head of banking surveillance at the Bank of Italy. Sarcinelli looked at the scheme and immediately rejected it. It would, he explained, cost the taxpayers 250 billion lire (about $250 million) – without any corresponding benefit. In November, Carlo Azeglio Ciampi, General Manager of the Bank of Italy, rejected the plan as 'impracticable'.

During 1978 and 1979, two of Sindona's biggest enemies, Enrico Cuccia and Giorgio Ambrosoli, received a series of death threats. Cuccia, head of Mediobanca, a state-controlled merchant bank, was one of the most respected and powerful financial figures in Milan. Though Sicilian like Sindona, he was accepted as a pillar of the establishment. Of Cuccia's power, industrialist Leopoldo Pirelli used to say: 'What Cuccia wants, God wants.' It was Sindona's belief that if Cuccia backed a rescue plan, it would definitely succeed.

Ambrosoli, a Milanese lawyer in his forties, had been appointed in 1974 by the Bank of Italy as liquidator of Banca Privata. By late 1978, he had compiled a draft report – running to more than 2,000 pages – on his findings. Equally threatening to Sindona was the fact that Ambrosoli was sharing his findings with a US prosecutor, John Kenney, who was probing the Franklin National affair and was involved in the consideration of Italy's request to extradite Sindona.

In December 1978, a Sindona ally contacted senior Bank of Italy officials and asked them if they could arrange a meeting between Ambrosoli and Sindona's lawyer. The request was denied.

The first threat to Ambrosoli came in an anonymous phone call on 28 December. 'You were in America and said things that weren't true,' the caller told Ambrosoli. 'You must return to New York on January 4 with the true documents, because if the extradition of Sindona is approved you will die.'

In January, three Franklin National officials were convicted in New York of falsifying the bank's earnings – and the threats to Ambrosoli continued. In early March, Sindona was indicted by the US Justice Department on ninety-nine counts of fraud, perjury and misappropriation of bank funds.

The Bank of Italy's decisions to move against Italcasse and Banco Ambrosiano – and to reject Sindona's rescue plan – were courageous, some would say foolhardy. Italcasse, Ambrosiano and Sindona were all connected to powerful politicians, and Sindona was also linked to the underworld. These events set off a fuse, and the explosion was not long in coming.

On 24 March 1979 Judge Antonio Alibrandi, a right-wing magistrate in Rome, indicted Paolo Baffi, Governor of the Bank of Italy, and his surveillance chief Mario Sarcinelli on charges of failing to pass on to judicial authorities information about possible crimes committed by banks under their supervision. Sarcinelli was arrested and detained in Rome's Regina Coeli prison. Baffi was spared from arrest only by his advanced age. (The charges were eventually found groundless and both men were fully exonerated – but only after being forced out of office.)

44

Soon there was another victim. In March Ambrosoli presented an enormous report on his findings up to that date, including evidence that Sindona had purchased Franklin National not with his own money, but with that of depositors in his Italian banks. In addition, Ambrosoli said that in connection with the 1972 deal in which Calvi had bought Banca Cattolica del Veneto from the Vatican (via Sindona), a secret payment of $6.5 million had been divided between 'a Milanese banker and an American archbishop'.

In July, Ambrosoli shared some of his findings with American investigators visiting Milan to gather material to be used in Sindona's trial, scheduled for September.

Ambrosoli knew that he was running a risk long before he received the first anonymous threat. When he first agreed to be liquidator of Banca Privata, he wrote: 'I will pay a very dear price for this assignment.' But, he continued: 'I knew that before I accepted it and I have absolutely no regrets. For me, it has been a unique occasion for doing something for my country.'

He paid the price on the morning of 12 July 1979. A few minutes after midnight he was accosted by three men in front of his house. Four pistol shots were fired, and he was dead. Two years later Sindona was charged with having sent the assassins.

Though Giorgio Ambrosoli had been martyred in the service of his country, few public officials bothered to attend his funeral. One of the few present was a fellow victim in the war against financial criminals: former Governor Paolo Baffi.

Sindona's legal problems in the United States remained, with his trial scheduled to begin 10 September. So Sindona made one more attempt to rescue himself. On 2 August, he disappeared from New York in a phoney kidnapping. With the help of underworld cronies, Sindona disguised himself and left the country on a fake passport. Several days later he arrived in Sicily. From a hideout in Palermo Sindona sent out extortionary letters to various bankers and politicians, including Roberto Calvi, in an effort to collect money as well as documents that could be useful in his case. During this episode, one of Sindona's helpers, a Sicilian-American doctor named Joseph Miceli Crimi, visited Licio Gelli at his home in Arezzo to solicit help.

Among those threatened during the fake kidnapping was Enrico Cuccia. In September, the banker received an anonymous letter saying in part: 'It's your fault that our New York friend has been ruined, and he's now in danger of his life. If they kill him we will destroy your family and then you.' The letter went on to say: 'We will follow you wherever you go for a hundred years.' The next month, a firebomb was thrown at

Cuccia's house, followed by an anonymous call to Cuccia's daughter: 'Tell your father,' the caller said, 'that if he doesn't do what we want we will burn you all alive; we are friends of the New York gentleman he knows.'

Sindona reappeared in New York on 16 October, thin and haggard, his leg injured, and recounting tales of how he had been tormented by his 'captors'. But Sindona had not yet given up. Through his New York lawyer, he appealed to his old friends in the Vatican to make statements that could be used on his behalf. Cardinals Giuseppe Caprio and Sergio Guerri and Archbishop Marcinkus all agreed, and gave videotaped depositions at the American Embassy in Rome. But these prelates were overruled by Cardinal Agostino Casaroli, the Vatican Secretary of State, and could not be used in court. 'The psychological effect on the jury,' Sindona said later, 'was disastrous.' The Vatican, he said bitterly, 'abandoned me'.

In March 1980, Sindona was convicted on sixty-five counts of fraud, misappropriation of bank funds and perjury. In June, following a failed suicide attempt in prison, Sindona was sentenced to twenty-five years in prison and fined $207,000.

A sort of epitaph on the failed financier was delivered by Guido Viola, a Milanese magistrate who has spent years investigating Sindona. 'Sindona,' said Viola, 'was nothing but a chicken thief… a vulgar thief who robbed in order to build and enlarge his papier mâché empire.'

No one knows for sure who was behind the Ambrosoli killing and the Baffi/Sarcinelli affair, but these events wreaked considerable damage at Via Nazionale in Rome. The Baffi/Sarcinelli affair had provoked cries of outrage in Italy and among central bankers and finance ministers in other countries. Petitions were circulated and open letters were published, signed by such luminaries as Paul Volcker, Chairman of the US Federal Reserve, and G. William Miller, US Treasury Secretary. But it was too late: the damage had already been done. Baffi and Sarcinelli were out of office, and Ambrosoli was dead. And the combined impact of those events was that the Bank of Italy was weakened and demoralised. Commenting on it years later, Sarcinelli said: 'The staff was intimidated. They became cautious.' Asked what they feared, he said: 'Maybe having a repetition of what happened to me – perhaps not with the same details. Also, when you have reason to believe that there are connections not only to politicians but to secret services and "powers", some of them probably worried about their physical safety.'

Whether Calvi himself or others were responsible, the Ambrosoli chairman certainly benefitted. For during the next few years, the Bank of Italy's probes of Ambrosiano proceeded slowly and cautiously. 'They changed the orientation of their surveillance from preventive to *ex post facto*,' says Giuseppe D'Alema, a Communist Member of Parliament. 'And instead of sending inspectors, they asked for information through letters. The Bank of Italy,' he concludes, 'no longer felt free.'

10

The Puppetmaster

As the Bank of Italy became less of a threat to Calvi, his power and influence continued to grow.

By the end of 1978 the Ambrosiano group was the largest private banking group in Italy for the second consecutive year. The total deposits of Calvi's three main Italian banks – Ambrosiano, Banca Cattolica del Veneto and Credito Varesino – stood at 8,748 billion lire (about $8 billion). His nearest rival, Carlo Pesenti, controlled two big banks – Istituto Bancario Italiano and Banca Provinciale Lombarda – with total deposits of 6,366 billion lire. The third-ranking private banker was Giovanni Auletta Armenise, who controlled Banca Nazionale dell'Agricoltura.

Late in 1979 Calvi persuaded Pesenti and three other prominent businessmen to join the board of La Centrale, his Italian holding company. They were: Alberto Grandi, chairman of the Bastogi holding company, which Sindona had tried to take over in 1971; Giovanni Fabbri, a leading publisher and paper magnate; Luigi Lucchini, a major steel-maker from Brescia with a large holding of Ambrosiano shares.

When these four tycoons joined forces with Calvi, some observers described it as a grand coalition of 'Catholic financiers', since most of them were, like Calvi, linked to the Vatican. These 'Catholic' businessmen were contrasted with so-called 'lay' financiers, such as Gianni Agnelli of Fiat and Carlo De Benedetti of the Olivetti office equipment company. But the term 'Catholic' did not just refer to connections with the Church. The word also connoted a kind of mentality: mysterious, Byzantine, reactionary. Calvi, in the words of one Italian weekly, was constructing a 'holy alliance' - a 'Counter Reformation' style of capitalism which was characterised by intrigue and secrecy.

It was not only Roberto Calvi who grew in importance in the late 1970s; so, too, did Licio Gelli. Almost every day the 'Venerable Master' of the P2 Lodge enrolled new members into his secret organisation, extending his influence still further through the upper echelons of the Italian establishment. During the first few years of Calvi's acquaintance with Gelli, the two men seldom saw each other. But after Calvi became chairman of Ambrosiano in 1975, and his need for 'political protection' increased, their meetings became more frequent. The Bank of Italy's inspection, in 1978, made Calvi feel even more vulnerable and he began to rely increasingly on Gelli's help.

Licio Gelli had a shadowy past and no one has been able to explain fully how he obtained his power or to what ends he used it. Born in 1919, Gelli grew up in the Tuscan city of Pistoia. In 1936 he lied about his age so he could volunteer to fight for Franco in the Spanish Civil War, with troops sent by Mussolini. Throughout World War II Gelli appeared to be a committed Fascist. At the same time, however, he had links with left-wing members of the Resistance. In the closing months of the war partisans were ready to execute Gelli for having collaborated with the Nazis. He was mysteriously spared when a Communist official interceded. This episode, coupled with other puzzling pieces of evidence, has led people to conclude that Gelli was a 'true Fascist' who saved his life by betraying his comrades; while others have argued that Gelli was a leftist all along (perhaps even a spy for the Soviets) who had only pretended to be a Fascist. There is a third school of thought: that Gelli was simply an opportunist who manipulated both the left and the right during and after the war in the pursuit of personal wealth and power.

Soon after the end of World War II, Gelli moved to Rome and became an assistant to a Christian Democratic Member of Parliament. It has been said that Gelli's experiences in Rome taught him the ways in which the *sottogoverno,* the 'undergovernment', operates. In their essay *Story of a Puppetmaster,* Pino Buongiorno and Maurizio De Luca write:

'It was in those corridors of a completely Christian Democratic Rome that Licio Gelli immersed himself and quickly and joyfully learned the secrets of *sottopotere* [underpower]: the art of the recommendation, of the right telephone call, of the debt to call in at the opportune moment...'

Later, Gelli moved back to northern Italy, where he went into the mattress business and later the clothing business. He joined a masonic lodge in 1963 and, according to an account in the weekly magazine *L'Europeo,* Gelli's masonic brothers from that period 'remember that he was constantly present at meetings of the lodge...and above all remember his ability to transform simple acquaintanceships into friendships.' Within a few years, Gelli was given permission to head a lodge of his own, a special lodge with membership restricted to VIPs. In order to protect the privacy of the members, it was a 'covered lodge', meaning that only Gelli and the head of Italian freemasonry knew who all the members were.

Gelli's deputy in the P2 Lodge, the businessman Umberto Ortolani, was himself well connected in business, political and Catholic circles. One of Ortolani's closest friends was Cardinal Giovanni Lercaro of Bologna – it is said that Ortolani even carried a picture of the Cardinal in his wallet. In 1963, on Lercaro's recommendation, Ortolani was made a Vatican nobleman: a 'Gentleman of Honour of His Holiness'. Ortolani had emigrated to Uruguay, where he owned a bank called Banco Financiero Sudamericano – 'Bafisud' for short.

Licio Gelli not only had a knack for turning acquaintances into friends, he also had a remarkable gift for finding those acquaintances in high places and persuading them to join his lodge. One of his first big coups came in 1970, when he became friendly with Giuseppe Saragat, then President of Italy. Though Saragat did not join Gelli's lodge, he did accept an invitation to spend a weekend at Gelli's home in the Tuscan city of Arezzo.

Beyond his undeniable charm, Gelli offered more tangible attractions to members, and would-be members, of the P2 Lodge. If a lodge brother was an executive of a big bank or corporation, Gelli might be able to help his 'brother' obtain a coveted promotion. If the brother had legal problems, Gelli could intercede with a friendly magistrate. If a newspaper was publishing negative articles about a P2 member, Gelli could arrange for positive stories to appear in another newspaper. Gelli, in fact, turned his lodge into a clearing house for favours: the 'brothers' helped each other, with Gelli acting as the intermediary.

As Licio Gelli proved how helpful he could be, his friends and lodge brothers could be numbered in the hundreds, as could those seeking his assistance. Gelli held court in a three-room suite at the Excelsior Hotel, on the Via Veneto in Rome.

In his book *Gelli*, Gianfranco Piazzesi writes:

'Licio Gelli had transformed his suite at the hotel into a small masonic office. He had an apartment with two separate entrances. Like the offices of specialists in sexual problems, the clients did not meet each other. A porter at the hotel, who had the list of those who were to arrive during the day, and who knew the hour of the appointments, watched the traffic discreetly, in order to avoid dangerous traffic jams.'

Columnist Enzo Biagi has written that these were not visits but 'pilgrimages...from people who sought a refuge, a protection, a smile'. Biagi has also noted that the slogan of the mattress company Gelli had once run was 'The whole world in your dreams.'

What did Gelli obtain in exchange for the favours he distributed so widely? Every favour created an obligation for the recipient to supply favours in return or, perhaps, share some of his bounty with the P2 leader. If Gelli helped a brother obtain a loan, he would, for example, expect a commission. If the recipient of Gelli's help was too gauche to reciprocate, Gelli did not hesitate to use his favourite weapon: his files. Over the years, the P2 leader collected a vast number of compromising documents, which could be used for manipulation and blackmail. The material came from two main sources: Italy's intelligence agencies (the leaders of which were P2 members) and from the recipients of Gelli's favours. The care the P2 leader lavished on his archives earned him the nickname *'Il Cartofilo'* – the paper-lover. Gelli's technique of manipulation has been described as follows by Pino Buongiorno and Maurizio De Luca:

'He would sit in the corner of the room, his left arm resting on a desk with several drawers. Every now and then he would open one and pull out some files...He would give a glimpse of the files – sometimes winking, sometimes in a threatening way – to his guests...Almost always, after every visit, the files were enriched by other papers, new secrets.'

Sometimes, the strangest things would appear from Gelli's desk. Vanni Nisticò, the former head of the Socialist Party's press office, has recalled a meeting with Gelli in his suite at the Excelsior. 'When he saw me,' said Nisticò, 'he went to get a large envelope and pulled out some photographs and showed them to me. I was breathless: they were some snapshots of Pope John Paul II completely nude next to his swimming pool. And Gelli said: "Look at the problems the secret services have. If it's possible to take these pictures of the Pope, imagine how easy it is to shoot him." I don't know,' Nisticò concluded, 'what use he then made of those pictures.'

By the late 1970s Gelli's lodge brothers included leaders of Italy's armed forces, intelligence agencies and state-owned industries. There were also dozens of members of parliament, including cabinet ministers; magistrates; and senior officers of the Carabinieri, the country's paramilitary police. From the private sector, Gelli's membership list included industrialists, bankers, publishers and leading journalists.

Gelli's power was not confined to Italy. He had a number of friends in the United States, mainly on the right-wing of the Republican Party. One US contact was Philip Guarino, an official of the Republican National Committee active in raising funds from the Italian-American community. Gelli asked Guarino to get him an invitation to Ronald Reagan's presidential inauguration in January 1981.

Gelli's largest collection of 'friends' outside of Italy was, however, in Latin America, where he and his deputy Umberto Ortolani had what amounted to a wholly-owned subsidiary of the P2 Lodge. Using Uruguay as his Latin-American base, Gelli purchased a sumptuous villa in Montevideo, which included a secret room containing a large portion of his archives. In Buenos Aires, Gelli held court at one of the top hotels, receiving supplicants just as he did in Rome.

Although Gelli boasted of friendships with businessman and right-wing political leaders throughout Latin America, his strongest connections were in Argentina, a country closely linked to Italy. It has been estimated that up to half of Argentina's population of thirty million is of Italian origin and Italy has long ranked as one of Argentina's leading foreign investors and trading partners. With a few strategically placed friends in both Italy and Argentina, Gelli could make a fortune as a middleman. Gelli's penetration of the Argentine power structure came from his friendship with Juan Dominigo Perón, the dictator who had been deposed in 1955. He first met Péron in 1971, when Perón was in exile in Spain and was fighting to make a comeback. The P2 leader took part in this campaign, and when Perón returned to Buenos Aires in 1973, Gelli was a guest of honour at Perón's inauguration as president. Giulio Andreotti, the former Italian Prime Minister who represented Italy at the ceremony, said later that he was 'struck by his [Perón's] almost reverential regard for Gelli...' adding: 'I saw Perón kneel in front of Gelli.'

Soon after the inauguration Gelli was able to add a number of important figures in Argentine society to his P2 membership list. These included: José López Rega, Minister of Social Welfare and widely regarded as the power behind the throne. He was nicknamed *'El Brujo'* – 'the magician' – because of his fascination with sorcery and the occult. Lopez Rega was also the organiser of the 'AAA' (Alianza Anticomunista Argentina), a death squad later blamed for hundreds of 'disappearances'. Admiral Emilio Massera was head of the navy, and also implicated in the death squads. A British journalist with long experience in South America describes Massera as 'a man of extreme ruthlessness, willing to use the most repulsive torture techniques against his opponents, a man totally without scruples, one of the few deeply evil men I have ever met'. General Carlos Suarez Mason, a military hardliner, was connected with López Rega's 'AAA' and later president of Yacimientos Petroliferos Fiscales (YPF), Argentina's state-owned oil company. José Bar Gelbard was Minister of the Economy and a business and political partner of López Rega.

Not long after his inauguration, Perón made Gelli an Argentine diplomat, appointing him a special economic counsellor in the Argentine embassy in Rome.

In 1974, Perón died and was succeeded on 1 July by his vice president (and widow), Isabelita, though it was clear to everyone that José López Rega was making most of the decisions. In December of that year, Gelli and López Rega flew to Libya with a large retinue of Argentine functionaries to discuss trade between the two countries. From those discussions a major trilateral deal resulted, involving Argentina, Libya and Italy. Argentina would obtain arms from Italy and oil from Libya. In exchange, it would ship meat and Argentine-made Fiat products. It was later alleged that Argentina paid far above the market price for the oil – with López Rega pocketing the difference.

In June 1975, Argentina military leaders forced Isabelita to dismiss Lopez Rega, and *'El Brujo'* fled the country. In March 1976 Isabelita Perón herself was overthrown by a military junta.

But Gelli easily survived the coup, since one of the members of the three-man junta was his old friend Admiral Massera, the chief of the navy. Not only did the P2 leader survive the *coup d'état,* he prospered from it: the new rulers of the country soon decided to spend billions of dollars importing arms – and one big supplier was Italy. Together with Admiral Massera, Gelli went into the arms business. In 1976, the year of the coup, Gelli assisted in an Argentine purchase of six frigates from an Italian manufacturer, the state-owned Cantieri Navali Riuniti.

As already noted, Gelli's power in Italy and Latin America was reaching its peak just as Calvi was coming under threat as a result of the Bank of Italy's inspection of Ambrosiano in 1978. It is not clear that Calvi realised the risk he was running by becoming enmeshed with the P2 leader. Not for nothing did Gelli have another, more ominous, nickname, based on his manipulative tactics: *'Il Burattinaio'* – the puppetmaster. Gelli was willing to provide help – but that also gave him the right to ask Calvi to help other P2 brothers.

Probably the first major example of Calvi helping a P2 brother at Gelli's request was when the banker agreed to finance the Rizzoli company. Rizzoli Editore was by far the largest publishing company in Italy, active in book-publishing, newspapers, magazines, films and television. Since 1974, the company's stable of publications had expanded to include *Corriere della Sera,* the most prestigious and largest-circulation newspaper in Italy. According to some estimates, the Rizzoli company controlled roughly a quarter of the Italian press. But though the company was large and important, it was also in a financially precarious state. It had expanded rapidly, financing this growth with expensive bank debt, and many of the new ventures were unprofitable. Banks became increasingly reluctant to extend more credit.

Andrea Rizzoli and his son Angelo explained their plight to Gelli's deputy, Umberto Ortolani, who introduced them to the P2 leader in the autumn of 1975. Gelli and Ortolani immediately saw a splendid opportunity: if they could procure financing for the Rizzoli company, the P2 lodge could acquire enormous influence in the Italian media. As Andrea Rizzoli recalled later in an interview: 'One day, Ortolani phoned me from Rome and told me: "I know that you have some financial problems, I could be of help to you." In essence, he told me that if I were to enroll in masonry, all my troubles would be resolved. I am not religious but I have a religion that is all mine, and it's this: a publisher must have as his only goal the truth. And so I didn't feel like accepting the pressures of Ortolani, I didn't want to have to choose between being a bad mason and a good publisher or a good mason and a bad publisher.'

Evidently his son Angelo, who was beginning to play an active role in the company, had fewer qualms about accepting help from the P2 leaders. Ortolani joined the board of Rizzoli and, in 1977, persuaded Banco Ambrosiano to grant major new financing to the company. According to Gelli's list, Angelo Rizzoli, Bruno Tassan Din, the managing director, Franco Di Bella, the new editor of *Corriere della Sera*, and the editors of several other Rizzoli publications joined the P2 Lodge. As Tassan Din later said: 'In appearance, we didn't have any more problems, but we had lost financial independence and the Rizzoli family had lost control.'

In making the loan to the ailing Rizzoli company, Calvi had violated every principle of prudent banking. But it was evidently the price he had to pay for Gelli's protection. It was, in fact, only the first of a long series of questionable loans Banco Ambrosiano was to make which seem in retrospect to have had no rationale other than fulfilling the wishes of Licio Gelli and Umberto Ortolani. The most extreme example of Calvi appearing to subordinate the interests of the bank to the interests of the P2 Lodge was the rapid and dramatic expansion of Banco Ambrosiano in Latin America.

11

Latin American Spree

The famous 'square mile' that is the City of London is not only the financial centre of the United Kingdom, but also the world's leading international banking centre. More than 400 foreign banks are represented in the City, ranging from giant institutions like Deutsche Bank and Citibank to relatively obscure banks from Third World countries. London's only serious rival is New York City, with nearly 300 foreign banks.

Although Banco Ambrosiano was one of the largest banks in Italy, it had neither a London branch nor a New York branch, which was a fact that often puzzled Calvi's subordinates. Michel Leemans says he used to ask Calvi why the bank was in places like Luxembourg and the Bahamas without being in London or New York. 'I always told him we are not in a serious financial place,' says Leemans. 'But he always postponed the issue.'

When Calvi decided, in the late 1970s, that the time was ripe to open some new banking offices overseas, he ignored the big banking centres. Instead, he chose Latin America.

Calvi had been travelling frequently to the Caribbean since the early 1970s, when he set up Banco Ambrosiano Overseas in the Bahamas. He owned a home at Lyford Cay and he and his wife spoke of moving to the Bahamas on his retirement. In 1978, they obtained permanent residence status there. Work was begun on a huge new headquarters for the Bahamas bank – Ambrosiano House – said to be the largest building (other than a hotel) to be built there in several years. The top floor of Ambrosiano House was to contain two penthouse apartments, one of them intended for the Calvis.

Calvi's trips to the Caribbean were sometimes combined with visits to the United States and Canada. After he set up the 'ghost companies' in Panama there were also brief forays to Central America. But around 1977 the banker began to take a closer look at Latin America, speaking

55

of the region as a land of opportunity. Sounding more like a sixteenth-century explorer than a twentieth-century banker, Calvi spoke of Latin America as an 'El Dorado' where great fortunes could be made. To his family and some of his colleagues, Calvi's enthusiasm seemed genuine. He told his wife that the region's vast natural resources could give it great importance in the years ahead. 'He thought the future of the world was in Latin America,' says Clara Calvi.

Calvi may have been sincere in what he said, but it seems hard to believe that Licio Gelli did not influence Calvi. Latin America was, after all, an area where the P2 leader enjoyed enormous influence. What is more, Calvi's sudden enthusiasm for Latin America came at a time when he was becoming increasingly involved with Gelli. To cite just one example: Ambrosiano's major loan to the Rizzoli company in 1977 was arranged by the P2 leaders around the same time Calvi made his first big investment in Latin America. Indeed, a strong case could be made to show that the real force behind Ambrosiano's Latin-American spree was not the bank's chairman, but the leader of the P2 Lodge.

Calvi's first banking investment in Latin America occurred in 1976, when his Bahamas bank purchased 5.5 per cent of the shares of Banco Financiero Sudamericano ('Bafisud'), the Uruguayan bank controlled by Umberto Ortolani. Calvi was not the only P2-connnected banker to buy shares in Bafisud. The state-owned Banca Nazionale del Lavoro, the largest bank in Italy, also invested in Ortolani's bank. It was later revealed that five top executives of BNL, including general manager Alberto Ferrari, were among those alleged to be members of the P2 lodge.

Around the same time, Calvi paid several visits to Nicaragua, where he met with President Anastasio Somoza. Somoza was regarded as one of the most corrupt dictators in Latin America, having pocketed millions of dollars in international aid intended to help the country recover from the devastating 1972 earthquake. What is more, Somoza was facing increasing opposition, soon to explode into civil war, from the Sandinista guerillas. In spite of Nicaragua's drawbacks, Calvi applied for permission to open a banking subsidiary in the country and Somoza readily agreed. The new bank would have the status of an offshore bank – meaning that it was limited in the amount of domestic business it could do. It opened on 29 September 1977, with the name Ambrosiano Group Banco Comercial.

Carlo Calvi insists that Licio Gelli had nothing to do with his father's choice of Nicaragua. And, in fact, the only apparent connection was that Italian construction magnate Mario Genghini (whose name was also on Gelli's P2 lists) was one of the biggest foreign investors in

Nicaragua. According to Carlo, his father was attracted to Nicaragua by the fact that he would have more freedom to operate there than he would 'in a more developed market'. Ambrosiano, he says, even 'wrote the legislation for offshore banking', noting that 'you can't do that everywhere.' Indeed, Somoza was such an agreeable host that he issued Nicaraguan passports to Calvi and his wife. A Latin America expert says bluntly: 'Somoza was a crook. In return for a few friendly services and loans to the right people, Calvi could be assured of favourable treatment.' (In fact, a Somoza relative was later reported to be a borrower from Calvi's Bahamas bank.)

What did the new bank do? Calvi claimed the new bank would promote trade between Italy and Central America. In fact virtually all of its loans were to ghost companies, from Calvi's Bahamas bank.

Licio Gelli may or may not have played a role in the creation of Calvi's Nicaraguan bank, but he certainly helped Calvi to penetrate Peru. Gelli introduced him to top Peruvian officials and helped him finance arms deals and other ventures. According to Sisti and Modolo, Calvi first visited Peru in 1977, attracted by new government policies aimed at encouraging foreign investment. Through an Ambrosiano-controlled company, Central American Service, Calvi obtained a 300,000 hectare (approximately 750,000 acres) concession in the Madre de Dios area to prospect for gold, uranium and oil. He also offered to finance the import of Italian-made arms – frigates and Augusta/Bell helicopters – by the Peruvian military.

In 1978 the Nicaraguan civil war forced Calvi to look for a new Latin American base. In early 1979, according to a report in the *Financial Times*, Calvi visited Peruvian Finance Minister Javier Silva Ruete, and made a big play for permission to open an offshore bank. Approval was granted and the new bank, Banco Ambrosiano Andino, opened in October 1979 – three months after the Sandinistas defeated Somoza. Calvi then transferred the bulk of the ghost company loans from his banks in Managua and elsewhere to Lima. Banco Andino was thus able to start with a balance sheet total of $600 million.

Banco Andino opened with a great fanfare. It would, according to Ambrosiano's publicity statements, specialise in lending to the Andean Pact countries. An article entitled 'Into the Andes with Calvi' in an Italian weekly said that the new bank represented 'a new chapter in the foreign expansion of the Banco Ambrosiano group'. Calvi, the article continued, was 'constructing a grand multinational bank which will operate in the Andean area.' Andino was a 'multinational' bank because part of the shares were to be owned by South American banks.

It was a sham. Some of the shares of Banco Andino *were* owned by

South American banks – but Andino had lent those banks the money to pay for the shares. For example, Banco de la Nación, a Peruvian government-owned bank, purchased two per cent of the shares of Andino, financing the purchase with money Andino had deposited with Banco de la Nación. As for specialising in 'the Andean area', the bulk of Andino's loans were to the Panamanian ghost companies – and the Andes mountain range does not stretch as far north as Panama. The executives of Ambrosiano's Nicaraguan and Peruvian banks led an agreeable and uncomplicated life. All the decisions were made for them in Milan. Regularly Ambrosiano executives in Europe would send telexes saying, for example, that X million dollars was being deposited with Andino, and that Y million dollars should be credited to, say, Bellatrix (one of the ghost companies). Years later, the process was described like this:

'...it would appear that Ambrosiano Group Comercial SA [in Nicaragua] is managed in, let us say, a 'trusting' manner. Telexes in which tens of millions of dollars were credited to phantom companies were signed simply "Giacomo", "Licia" or "Angelica". Giacomo is Giacomo Botta, central manager of Banco Ambrosiano SpA and the senior man in the foreign services, Licia and Angelica are his secretaries. From Milan they travelled regularly to Monte Carlo from where, on a direct telex line, they imparted to Banco Ambrosiano Overseas [in the Bahamas]...which kept the books on behalf of Ambrosiano Group Comercial, those instructions...A similar system was employed for managing Banco Ambrosiano Andino...'

Calvi's third Latin American bank was opened in Argentina in 1980. Bearing the grand name Banco Ambrosiano de América del Sud, it had impressive headquarters in Buenos Aires. Just as Banco Andino had been touted in the press as an important new 'multinational bank', Calvi's Argentine bank was said to be a significant contribution to Latin American development. This time, however, the hand of Licio Gelli could be clearly discerned behind the favourable publicity. For the most fawning coverage was in newspapers belonging to the Abril group, an Argentine publishing company recently purchased, with Gelli's assistance, by Rizzoli.

Unlike Calvi's first two Latin American banks, which had offshore status, the Argentine bank was licensed to do business locally. Gelli evidently hoped to use the new bank to exploit his local contacts. In fact, one of Gelli's prime Argentine contacts, Admiral Massera, took an office in the same building as the new bank, after his resignation from the ruling junta.

Throughout Calvi's Latin American expansion there were two serious threats to him hovering in the background: the Italian magistracy was investigating his capital exports while his ghost company scheme to control Ambrosiano was beginning to cause financial strain.

The ghost company scheme was inherently risky because it involved a major gamble on the value of the lira against the dollar. That is because Ambrosiano stock (and the dividends earned by the ghost companies that held that stock) was quoted in lire, while most of the loans taken out to pay for the stock (and the interest payments on the loans) were in dollars. If the dollar rose sharply against the lira, the ghost companies would be unable to pay all the interest on the debts, except by taking out new loans. Full repayment of the loans would be impossible since the loans would exceed the value of the Ambrosiano shares.

Calvi's legal and financial problems fed off of each other in a vicious circle. Gelli offered Calvi 'protection' from judicial inquiries, but apparently the price of that protection was that Calvi had to take money out of Ambrosiano's coffers to pay bribes and make questionable loans to P2 brothers. This, of course, exacerbated the financial strain. If these questionable payments were discovered, they could lead to new legal investigations of Calvi, requiring him to make still more protection payments – making the vicious circle complete. By ensnaring Calvi in this way, and profiting in every conceivable way from the banker's misfortunes, Gelli showed how well he deserved his nickname of *'Il Burattinaio'* – the puppetmaster.

Calvi's first big loan to a P2 brother was, as noted above, the 1977 Rizzoli deal. But others soon followed. In 1978 Ortolani's son Amadeo visited Ambrosiano to apply for financing for a company he controlled called Voxson, a Rome-based manufacturer of radios and television sets. Roberto Rosone, then the head of Ambrosiano's domestic business, says that he flatly rejected the application – only to be overruled by Calvi a few hours later.

A much larger dubious loan was granted later that year to a P2 brother: Mario Genghini, head of a big construction company and, like Calvi, an investor in Nicaragua. Genghini was in serious financial straits because of a disastrous construction project in Saudi Arabia. Genghini asked Rosone for a $5 million loan. Rosone turned him down, on the grounds that Genghini could offer no guarantees. The builder then went to the fourth floor to see Calvi. Rosone was flabbergasted by the chairman's reaction. 'Give him $20 million,' said Calvi. 'But $20 million is madness,' Rosone replied. 'You don't have the slightest idea of how much Genghini is worth,' Calvi answered in a disparaging tone. 'He's the owner of half of Nicaragua, thousands of acres of teak...' The loan was granted.

When the Genghini empire later crashed, Ambrosiano was exposed to the tune of 150 billion lire – more than $100 million. In November 1981 the bankrupt builder fled Italy. He was arrested a year later in the Hôtel de Paris in Monte Carlo.

In late 1979 the ghost company scheme was hit by a potentially devastating blow. The Carter administration had been under strong international criticism because of high US inflation rates and the weakness of the dollar. Late in October 1979 President Carter announced a tough programme to curb inflation and prop up the dollar – and the foreign exchange and money markets went wild. The dollar soared in value against almost every other currency, including the lira, and US interest rates rose to their highest ever levels. If the ghost companies were to service their debts, Calvi would have to raise tens of millions of dollars in new loans. Once again, Gelli was ready to help. Although the P2 leader was part of the problem, he was also part of the solution. Gelli appears to have used his influence to obtain vast amounts of financing for Calvi from Italy's largest company and its largest bank.

Ente Nazionale Idrocarburi (ENI), Italy's state-owned oil company, became a big lender to Ambrosiano's foreign subsidiaries in 1978, through ENI-owned banks in the Caribbean. In 1979 and 1980, the volume of ENI loans to the Ambrosiano group soared. Although there is no proof that Gelli 'persuaded' ENI to lend so much, there are strong grounds for suspicion.

In July 1979, the chairman of ENI, Giorgio Mazzanti, who had been appointed to that post with the backing of the Socialist Party, announced a three-year contract to import crude oil from Saudi Arabia's state oil company, Petromin. In the oil business, according to an industry executive, typical commissions on such deals ranged from $\frac{1}{2}$ to 2 per cent. ENI, however, agreed to pay 7 per cent to a shadowy Panamanian company, for a total of 120 billion lire (about $100 million). Later that year, rumours began circulating that part of the exorbitant commission had been kicked back to various people in Italy, touching off a scandal known as the 'ENI/Petromin Affair'.

In October 1979 Mazzanti attended an OPEC meeting in Vienna, and received a phone call telling him that a certain Licio Gelli wanted to see him. Gelli had long been trying to recruit Mazzanti into his lodge, but had never been able even to obtain an appointment. After returning to Rome from the OPEC meeting, Mazzanti agreed to visit Gelli at his suite in the Excelsior Hotel. During the meeting, Gelli showed the ENI chairman an 18-page document labelled 'Arabia Saudita' (Saudi Arabia), giving an extraordinarily detailed account of the ENI/Petromin deal. On 30 November – at the peak of the scandal –

Mazzanti agreed to join the P2 Lodge.

In the wake of that meeting ENI increased its lending to Ambrosiano, until it reached a total of some $200 million, making ENI by far the largest creditor of the Ambrosiano group.

Among Italian banks, the largest lender to the Ambrosiano group was another P2-connected institution, the state-owned Banca Nazionale del Lavoro, the largest bank in Italy, which, as noted above, was linked to P2. Gelli's records show that General Manager Alberto Ferrari enrolled in 1975, around the same time as Calvi.

In addition to the ENI and BNL lending to Ambrosiano, there were other links among those institutions, the P2 Lodge and the Socialist Party.

Gelli's list of presumed P2 members included Calvi, ENI Chairman Mazzanti, senior executives of BNL, and several officials of the Socialist   Party.

The Socialist Party chose ENI chairman Mazzanti and BNL chairman Antigono Donati. Calvi later said that he paid $15 million to the Socialists in exchange for political protection. He said he made the payment through Ortolani's Uruguayan bank, Bafisud.

BNL and Ambrosiano both owned shares in Bafisud, and a BNL official says that Ortolani regularly passed himself off as a South American representative of BNL.

One common denominator in several of these institutions was Pierre Siegenthaler. Siegenthaler was the President of Banco Ambrosiano Overseas in the Bahamas; a board member of Tradinvest, an ENI-owned bank in the Caribbean that did much of ENI's lending to Ambrosiano; a board member of Bafisud; and head of one of the Panamanian ghost companies (Lantana) which ultimately received funds borrowed from ENI, BNL and other Ambrosiano creditors.

Licio Gelli appears to have constructed an intricate machine for collecting and distributing money, favours and 'protection' among four of the most important institutions in Italy: the largest company (ENI), the largest bank (BNL), the largest private banking group (Ambrosiano), and the second largest party in the governing coalition (the Socialists). If this interpretation is correct, it means that Gelli had conceived and carried out a protection racket on a scale that would put the biggest Mafia chieftains to shame.

12

The P2 Lists

Terrorism, one of the scourges of the 1970s, afflicted Italy more than perhaps any other industrialised country. Hundreds of attacks were carried out against politicians, policemen, journalists, magistrates and others deemed to be representatives of the establishment. As the years went by, the attacks became bolder and less descriminating, reaching a peak in August 1980, when a bomb planted at the Bologna railway station by right-wing terrorists killed 84 people and injured more than 200.

One man marked for assassination was Emilio Alessandrini, the Milan magistrate who had begun investigating Banco Ambrosiano in early 1979. With the bizarre logic often employed by terrorists, Alessandrini was singled out because of his integrity and competence. In her book *The Terror Network*, Claire Sterling notes that the left-wing terrorist organisation Prima Linea ('Front Line') '"accused" him of "having contributed to restore the state's democratic and progressive credibility."' On the morning of Monday 29 January 1979 Alessandrini was murdered by five killers from Prima Linea.

Upon the death of Alessandrini, the Ambrosiano case was transferred to another investigating magistrate, Luca Mucci. Mucci, an expert in 'white collar' crime, was a careful and thorough magistrate, well-equipped to determine whether Calvi's exports of roughly 25 billion lire (about $20 million) were in violation of Italy's foreign exchange laws.

Mucci began his work by examining the material his predecessor had received from the Bank of Italy and saw that it included only brief extracts from the so-called 'Padalino Report' (the inspectors' report on Banco Ambrosiano). So he asked the central bank to send him a complete copy. Mucci then asked the Guardia di Finanza, the police squad attached to the Ministry of Finance, to conduct an investigation of Calvi's suspicious share transactions, which had been the means for exporting capital from Italy. The Guardia di Finanza submitted its report to Mucci on 22 June 1979, concluding that Calvi had done nothing illicit. What Mucci did not realise was that his probe was being systematically obstructed and delayed by Licio Gelli through his contacts in the Guardia di Finanza.

Mucci, however, persisted in his work. In September 1979 the magistrate ordered the Guardia di Finanza to conduct a second investigation. This time an official went to Lugano in Switzerland to investigate links between executives of Ambrosiano's Swiss bank, Banca del Gottardo, and one of Calvi's suspicious share deals, the so-called 'Toro Operation'. The official discovered that Gottardo executives were connected to ghost companies in Panama and Liechtenstein that had bought shares from Calvi. On 16 October Mucci wrote to the Italian Foreign Exchange Office asking whether Calvi controlled those ghost companies. Later that month, he invited Calvi to visit his office to answer questions about the questionable share dealings.

Mucci's interrogation of Calvi in October 1979 was just one of what was to be a long series of encounters between the banker and the magistrate in Mucci's cramped office in the marble Palazzo della Giustizia. And just as the Bank of Italy inspectors had found Calvi to be evasive and unhelpful, Mucci was disappointed in the banker's answers. One magistrate who interrogated Calvi said later that when the banker was nervous his moustache would twitch and he would begin to twist it with his fingers. That, said the magistrate, was the sign that Calvi was lying – and it was time to stop the interrogations for the day.

On 12 June 1980 Mucci received a new report from the Guardia di Finanza. Unlike the one the previous year it did not clear Calvi. In fact the new report contained evidence that Calvi and some of his associates had committed a number of serious crimes: illegal capital exports, falsification of bank records and fraud.

Two weeks after receiving this damning report, he ordered the banker to hand over his passport. This was a major blow to Calvi for several reasons. It meant that Mucci felt his case against Calvi was strong; news that Calvi had lost the passport would seriously undermine the banker's public image; and Calvi would be prevented from travelling abroad to manage his ghost company scheme. So the banker resolved to do everything possible to have the document returned – even if only temporarily.

On 7 July Calvi's lawyer, Valerio Mazzola, visited Mucci to ask for the temporary return of the passport, but the request was turned down.

Licio Gelli then mobilised friends in political and judicial circles on Calvi's behalf. Letters from powerful people flowed into Mucci's office. There were later allegations that large sums of money were paid into Swiss bank accounts.

Calvi was so desperate that he visited Mucci personally to plead for the return of the document and, according to one account, the normally stoical banker broke down in tears. Calvi said he had to attend the joint annual meeting of the International Monetary Fund and the World Bank, to be held in Washington in the autumn. He added he wanted to combine that trip with a visit to Banco Ambrosiano Overseas in the Bahamas.

Mucci discussed Calvi's request with his colleague Mauro Gresti, who suggested that Calvi send another Ambrosiano official to the IMF–World Bank meeting in his place. Calvi replied that other major banks normally sent their chairmen. Eventually, Mucci and Gresti agreed to restore the passport temporarily.

An investigation conducted several months later cleared Mucci and Gresti of any impropriety; it was found that Gelli's lobbying had nothing to do with their action. But this did not stop Gelli from claiming credit for the decision, which further enhanced his image in Calvi's eyes.

Gelli was indeed powerful and nothing delighted him more than flaunting his power. He would drop names of top politicians, pick up the phone in the presence of visitors to arrange appointments with cabinet ministers, and show off confidential papers he had collected from his friends in Italy's intelligence agencies. He seemed to be omnipotent. But he was not. A handful of investigating magistrates had been on Gelli's trail since 1979 when the journalist Mino Pecorelli, editor of a scandal sheet called *OP*, began publishing information on Gelli. The P2 leader had often used Pecorelli in the past as a tool in his campaigns of extortion. Now, however, Pecorelli had apparently decided to turn the tables on Gelli. In a February 1979 issue of *OP*, Pecorelli told how a certain Fascist had betrayed many of his comrades at the end of World War II in order to save himself from partisan reprisals. In March another article appeared that could be damaging to Gelli: alleging that secret service dossiers that were supposed to have been destroyed in 1974 had actually 'disappeared abroad'. The issue of *OP* containing that story appeared on 20 March 1979. Within hours Pecorelli was murdered.

In 1980 Gelli became reckless. His power was enormous – but always exercised in the shadows. He decided, for the first time, to assume a more public role. In October 1980 he arranged for a journalist from *Corriere della Sera* to interview him about his political 'philosophy'. The little-known masonic leader expounded on Italy's political malaise, asserting that the best solution was to replace the country's party-dominated parliamentary system with a de Gaulle-style 'presidential republic'.

But neither the disclosures by Pecorelli nor the interview with *Corriere della Sera* proved to be Gelli's undoing. He was ultimately exposed because of his ties with Michele Sindona. Early in 1981 two Milanese magistrates, investigating Sindona's ties with the Mafia, travelled to Palermo to interrogate one of the people who had helped Sindona during his fake kidnapping in 1979. Joseph Miceli Crimi, a Sicilian-American physician, was asked by the investigating judges why, during the period when Sindona was hiding in Palermo, he had suddenly visited Arezzo, some 600 miles to the north in Tuscany. 'I went to Arezzo,' he replied, 'because my dentist lives there, and I was suffering from a toothache that summer.' The magistrates were far from satisfied with that answer and pressed for the real reason for the trip.

On 14 March 1981 Miceli Crimi broke down: 'The truth is that I went to Arezzo because Licio Gelli is there; Gelli is my masonic brother and a close friend of Michele Sindona.' The magistrates quickly ordered a search of Gelli's home in Arezzo and his office in the nearby town of Castiglion Fibocchi, which was carried out on March 17. Buongiorno and De Luca describe the search in *Story of a Puppetmaster*.

'In Gelli's office was a secretary, Carla Giovannini, longtime trusted co-worker of Gelli. Behind the desk, the men from the Guardia di Finanza saw a safe. On the table was the secretary's purse. "Let me see", ordered a junior officer. From the purse came out a key that opened a desk drawer. In the drawer were another two keys: one was the key to the safe. They opened it. Inside were the complete lists . . . of the lodge . . . In addition there were dozens of photographs and membership applications with illustrious names . . . . Near the safe was a leather bag with a label attached marked "fragile". It was opened with the second key found in the desk. It contained 32 sealed envelopes full of photocopies of State documents, notes of transfers of money abroad in favour of senior magistrates, politicians, leaders of public corporations, and detailed reconstructions of scandals.'

Officials who studied the P2 material found that Gelli appeared – on the basis of the list – to have recruited into his lodge powerful figures from almost every sector of the establishment:

Politics: forty-three Members of Parliament, including three cabinet ministers.

The military: the head of every branch of the armed services.

The intelligence agencies: General Giuseppe Santovito, head of military intelligence, General Giulio Grassini, head of civilian intelligence, and the civilian co-ordinator of intelligence.

Business and finance: senior officers of public- and private-sector banks and corporations.

The mass media: top officials of the Rizzoli publishing group; RAI, the state-owned broadcasting company; and other media organisations.

The presence of so many military men and intelligence officials on Gelli's lists prompted speculation that the purpose of the lodge was to launch a *coup d'état*. Others, however, rather cynically dismissed that notion with the argument that a coup would be pointless because Gelli already appeared to have accomplished it.

Perhaps as amazing as the lists of names was the evidence that Gelli had been involved in a long series of scandals stretching back over the previous decade: including the Sindona affair, the ENI/Petromin scandal and now the Calvi case. In addition, Gelli's 'friends' included a number of people linked to acts of right-wing terrorism and conspiracies to overthrow the Italian government.

In subsequent months political analysts and observers had to grope to find words to capture the importance of Gelli's P2 Lodge. Referring to Gelli's involvement in so many scandals, Luigi Spaventa, a left-wing Member of Parliament, said: 'I'm totally against finding "the big plots".
Unfortunately, I'm becoming convinced. In all the dirty affairs of this country, you always find one common denominator: Gelli.' Other observers defined the P2 Lodge as a 'state within the state'. It was quite extraordinary how the puppetmaster was able to manipulate people whom everyone had assumed were far more powerful than he.

The P2 scandal did not erupt for several weeks after the search of Gelli's files on 17 March. Only a few magistrates and other officials knew the contents of his lists and dossiers. Copies of the lists were handed over to Prime Minister Arnaldo Forlani, who decided to lock them in a desk drawer and not release them publicly. This meant that Gelli still had time to try to limit the scope of the scandal by employing his old manipulative tactics. He seized upon a bold plan: if he could persuade Calvi to buy control of the Rizzoli group, Gelli could use Rizzoli to bargain for political protection.

Calvi had been trying to distance himself from the P2 leader for a number of months, according to the banker's family. Anna Calvi has told Italian magistrates: 'Some months before the explosion of the story of the P2 lodge . . . my father had already begun to refuse to accept phone calls from either Gelli or Ortolani. He said I should answer that he wasn't in, or say that he was ill or in bed.'

Upon the discovery of his files, Gelli had fled Italy and gone into hiding. But he persisted in contacting Calvi, and still enjoyed considerable influence over him. As far as the banker knew, Gelli still had the power to obstruct legal probes of Calvi's banking dealings, so if he wanted this protection he would have to do Gelli's bidding. Calvi's assumption, however, was wrong. The material seized from Gelli's office included a file labelled 'Roberto Calvi', which contained evidence of how Gelli had interfered with the investigation of the banker. Now that they knew how Gelli operated, the judicial authorities were no longer vulnerable to his manipulative tactics.

On 3 April 1981 the Calvi case was handed over to a new investigating magistrate, Gerardo D'Ambrosio. D'Ambrosio was evidently so incensed by the P2 leader's tactics that he took a much tougher line with Calvi.

On 29 April Calvi called together Leemans and Rosone and told them that he had made an agreement for La Centrale to pay 115 billion lire for a 40 per cent stake in the Rizzoli publishing company. Roberto Rosone, for one, could not believe his ears: the price seemed exorbitant. He grabbed a pencil and made a quick calculation: 96,000 lire a share, at a time when the publisher was in disastrous financial shape. Calvi, however, insisted that the price was a bargain.

Another executive asked whether the deal was even legal. He remembered hearing about a recent government decree that forbade banks from owning newspapers. One director suggested that there could be a political backlash from parties that had been hoping to control Rizzoli for themselves, and would now be foiled by Calvi's deal. Calvi reassured them, saying that everything had already been cleared with political leaders in Rome.

There is no proof that the Rizzoli deal triggered the events that followed. Calvi, however, evidently believed that it did. Using the Italian equivalent of 'the straw that broke the camel's back', the banker later called the deal 'the drop that made the pot overflow'. On other occasions, he said: 'All my problems began when I bought Rizzoli.' Calvi was referring to a decision taken the following month by magistrate Gerardo D'Ambrosio. In late May, D'Ambrosio indicted eleven financiers on charges that they had illegally exported about $20 million worth of lire through a series of suspicious share operations. They included nine men from the Ambrosiano group and two from the 'Bonomi-Invest' group. The most prominent of the eleven was Roberto Calvi.

13

Arrest and Trial

At about 7 a.m. on Wednesday 20 May 1981 a captain of Guardia di Finanza, accompanied by three junior officers, arrived at Via Giuseppe Frua 9, in a wealthy residential quarter of Milan. They pressed the buzzer on the intercom, and a porter led them to the gentleman who lived on the eighth floor. 'Signor Calvi,' said the captain, 'you are under arrest.'

That same morning six of the other co-defendants in what came to be known as 'the Calvi trial' were put in prison.

When word of the arrests spread the switchboard of Ambrosiano was inundated with phone calls asking for details. In the executive suite there was confusion since Calvi had never groomed an alter ego. 'He was number one and there was no number two,' explains an Ambrosiano official. 'And so there was panic.' The financial community was shocked by the round-up of bankers. In the words of the weekly magazine *L'Europeo:* 'The world of high finance has been struck by an unprecedented earthquake.'

But the shock of Calvi's arrest was quickly overshadowed by another event later that day: the public release of Gelli's list of 962 names, the presumed members of the P2 Lodge. That the two events should occur the same day was appropriate. For Calvi was the most prominent banker on Gelli's lists and the decision of the judicial authorities to arrest Calvi, rather than just order him to appear at the trial, was probably based on his close relationship with Gelli.

The disclosure of the P2 lists caused the collapse of the government of Prime Minister Arnaldo Forlani within days. In itself this was not remarkable, since Italy had averaged about one government crisis a year since World War II. What was extraordinary was that Forlani was succeeded by the first prime minister since the 1940s from a party other than the Christian Democrats. After years of being implicated in scandals the

Christian Democrats agreed to hand the post to someone from another party: Giovanni Spadolini of the small Republican Party, a party which was seldom tainted by scandals. Spadolini described the P2 scandal as 'a moral emergency'.

Clara Calvi was in her bedroom when the Guardia di Finanza came to arrest Roberto. 'My husband came in and said, "They are coming for me." I said I wanted to come with him,' but she was rebuffed by the captain. She was alone with her daughter in Milan and had no idea what to do to help her husband. She called Ambrosiano officials and the lawyers the bank had retained for her husband, but, she says, they were unable to give her any advice.

She and Anna visited Calvi in prison and he told them of various steps they could take to help him in his case. He told them that politicians whose parties had benefitted from Ambrosiano's generosity in the past should be mobilised to use their influence on his behalf. He also said that pressure should be put on IOR, the Vatican bank. Calvi told his family that the two share deals for which he had been arrested were not done on his own account, but on behalf of IOR. Proof of IOR's involvement was in documents in the possession of Banca del Gottardo, Ambrosiano's Swiss bank. But Swiss bank secrecy laws prevented Gottardo from releasing the papers unless IOR gave permission. The banker said that pressure should be applied to IOR's top two officials, Archbishop Marcinkus and Luigi Mennini. During one prison visit, he even handed his wife and daughter some papers on which he had written 'This trial is named IOR.' When Clara and Anna left the prison they were spotted by Luigi Mennini's son Alessandro, who was an executive of Ambrosiano. 'When he saw the papers in my daughter's hand he tried to grab them,' Clara Calvi later said. 'But I sat on them and wouldn't let go.' She claims that Mennini then told her: 'You must not mention this name [IOR] – not even in confession.'

What Calvi was asking of his family was that they conduct a sophisticated lobbying campaign on his behalf – something they had no experience in doing. This was the sort of thing Licio Gelli had been adept at, but he was now in exile and, in any event, no longer entirely trusted by Calvi.

Very soon, however, a new 'fixer' appeared offering to help the Calvi family out of their predicament. His name was Francesco Pazienza and he was a glib, flamboyant man in his thirties. In March 1981 Calvi had retained him as a 'consultant' to Ambrosiano – at the enormous fee of 600 million lire a year (about

$500,000). He was, in a way, a younger version of Gelli: a shadowy character who boasted of connections with politicians, intelligence agencies and the press.

Pazienza phoned Clara Calvi within days of her husband's arrest and arranged a trip to Rome. Also accompanying them to Rome were his partner, Maurizio Mazzotta, and a right-wing publisher named Giuseppe Ciarrapico, said to be closely connected with Giulio Andreotti, the former Prime Minister. On the way to Rome, Ciarrapico told Signora Calvi that she should point out to the politicians they were going to meet that her husband had been extremely generous to their parties. Referring to an alleged payment of 30 billion lire to the Socialist Party, Ciarrapico told her to say to the head of the Party, Bettino Craxi: 'Signor Craxi, 30 billion lire is really not a joke.' Ciarrapico later denied giving such advice.

Clara Calvi visited Andreotti, Craxi and Christian Democratic leader Flaminio Piccoli, and found their responses disappointing. Piccoli only told her: 'Relax, have faith in justice.' She later said: 'I went to the leaders of the parties who had received a lot from him [Calvi], but none of them moved.'

While Clara Calvi was attempting to lobby the politicians, her son, who lived in Washington, tried to put pressure on the Vatican bank. He flew to the Bahamas, where he found papers in a bank vault which, he says, supported his father's claims about the Vatican's involvement in his share dealings. 'I called Marcinkus from the Bahamas a couple of times,' says Carlo Calvi. 'I basically said that since he had this convenient set-up, he should do something to help us.' But Marcinkus's reply was: 'Ambrosiano's problems are your problems.'

Soon after that, Pazienza flew to the United States and contacted Carlo Calvi. He told Carlo that Archbishop Giovanni Cheli, the Vatican's observer at the United Nations, might be able to help since, Pazienza explained, Cheli was hoping to take Marcinkus's place as head of IOR. Later, Carlo Calvi described the visit to the weekly magazine *Panorama*:

'I took a plane and went to New York with Pazienza. As soon as I arrived, Pazienza took me to an apartment in Manhattan where waiting for me was a noted Mafioso – a former friend of Sindona and Gelli – and a priest... Well, these two men told me to be polite to Monsignor Cheli and above all to pay attention to his advice. And so, all together – that is, Pazienza the Mafioso, the priest and I went to the UN where Cheli received us in his office. Cheli, in diplomatic language, told me in substance what Marcinkus had told me on the phone: to tell my father to be quiet, not to reveal any secrets and to continue to believe in Providence.'

Upon his arrest, Calvi had been taken to a prison in the town of Lodi. A squat, yellow building with only about a hundred inmates, it was far more comfortable than most Italian gaols. Often used to house 'white collar' criminals, it had earned the sobriquet 'the prison of the VIPs'. But this was little consolation to Calvi. He was, according to relatives and colleagues, shocked and degraded by the experience of imprisonment. For a decade, Calvi had moved in the rarefied world of international high finance, with executive jets, chauffeur-driven limousines and suites at the best hotels. After reaching the chairmanship of Ambrosiano, Calvi was treated with extraordinary deference by his employees: even some of the top officials of the bank addressed him as 'Presidente', rather than simply 'Signor Calvi'.

On the morning of 20 May 1981 the executive perquisites and the obsequious treatment vanished. Calvi was photographed and finger-printed like a common criminal. His necktie and shoelaces were removed. The prison guards, some of them barely out of their teens, did not address him as 'Presidente' or even 'Signor Calvi'. Instead, they would snap 'Calvi!' as if calling a dog. Even more insulting, the gaolers used the familiar *tu* form, rather than the polite *Lei* to which Calvi was accustomed.

Calvi was an intensely private person and being forced to share a cell with two of his fellow defendants made it almost impossible for him to sleep. Michel Leemans, one of the first executives of the Ambrosiano group to visit Calvi in prison, recalls that 'he was destroyed because he had not had a normal night's sleep'.

On Friday 22 May, two days after his arrest, Calvi was visited by the magistrate who had put him behind bars, Gerardo D'Ambrosio, for the first of a series of interrogations. Although Calvi had the right to remain silent, he agreed to be questioned. The interrogation began at 4.30 p.m. with the magistrate asking Calvi to explain one of his questionable share deals. D'Ambrosio found the banker evasive, and soon moved on to another topic: Calvi's relations with Licio Gelli. What the banker did not realise was that D'Ambrosio had in his possession copies of material seized from Gelli's files, and so he walked right into the trap. 'I never had any relationship with Gelli,' Calvi said. He then corrected himself, with an only slightly less sweeping lie: 'I have known Licio Gelli for about two years, but I never had any specific relationship.' At this point, D'Ambrosio pulled out the first of a series of documents found in Gelli's files that linked the banker to the P2 leader.

Throughout the evening the cat and mouse game continued. D'Ambrosio would ask a question, Calvi would make a flat denial, the magistrate would produce a document that showed Calvi was lying. Eventually Calvi realised the game was lost and said lamely: 'I'm absolutely not capable of giving explanations.' At 9 p.m. D'Ambrosio terminated the session.

It was only a temporary respite. The following afternoon the magistrate returned, bringing with him papers relating to Calvi's legal case that had been found in Gelli's files. The last of these was eight typed pages dating from the summer of 1980. Calvi identified it as 'a memorandum made for my own use, to summarise the things I could remember of my case. I never made us of it,' he claimed, 'and I absolutely cannot explain how its contents ended up in Gelli's hands.'

The morning of Friday 29 May was the time set for the arraignment of Calvi and his co-defendants – the official reading of the charges against them. By 9.30 a.m. the courtroom chosen for the hearing was overflowing with reporters, television crews, friends and relatives of the accused and curiosity-seekers. The panel of three judges quickly decided to transfer the proceedings to a larger hall. The new courtroom was ornately decorated but it contained a grim reminder of the kind of trials sometimes held there. Along one wall was a metal cage and just a few weeks earlier it had been filled with members of the Red Brigades terrorist organisation. Some of the relatives and friends of the defendants in the 'Calvi Trial' shuddered when they saw the cage, and whispered the hope that the judges would spare the defendants the indignity of being caged during this trial.

At about 11.30 a.m. the defendants entered the courtroom. Calvi and the others who had come from the Lodi prison wore no handcuffs. The accused who had been held at Monza prison were manacled. It was soon decided to remove the handcuffs on the ground that 'bankers are not considered dangerous'.

The 'Calvi Trial' began on 10 June, in a hot and stuffy courtroom. In spite of the discomfort the defendants were poised and mannerly. Echoing the famous observation of F. Scott Fitzgerald that 'the rich are different', the Communist Party newspaper *L'Unità* noted that the financiers were not like most defendants. 'The rich behave themselves even when they find themselves among the accused – even imprisoned,' said the newspaper. 'They do not fidget, they do not raise their voices, they do not wave to relatives and friends in the crowd. They consult documents, notes, speak with their lawyers … there's the atmosphere of a board meeting.'

In the afternoon, Calvi took a seat in the witness's chair to deliver a statement explaining the 'Toro Operation'. He was dressed in the most sober manner as befitted a banker: black suit, black shoes and socks, dark tie and blue shirt. He crossed his legs to support a pile of papers on his lap, papers he consulted from time to time while making his statement. According to one press report, Calvi seemed a bit like a student 'worried about not upsetting the professor on the very day of the final examination'.

It soon became clear, from the tone of the judges' questions, that they were not satisfied with Calvi's explanations. Calvi's style of answering the judges' questions also undermined him. He spoke in the same contorted fashion that had irritated the Bank of Italy inspectors and the investigating magistrates. 'He gave a vey bad impression,' recalls Michel Leemans. 'He could be asked a very simple question – like whether it rained on a certain day – and he would say: "Looking at it from this point of view, we may realise . . ." He gave the impression of being confused, and then created the impression of being deliberately confused.'

Towards the end of June it was clear to Calvi's lawyer, Valerio Mazzola, that his client was likely to be convicted, but Mazzola feared that Calvi did not realise how badly the case was going. So the lawyer asked Leemans to break the news to Calvi. 'I went to talk to Calvi during a recess,' says Leemans. 'I said that from talking to various people I had the impression that he would have problems; that there was a good chance he would be convicted.' But Calvi refused to accept what Leemans was saying. 'He said: "No, you do not understand, you are not Italian. No, not really." He had a mental block; he refused to accept the possibility of being convicted.'

Around this time the judges rejected Calvi's third application for bail. The trauma of imprisonment was wearing him down. He became increasingly moody and suspicious. He refused to leave his cell during the exercise period, perhaps in fear of an attempt on his life. When his wife and daughter visited, Calvi told them that if the Vatican bank and his political allies did not help him, he would begin divulging what he knew about their questionable dealings. 'My father repeated more than once . . . that he would say everything he knew about IOR and about economic and political questions in the courtroom,' Anna Calvi later said.

Officials of the Rizzoli group approached Anna and informed her that if her father talked to the magistrates investigating the P2 Lodge, he might be able to get out of prison on bail. And so she went to see her father, says Carlo Calvi, 'to convince him that this was a good idea'.

At about 7 p.m. on 2 July three magistrates investigating the P2 scandal, Pierluigi Dell'Osso, Luigi Fenizia, and Guido Viola, received a message from Calvi: he was ready to talk. A few hours later they arrived at the Lodi prison and the interrogation began just before 10 p.m.

Calvi began by telling the magistrates: 'You must get me out of here, I can't take it any more.' He made it clear that in exchange for his freedom, he would tell them about his secret payments to the Socialist Party, his relations with the Rizzoli group, and about documents found in Gelli's files relating to the ENI/Petromin scandal. The magistrates, however, responded that they had no power to release Calvi from prison, since they had nothing to do with his trial. On hearing this news, the cold, reserved banker, 'the man with the eyes of ice', began to weep.

After regaining his composure, Calvi said he was still willing to talk. On his relations with the P2 Lodge, Calvi confirmed that Gelli and Ortolani had considerable influence over him. Ortolani, he said, 'made me understand that in my position I had particular need of protection and support – at political, financial and administrative levels – which he said that he and Gelli were able to guarantee me. With time, Ortolani was able to insert himself more and more in my banking activities, sometimes suggesting interventions, agreements with other financial groups, even persuading me to finance the Rizzoli group.' Calvi went on to say that the P2 leaders persuaded him to finance political parties, particularly the Socialists.

As the interrogation proceeded, the magistrates pressed Calvi for more details of the relations with the P2 Lodge and the banker's composure crumbled once again. Calvi then made an extraordinary statement, implying that he had become little more than the puppet of his erstwhile protectors: 'I'm just the last wheel on the cart,' said Calvi, 'try to understand. Banco Ambrosiano is not mine. I'm simply in the service of someone else.' 'But who controls you?' asked the magistrates. 'Who does the bank belong to?' 'I cannot tell you any more.' The interrogation ended at 3 a.m.

Calvi's willingness to talk to the magistrates about the P2 Lodge and his payments to political parties had little, if any, positive effect on his case. On 3 July the prosecutor told the court that he would seek a stiff sentence for the Ambrosiano chairman: three and a half years in prison and a fine of 32.6 billion lire (nearly $30 million).

The interrogation did, however, have another effect. According to members of the Calvi family it provoked threats from politicians in Rome, particularly the Socialists. The Socialists, says Clara Calvi, told her husband that if he did not retract his statements he would spend the rest of his life in gaol. And, in fact, when the P2 investigators visited Calvi on 5 July he retracted some of his previous statements.

On the morning of 9 July the courtroom quickly filled for that day's session of the trial. By 9.15, however, Calvi had not yet appeared, and the spectators began to wonder why. Valerio Mazzola, Calvi's lawyer, explained to the court that his client was ill and had been taken to hospital. A few minuted later, another defence lawyer stunned the courtroom with an announcement: Calvi had attempted suicide. In the early hours of the morning, it was announced, Calvi had taken an overdose of barbiturates and slashed one wrist. 'Everyone rushed to the telephones,' recalls Michel Leemans. 'Then people said: he did it, or he tried it, or it's a fake. And they asked what the impact would be.'

Was the suicide attempt genuine? One of Calvi's cellmates said that the cut on Calvi's wrist was superficial and the acting director of the prison was quoted in the press as saying that Calvi had not taken 'an excessive dose' of pills. He added: 'We're dealing with a suicide attempt that failed at birth.'

Calvi's family believes that the suicide attempt was probably feigned, with the intention of preventing the magistrates who were probing the P2 Lodge from interrogating him in prison about his loans to the Socialists. 'He was never in danger of his life,' says Carlo Calvi. 'He was never in a serious condition.' In one interview, however, Clara Calvi clearly referred to it as a 'suicide attempt', adding that it came at a time when her husband 'felt betrayed by everyone'. In fact, because of lingering suspicions within the family that the attempt might have been genuine, Carlo Calvi says that the family chose not to risk upsetting Calvi by asking him about it.

If the suicide attempt was intended partly to win sympathy from the banker's political protectors, it succeeded. It was followed by rousing defences of Calvi, by some of the most powerful politicians in the country, the leader of each of the three biggest parties of the governing coalition: Christian Democrat Flaminio Piccoli, Socialist Bettino Craxi and Social Democrat Pietro Longo. They portrayed the Calvi trial as a sort of witch hunt of bankers. Craxi, for example, stood up in Parliament on Friday 10 July and claimed that the trial was being conducted in an atmosphere of 'intimidatory violence', and that the legal authorities were making 'political use of judicial papers'.

To a certain extent, the politicians' arguments were valid. Calvi was being treated very harshly by, for example, being denied bail. One source close to the trial says he felt that Calvi had been 'demonised' by his involvement in the P2 scandal. But what these politicians failed to mention in their stirring speeches was that their parties had received privileged financial treatment at Banco Ambrosiano. Indeed, some opposition politicians were unable to restrain their disgust at the speeches by Calvi's protectors. One member of the Radical Party blurted out in Parliament: 'Yes, yes, it's all the fault of the judges. Great person, Calvi!'

Just before 10 a.m. on 20 July the three judges met to consider their verdict. By the late afternoon the courtroom was full, with only one notable person absent: Calvi. He was still in the prison hospital, recovering from a case of pneumonia. At 6.50 p.m. the judges returned to announce their decision: Calvi and three others from the Ambrosiano group were guilty; the remaining defendants were acquitted – two of them for 'lack of proof'. Of the four men found guilty, Calvi received the stiffest sentence: four years' imprisonment and a fine of 16 billion lire (over $10 million).

As the judges later explained, they regarded Calvi as 'the sole co-ordinating brain' of the Toro and Credito Varesino operations. In addition, they were highly critical of the way he explained himself in court. 'Calvi's method of responding,' the judges wrote, '[was] never anticipatory . . . [he waited] for the facts and evidence that in a "crescendo" were put to him . . . [contributing] to the judgment that many of his denials and explanations were unreliable.'

Calvi was ordered to be released, pending his appeal against conviction. On 22 July, Clara Calvi went to the hospital to take her husband home in their armoured Mercedes SEL. In front of the Mercedes was a yellow Alfetta with two bodyguards. Behind was a white Alfetta with two more guards.

14

Investing in the *Sottogoverno*

Calvi's arrest and trial – and his involvement in the P2 scandal – had touched off widespread speculation about how long he would remain chairman of Banco Ambrosiano. Some people did more than just speculate. In June, a trade union representing Ambrosiano employees circulated a bulletin calling for the suspension of bankers involved in the P2 scandal.

Within the bank, Calvi's nominal deputy was Carlo Olgiati, deputy chairman and general manager. But the man widely regarded as the most likely successor was Roberto Rosone, head of the bank's domestic activities. Indeed, he was sometimes called 'Roberto the Second' and he even sported a moustache similar to the chairman's. In most other ways he was very different from Calvi. Born in 1928, Rosone grew up in humble circumstances. His father was a tram driver and the family lived in a working-class district of Milan. In 1946 Rosone obtained a letter of recommendation from a priest and was hired by Ambrosiano as a messenger. He studied accounting at night school and rose slowly through the ranks of the bank. He sometimes complained bitterly that, unlike Calvi, he was never singled out to skip a few rungs of the corporate ladder. In personality, Rosone was the exact opposite of his boss: emotional, expansive and gifted with an engaging sense of humour. He was regarded as a good banker, though without any international experience.

When Calvi was arrested, Rosone decided that the chairman had to go – at least until the legal process was completed. He has claimed that he did not take this view out of ambition or disloyalty, but rather in the belief that confidence in Ambrosiano would be undermined as long as there was a cloud over its chairman. 'I was truly tired of . . . reading in certain papers every morning what was written about Calvi,' Rosone later said in an interview. 'There was a kind of daily bombardment that made it impossible to manage the bank with the slightest tranquility. If I have a tobacco shop, I don't give a damn who comes in to shop. But a bank, no. A bank sells confidence, only confidence.'

Rosone enlisted the support of his nominal boss, Carlo Olgiati, and even visited the former Ambrosiano chairman Ruggiero Mozzana (who had resigned from that post in 1975). Though Mozzana was nearly eighty and seriously ill in a clinic, he agreed to back Rosone. Mozzana said he would even return to the chairmanship if necessary. In July, Rosone and Olgiati sent a message through an intermediary to Carlo Azeglio Ciampi, Governor of the Bank of Italy. (Ciampi had succeeded Paolo Baffi in 1979.) They asked the Governor to support their campaign to oust Calvi from the chairmanship.

Ciampi and his deputy, Lamberto Dini, were sympathetic to Rosone's point of view. They held a series of meetings with Calvi after his release from prison, but were unable to persuade him to step down. One source says that Treasury Minister Beniamino Andreatta met with central bank officials to discuss the possibility of taking over the management of Ambrosiano by appointing special commissioners. This option was rejected, says this source, out of the fear that Calvi could successfully challenge it in court – making his position even stronger.

On 28 July, eight days after he was sentenced to prison, Calvi chaired a meeting of the board of directors of Banco Ambrosiano. Calvi was nervous, according to Rosone, but the board members were even more nervous. In other words, Calvi dominated the meeting just as he always had.

Calvi began by thanking the board, management and employees of the bank 'for the activities [they have] performed, in this recent, difficult period, in the interests of the bank'. Then, according to the minutes of the meeting, board member Giuseppe Prisco, speaking on behalf of all the directors, expressed 'faith in the judiciary and the belief that the judgment of the next level will grant [Calvi's] appeal.'

The board then voted to reconfirm Roberto Calvi as chairman and managing director of Banco Ambrosiano. 'An eminent and disquieting banker has learned the rigours of justice,' journalist Eugenio Scalfari later commented, but 'his power has not been even slightly scratched.'

Also at that meeting Carlo Olgiati resigned and Roberto Rosone was named general manager and *vicepresidente* – deputy chairman. Calvi, however, very soon made it clear that he did not trust his new deputy. 'He took me aside and said: "I made you *vicepresidente* and yet you tried to get me out of the bank",' implying that Rosone was a potential Judas.

Not only did Calvi retain the chairmanship, he quickly regained his legendary self-control. 'You could hardly notice any difference in the man,' recalls a Milanese banker who saw him shortly after his release from prison. 'The control was just perfect.' Adds Leemans: 'He was able to take that and that and another blow and another and continue as if nothing had happened.'

Perhaps even more surprising was the buoyant price of Ambrosiano's shares. The price fell after Calvi's arrest, but quickly recovered when the trial was over and hovered around 50,000 lire (about $40) a share for most of the remainder of 1981. When this price was multiplied by 50 million – the number of shares outstanding at the end of the year – it showed that the stock market valued Banco Ambrosiano at about 2,500 billion lire (more than $2 billion) – extraordinarily high for a bank of its size.

In fact, Ambrosiano's solid record had enabled it to make a huge rights issue early in the year – nearly doubling the bank's capital and adding thousands of new shareholders. By the end of 1981, some 37,000 investors held stock in the bank, an increase of more than 8,000 over the previous year.

In retrospect, Ambrosiano's high share price seems 'incredible – almost absurd,' as author Gianfranco Modolo puts it. But at the time, investors knew nothing about the dubious loans to the ghost companies. Calvi was helped to conceal what he was doing by Italy's primitive accounting and auditing standards. The accounts of Ambrosiano and all the companies it controlled were published separately, rather than in consolidated form, which meant that investors were given a distorted picture of the 'group'. Perhaps even worse, the accounts of the parent bank in Milan were not scrutinised by independent auditors, but rather by the *'collegio sindicale'* – the 'board of auditors' – an internal committee that seldom challenged the information given to them by management. One accountant says disparagingly: 'The kind of thing the *collegio sindicale* does is count the cash in the vault.'

But it was not only the lax accounting and auditing standards that explain Ambrosiano's inflated share price. Another factor was that the shares were touted aggressively by Ambrosiano branch managers, many of whom were also shareholders in the bank and thus stood to profit from strong demand. A small depositor would often come to a branch to open a savings account or purchase government bonds and then be persuaded by the branch manager to buy Ambrosiano stock instead. 'It was a share that wasn't sold in the market – it was *pushed*,' says an Italian investment manager. 'My father was a depositor in the bank and the branch manager used to call him up every three or four weeks and tell him to buy the stock because in two or three weeks it would go up by 3,000 lire.'

Another reason why the Ambrosiano share price remained steady was that many investors believed the bank could profit from the strong political connections Calvi seemed to have. After all, his trial had inspired cries of support from some of the most powerful politicians in the country and he had remained chairman of the bank in spite of being sentenced to four years in prison. As one union official puts it: 'He was protected by three umbrellas: the Vatican umbrella, the Christian Democratic umbrella and even the 'lay' politicians' umbrella – Socialists were defending Calvi. That's why there wasn't a big sell-off of the shares.'

An American banker in Milan agrees, although he expresses the point a little differently. Some of the shareholders, says this banker, probably felt that by investing in Ambrosiano they were investing in the *sottogoverno* – the 'undergovernment' of secret power alliances that they believed really ran the country. 'The small shareholders,' he says, 'were all in it because they thought, "Calvi's got all these connections. Let's invest in the *sottogoverno*."' And, it could be added, they were 'short-selling' the official government.

15

Letters of Comfort

Calvi's ghost company scheme had been unravelling since the late 1970s. Ambrosiano's subsidiaries in Luxembourg, the Bahamas, Nicaragua and Peru had borrowed hundreds of millions of dollars from international banks, money which was then recycled to the 'ghost companies' to be invested in Ambrosiano shares. When the dollar rose in value against the lira and interest rates soared, the ghost companies could only pay the interest on their debts by borrowing more money – which, in turn, forced Ambrosiano's subsidiaries to raise more funds.

In 1980, for example, Banco Ambrosiano Holding in Luxembourg was lent $40 million by a group of seventeen banks led by Midland Bank, one of the UK's 'big four' banks. In early 1981, BAH borrowed $75 million from twenty-eight banks led by another of the big four, National Westminster. Other major sources of credit included ENI, the Italian state oil company, and the 'interbank' market – that is, short-term deposits from international banks.

While it was difficult for the ghost companies to service their debts, it was impossible for them to repay the debts in full. The gap between the debts and the value of the Ambrosiano shares they owned was probably about $200 million to $400 million by late 1981.

Of course, the other financial strain, as noted above, was the 'protection' money Calvi had paid to Gelli and various political parties – money taken from the coffers of the Ambrosiano group. And the more he paid, the more was demanded from him. 'He probably gave the impression that he could be relied on for any amount of money,' says an Italian official, 'so they kept asking for more.'

For years, Calvi had managed to conceal the ghost company scheme – not only from his shareholders, but from the Bank of Italy and all but a handful of his executives. He would shift money and shares from one phantom company to another, to make it difficult for anyone to prove that the offshore companies that owned a large part of Ambrosiano were

81

the same ones that had borrowed money from the foreign banks Calvi controlled. As one Italian businessman describes this tactic: 'He was a master of Chinese boxes . . . the kind you open and keep finding new ones inside. He had many Chinese boxes outside of Italy, and only he opened and closed them. Only he knew what was inside.'

The game was nearly exposed in 1978, when the accounts of Banco Ambrosiano Overseas (the Bahamas bank) were audited by Coopers & Lybrand, a leading international accounting firm. The men from Coopers asked for an explanation of BAO's loans to the Panamanian companies and were told that the companies were owned by the Vatican bank.   After Calvi's arrest in May 1981 the risk of exposure – and the potential financial damage – grew tremendously. Many international bankers became reluctant to provide fresh loans and deposits to the Ambrosiano group, because of all the controversy surrounding Calvi. Those who were willing to lend would often demand above-market rates or insist that the borrower be the parent bank in Milan – which was considered safer, since it was under the direct supervision of the Bank of Italy.

Calvi was thus forced to use the parent bank in Milan to raise new money for the ghost companies, which exposed it directly to the risks of the scheme. Until then, it could have permitted its foreign subsidiaries to default, and so in effect Ambrosiano would only lose whatever money it had invested in the share capital of the Luxembourg holding company.

When Calvi was convicted, the Bank of Italy began putting pressure on him to explain his foreign activities. One Italian official said later that after Calvi refused to resign from the chairmanship, 'We accelerated our inquiries. We thought that maybe he *couldn't* step down, because a basket of crabs would come out.'

Within the bank itself some of Calvi's subordinates clearly sensed that trouble was coming. In June 1981, just after Calvi's arrest, three senior executives in the foreign department – Filippo Leoni, Carlo Costa and Giacomo Botta – suddenly resigned from posts they held with Latin-American subsidiaries of Ambrosiano. In August, directors of Banco Andino in Peru flew to Milan and had a stormy meeting with Calvi. Giorgio Nassano, head of Andino, later told the *Financial Times* that he and his fellow directors threatened to resign immediately if Calvi did not provide them with guarantees that the loans to the Panamanian companies would be repaid.

The ghost company scheme, intended as a means to gain control over Ambrosiano, was now threatening to destroy it. If Calvi was to save it from collapse, he would have to find a way of raising money to repay the ghost companies' debts – perhaps by selling the Ambrosiano shares that they owned. Such a deal would be delicate and difficult under any circumstances. It would be impossible if the questions and suspicions from his subordinates continued to grow. He needed a way to allay their concerns, so he could work on a rescue plan.

Since the early 1970s Calvi had climbed to the top of Banco Ambrosiano and transformed it into a financial empire with the help of Michele Sindona, Licio Gelli and Archbishop Paul Marcinkus. Sindona had turned from a friend into a bitter enemy. Gelli had turned from protector into manipulator. The only one of the three who could help Calvi now was Marcinkus.

Calvi visited Marcinkus and explained his plight. He asked for some kind of guarantee that could be used to buy time to sort out Ambrosiano's financial problems. Marcinkus refused to issue an explicit guarantee, but he did agree to write a series of letters indicating that the Vatican bank stood behind the companies in Panama and Liechtenstein. In bankers' jargon, these are known as 'comfort letters' or 'letters of patronage'. Dated 1 September 1981 on stationery headed 'Istituto per le Opere di Religione, Città del Vaticano', the letters said in part that IOR 'directly or indirectly controls' eleven ghost companies and was 'aware of [their] indebtedness . . .' They were signed by Mennini, Marcinkus's deputy, and Pellegrino de Strobel, IOR's chief accountant.

The patronage letters worked. An official of Banco Andino says that when the general manager, Giorgio Nassano, returned to Peru after his clash with Calvi, he received 'a very strong comfort letter' giving IOR's total support to the Panamanian companies' debts, which by now totalled roughly $1 billion.

What the letters did *not* indicate was that Marcinkus apparently had no intention of honouring the debts. In fact, the Vatican banker obtained from Calvi a secret letter freeing IOR from any obligation to repay the loans. The letter assured the Archbishop that IOR would suffer 'no further damage or loss'.

Ironically, less than two months before the patronage letters were issued, Pope John Paul II had appointed a committee of fifteen cardinals to study Vatican finances, partly to avert Sindona-type scandals in the future. As one member of the council, West Germany's Cardinal Joseph Hoeffner, said some months later: 'The Holy See must stay out of financial, speculative games. [It must] avoid future scandals and adventures.' What Cardinal Hoeffner did not realise was that the game of the patronage letters was soon to embroil the Vatican in a scandal of far greater proportions than the Sindona affair.

16

The New 'Fixer'

The Vatican's patronage letters bought precious time, but they did not solve anything. Banco Ambrosiano was still in danger of collapsing, and its chairman still faced a four-year prison sentence. If Calvi was to solve either problem, he would have to work quickly.

Calvi's weakness for shadowy 'fixers' and 'middlemen' who claimed to be able to manipulate events had not been lessened by his disastrous experiences with Gelli. In fact, after his conviction, Calvi was more desperate than ever and thus more vulnerable to the blandishments of would-be 'protectors'.

Since early 1981 he had availed himself of the services of Francesco Pazienza, the 'consultant' who had taken Clara Calvi on visits to politicians during the banker's trial. After the trial, Pazienza introduced him to another 'fixer', Flavio Carboni, a man who was to play a crucial role in the remainder of Calvi's life.

Flavio Carboni, born in 1932, was a wealthy businessman from Sardinia, a property developer who led a playboy existence, complete with yachts, expensive cars, a private jet and a string of mistresses. Like Gelli and Pazienza, Carboni seemed to have a surprising number of friends in high places. Carboni's contacts were in politics, publishing, the Vatican, intelligence agencies and the criminal underworld.

In late July, shortly after Calvi's trial, Pazienza suggested that the banker unwind by taking a vacation in Sardinia. A few days later, Pazienza was strolling through a piazza in Rome, accompanied by Domenico Balducci (reputedly a Mafia boss), when he saw Carboni. The two had met the year before in the office of a Roman police official. They stopped to chat and Pazienza asked Carboni for help in renting a house in Sardinia, for the holiday he was taking with the Calvi family. The mention of Calvi's name aroused Carboni's interest; he was building a tourist complex in Sardinia and needed bank financing. Pazienza agreed to introduce him to the banker.

Roberto, Clara and Anna Calvi took their holiday in one of the most beautiful parts of Sardinia, just off Budelli Island. One morning Pazienza took the banker out on his cabin cruiser and the boat was soon flanked by another: Carboni's. For all that Calvi knew, it was the chance encounter of two friends. But there was nothing accidental about it. 'I had an appointment at sea with Pazienza,' Carboni later admitted. It was a friendly meeting, and Calvi agreed to see Carboni after his return to Milan.

As pleasant as Sardinia might have been, Calvi could not relax entirely. Several times during the three-week holiday he had to fly to Rome for meetings with Bank of Italy officials. Calvi was also becoming concerned about the physical safety of his family, and he urged his wife and daughter to leave Italy. Anna went to stay with her brother in Washington, but soon returned, insisting that she had to complete her university studies. Clara Calvi left Italy in late August, spent a month in London, then stayed for a few months in her son's home. In late November she moved back to London. She was not happy there, and insisted on making occasional weekend visits to Milan. But her husband would not let her return permanently because, she explains, 'he said I was in danger in Italy.'

Calvi's relations with Francesco Pazienza were becoming strained. The banker was disturbed by Pazienza's friendships with questionable people, and his habit of making aggressive remarks. According to Anna Calvi: 'He would use expressions like "I'll have that guy eliminated," "I'll have him beaten up" and so on.' She adds that Calvi's 'consultant' also upset her father by constantly demanding money. 'I remember one time, when my father and I were intent on having dinner, a phone call from Pazienza came. He was screaming at my father and my father was asking him "What do you want from me?"'

Eventually, Calvi forbade Pazienza to visit the family home or even telephone. But he continued to harass the banker at his office, according to Anna Calvi. 'My father told us that on one occasion... Pazienza came to his office and told him point blank: "Tell me where you keep your money and give me access to it, so that when you return to prison I'll be able to help your family." My father, according to what he told us, answered very sharply: "Look, I'm not planning to return to prison and I'll do everything to defend myself." More than once my father said of Pazienza that in some ways he was like Gelli.' Calvi was obviously ready to retain a new 'fixer' and he soon found one.

Towards the end of 1981 Calvi agreed to lend Flavio Carboni five billion lire for a construction project in Sardinia. But the relationship soon developed beyond that of lender and borrower. The Sardinian builder became a frequent visitor to the Calvi family homes in Milan and Drezzo and, recalls Anna, 'when Carboni was around, my father would withdraw with him and engage in long conversations.' He became the banker's confidant. Calvi said he felt persecuted by the Bank of Italy and by the Italian press. He said he was getting little co-operation from the Vatican, which he characterised as his closest business partner and thus obliged to help solve the bank's financial problems.

By mid-December, Carboni had assumed the role of Calvi's chief lobbyist, putting his connections at the banker's service. He called upon his influential friends in an effort to help Calvi rescue Ambrosiano and prevent a return to prison.

Why was Carboni doing all of this? Was he, as he has portrayed himself, a sort of 'good Samaritan', eager to help a friend in trouble? Was he hoping to earn some money to support his expensive life-style? Or was he a new puppetmaster, a successor to Gelli, intent on exploiting and manipulating the banker?

Calvi's family and colleagues were suspicious of his new companion. His deputy at Ambrosiano, Roberto Rosone, referred to characters like Pazienza and Carboni as 'people who make you afraid just by looking at them'. Carlo Calvi said of Carboni: 'It took me only a few minutes to see that he was a good-for-nothing. Unfortunately, Papà went around with strange types.'

17

Marriage of Bad Faith

The journalist Piero Ottone once wrote that there are 'two Italys': an Italy of clarity and an Italy of intrigue. Ottone, editor of *Corriere della Sera* until he was replaced in 1977 by a P2 member, believes the country is torn between two conflicting mentalities. The Italy of clarity takes its inspiration from Protestant, rationalist northern Europe. The Italy of intrigue has its roots in the country's Catholic and Mediterranean traditions. In the business world, companies and banks are often labelled as 'Catholic' or 'lay'. Whether or not one accepts the analysis, two Italian business leaders in late 1981 were widely regarded as epitomising each of those 'two Italys'. Roberto Calvi represented 'the Italy of intrigue', while Carlo De Benedetti exemplified 'the Italy of clarity'.

De Benedetti, the scion of a prosperous Jewish family in Turin, had made his reputation in the early 1970s when he acquired a small tanning company and built it up into a sort of mini-conglomerate. In 1976 Gianni Agnelli, the head of Fiat, made De Benedetti his deputy, but the two strong personalities apparently clashed, and De Benedetti left within a few months. In 1976 he joined Olivetti, the office equipment company, which was then having financial problems. Within a few years he had recapitalised the company, slashed overheads and boosted sales and profits. In the process, he acquired a reputation as one of the most gifted businessmen in Italy. Within the company his dynamism earned him the nickname *'forza della natura'* – 'force of nature'. Italian magazines regularly described De Benedetti (along with Calvi) as one of the most powerful men in the country. But the reputation of the Olivetti chief was based on more than his business skills. His *style* of doing business was remarkable – open, direct, and relatively apolitical – 'more American than Italian', as one businessman puts it. Says one of his associates: 'He has an image of "transparency". He speaks his mind clearly in a country that is a bit Byzantine.' It would be hard to imagine a more unlikely partner for Roberto Calvi.

Late in October 1981 Francesco Micheli, a young financier who worked with De Benedetti, visited Calvi to ask him whether he was interested in buying some convertible bonds belonging to De Benedetti – a fairly routine transaction. The Ambrosiano chairman, however, said he might be interested in discussing a closer relationship – for example, selling De Benedetti a large block of Ambrosiano shares.

De Benedetti was intrigued by the offer. Calvi was a controversial figure, but Ambrosiano appeared to be a dynamic and profitable bank. Several meetings were held and it was agreed that De Benedetti would buy one million shares, about 2 per cent of the shares outstanding, at a price of 50,000 lire per share, for a total of 50 billion lire (around $40 million). De Benedetti would assume the title of deputy chairman of Banco Ambrosiano and Micheli would take a seat on the board of La Centrale.

De Benedetti and his colleagues were fascinated by Calvi. 'Calvi was considered extremely powerful and capable – but compromised by the world of Sindona,' says a De Benedetti associate. 'On the human level, he was considered a mysterious man, a person fascinated with mystery and secrecy. He was considered a genius – whether a genius of good or evil. We asked how it was that a man who attempts suicide is permitted to remain chairman. We considered that as proof of his power.' He adds that 'the idea of putting these two characters together was absurd – but if it went well, it would be an extraordinary operation.'

There were potential advantages to both sides. By joining forces with De Benedetti, Calvi could improve his image and the image of the bank. The attraction of the deal to De Benedetti was that it could enable him to gain control of the Ambrosiano group for a relatively small investment: if Calvi were forced to resign or lost the appeal against his conviction, De Benedetti would be the most likely successor. 'Both of them were enthusiastic,' says a De Benedetti aide, 'but a little afraid.'

Before the deal was announced the two men met at Calvi's country home. In this meeting, according to a detailed account in the weekly magazine *Panorama,* De Benedetti posed a number of delicate questions to his new 'partner'. He asked Calvi about his relationship with Gelli, about his political 'godfathers', and he asked who really owned Banco Ambrosiano. In answer to the last question, Calvi claimed that the mysterious offshore companies that appeared on the list of the bank's stockholders had been set up by Italian families living overseas. De Benedetti didn't challenge the explanation that he was offered, but he didn't believe it. 'We considered Calvi the owner of the bank,' says one of his colleagues.

On 17 and 18 November De Benedetti made courtesy calls on

Governor Ciampi of the Bank of Italy, Treasury Minister Andreatta and a handful of top bankers, to give them some advance warning of the deal. Both Ciampi and Andreatta expressed enthusiasm, with the former saying he hoped De Benedetti would bring the same kind of 'transparency' to the management of the bank that he had brought to Olivetti.

On the afternoon of 18 November Calvi introduced his 'partner' to the Ambrosiano board of directors. None of them expressed an opinion, leaving De Benedetti with the impression that the board was totally dominated by Calvi. But when the deal was announced publicly, the financial world was stunned by this extraordinary 'marriage'. The *Financial Times* noted that 'most of Italy's financial establishment is . . . rubbing its eyes with something akin to disbelief.' Treasury Minister Andreatta was quoted in the press as saying: 'Capitalism sometimes has interesting surprises', while a Bank of Italy source referred to De Benedetti as 'Archangel Gabriel'. The most prophetic comment came from Enrico Cuccia, the powerful financier who had been the target of Sindona's threats: 'One of them', he said, 'is making a mistake. Only time will tell which one.'

Calvi was delighted by the arrival of the Olivetti chief. Carlo Calvi later said: 'I was there myself that day. He introduced me to De Benedetti, who said that we should soon get together and exchange ideas about business. Papà was beaming; he took my arm and said: "Did you see? Now you know a really capable person. You could work with him."'

Roberto Rosone, Calvi's deputy, reacted with unalloyed delight, even though this meant he had to make room for a second deputy chairman. In fact, he was so enthusiastic that Calvi accused him of disloyalty. After one clash, Rosone claims that he screamed at his boss: 'Get your ass out of here!', prompting Calvi's secretary, Graziella Corrocher, to whisper 'Bravo, Bravo.'

Within days of the 'marriage', Calvi's attitude changed abruptly from enthusiasm to hostility. He complained when De Benedetti granted an interview to a newspaper about the deal, although this had been agreed between the two of them previously. Calvi's daughter recalls that her father 'commented bitterly that De Benedetti didn't miss any opportunity to give interviews and to appear in public'.

The Olivetti chief and his aides were puzzled by Calvi's sudden change in heart. They suspected that the deal had met with the disapproval of Calvi's political 'godfathers'. Whatever the cause, the banker began to renege on various agreements he had made. He refused to answer questions about Ambrosiano's activities, and would not even provide his new 'deputy' with an office and a secretary. He said he was opposed to putting De Benedetti's representative on the board of La Centrale, claiming that such a move would look like 'a military occupation by De Benedetti'. Referring to his fruitless requests for information, De Benedetti later said, 'I ran into a wall of rubber.'

On the Saturday after the deal was announced, the two men met at Calvi's country home. The banker told the industrialist: 'You must be attentive to the reactions of the political and financial worlds, domestic and international.' De Benedetti replied: 'I have never been afraid of anything in either of those worlds.' Calvi, he later said, 'spoke and behaved like a frightened animal'.

Around the end of November, De Benedetti began receiving anonymous threats, in phone calls and in a cryptic letter. He took these seriously enough to report them to the Interior Minister, Virginio Rognoni. In early December, De Benedetti received a veiled threat from Calvi himself. 'Watch out,' the banker told him. 'I've learned that the P2 is preparing a dossier on you.'

On 13 December De Benedetti sent a long letter to Calvi, outlining a twelve-point plan for improving the management of the Ambrosiano group. Calvi's reaction was to ask the industrialist to sign a statement affirming that he was satisfied that he had obtained all the information he wanted about Ambrosiano. 'With a vaguely menacing tone,' De Benedetti said later, 'he told me that it would be better for me if I signed.'

Although Calvi refused to answer questions about the bank, De Benedetti managed to obtain information from other sources. He learned that Calvi's Peruvian bank, Banco Andino, had accumulated a loan portfolio totalling $800 million in only fifteen months and was told that all the borrowers were obscure foreign companies. Angelo Rizzoli, an official of the publishing company, sent a disturbing message through a friend. 'Tell De Benedetti to watch out,' the message said. 'The real proprietors [of Ambrosiano] are Gelli, Calvi and Ortolani. They made a hole [deficit] of 600 billion lire by buying shares of the bank with the bank's money . . .'

On 15 January 1982 a Calvi representative called on De Benedetti and suggested that he resign his post at the bank, adding that Calvi would arrange for his shares to be purchased. The following day the Olivetti chief received a detailed written offer for the shares: the price paid in November plus two months' interest. The transaction took place on 22 January.

On withdrawing from Ambrosiano, De Benedetti said that he had joined the bank to act as an entrepreneur – to develop it, to improve its management. Instead, he said, he had found himself struggling amid lawyers and registered letters, in a world of intrigue and *sottopolitica* ('underpolitics'). 'I'm happy to be out of it,' he said.

Roberto Rosone says that he was shattered by the news: 'I cried like when my mother died when De Benedetti left.'

The chairman of a large Italian bank later said of the 65-day partnership: 'It was a marriage of bad faith – each one wanted to destroy the other. And that's grounds for a Catholic annulment.'

18

New Questions

Within days of his 'divorce' from De Benedetti, Roberto Calvi took a new 'bride': Orazio Bagnasco. A Genoese businessman resident in Switzerland, Bagnasco had made a fortune in property leasing and through a property investment fund, called Europrogramme. In 1980 he had bought the CIGA chain of luxury hotels, which included Milan's Principe e Savoia and Rome's Excelsior (where Gelli held court). Bagnasco and some of his associates purchased about 1.28 per cent of Ambrosiano's stock, paying 28 billion lire. On 26 January, he joined the board as deputy chairman. Various friends and business associates of his bought large amounts of stock at the same time.

Calvi told his daughter that he was becoming annoyed by the comings-and-goings in the executive suite: 'I remember my father commenting, with a very displeased tone, that the bank was becoming a kind of tram, that one boarded and got off more or less as one pleased. My father repeated many times: "The bank is not a tram."'

But Calvi's new alliance did have several attractions. Bagnasco's willingness to invest about $20 million in the bank represented a major vote of confidence. Ambrosiano's new deputy chairman also had important friends in the political world, such as former Christian Democratic premier Giulio Andreotti. But perhaps most important of all, Bagnasco, unlike De Benedetti, seemed to have a remarkable lack of curiosity about the bank whose stock he was buying. In an interview with the business weekly *Il Mondo*, Bagnasco said he was not interested in knowing who owned the mysterious companies that held large amounts of Ambrosiano stock (the existence of the ghost companies had been reported in the press by this time). He also expressed great confidence in Calvi's management skills, in the health of the Ambrosiano empire and in the rigorous regulation exercised by the Bank of Italy. Any person, said Bagnasco, 'can decide whether to believe in Calvi, but no one can deny that he's known how to create an extremely solid empire. In his field, he has no rivals.' In short, Calvi seemed to have found an ideal 'bride': trusting, unquestioning and docile.

Bagnasco's faith in the bank did seem to be justified by the bank's strong financial performance. On 25 January it announced spectacular results for 1981. Ambrosiano's profits had more than tripled to 43 billion lire (over $30 million) and its 'sister' banks in Italy, Banca Cattolica del Veneto and Credito Varesino, had done extremely well. In fact, Credito Varesino reported the highest profits of any commercial bank in Italy: 71 billion lire.

The financial press said these results indicated that the controversies surrounding Calvi had little, if any, negative impact on Ambrosiano's performance. In early March one Italian magazine said that 'the solidity of the group seems to be beyond question', although it did suggest that Ambrosiano's stock might be overvalued. In April the *Financial Times* wrote that 'perhaps the most striking lesson of the last year is that with or without Calvi, Ambrosiano is doing fine.'

But behind the apparently rock-solid façade of the Ambrosiano empire was, as noted above, a nearly bankrupt institution. By early 1982, the ghost companies' debts to Ambrosiano's foreign subsidiaries totalled more than $1 billion – only about half of which was now covered by the value of the stock the companies owned. Even ignoring these dubious loans, the widespread faith in Ambrosiano's published accounts, and in the 'rigour' the Bank of Italy's supervision, was sadly misplaced. As noted earlier, Ambrosiano's accounts were not consolidated and not independently audited. As far as the Bank of Italy's supervision was concerned, it effectively stopped at Italy's borders. For example, it had no power to examine the books of Banco Andino, where the dubious loans were concentrated, since Andino was not a branch of Ambrosiano. Banco Andino was a foreign-incorporated bank controlled by a foreign-incorporated company (Banco Ambrosiano Holding in Luxembourg) which, in turn, was controlled by Banco Ambrosiano in Milan.

In spite of Calvi's ability to mislead the press and his stockholders, questions from other quarters were becoming increasingly persistent. In the autumn of 1981, after becoming deputy chairman, Roberto Rosone began to ask Calvi about the loans to the Panamanian companies. Calvi brushed him off with the same explanations he had used with Banco Andino officials: that the ghost companies' debts were backed by IOR. Calvi said forcefully: 'Behind those loans is the Vatican – the Pope.' In early 1982, Rosone pressed Calvi again, and, he says, 'Calvi silenced me with this sentence: "Rosone, do you mean that you have the slightest doubt about the central bank of the Vatican?" He said it just like that: the central bank of the Vatican.'

At the end of January, Giorgio Nassano, the head of Banco Andino, came to Milan again and, according to a report in the *Financial Times*, extracted a promise from Calvi that the ghost companies would repay their debts by 13 June.

Pressures on Calvi were also building up outside the bank. Since his release from prison, the Bank of Italy had been bombarding the Ambrosiano chairman with letters demanding that he explain what he was doing overseas. Calvi, however, kept most of the letters to himself rather than sharing them with his board of directors. Calvi's rationale was that the letters were marked "confidential" and addressed to him personally!

Exasperated by Calvi's refusal to provide information, the Bank of Italy decided to take more direct action. In February inspectors were dispatched to Peru to find out what Banco Andino was doing. When they arrived, though, they found the local banking authorities unwilling to help them. 'They were not welcomed very warmly by the Peruvian officials,' says an Italian official. Treasury Minister Andreatta is more blunt. The Peruvians, he says, 'treated them like criminals'.

Yet another regulatory agency was losing patience with Calvi: CONSOB (Commissione Nazionale sulle Società e la Borsa), which supervises the stock market and listed companies. CONSOB had been created after the Sindona collapse in an effort to clean up the stock-market and improve standards of financal disclosure. Guido Rossi, the head of the agency, felt strongly that Ambrosiano should list its shares on the Milan exchange – rather than being traded on the 'restricted market' – since this would force it to disclose more information to shareholders. Listing would, for example, oblige the bank to publish consolidated accounts and appoint independent auditors. For about a year, says Rossi, Calvi resisted these pressures because 'he was aware that CONSOB's controls would increase. He was very much afraid of being asked to prepare a consolidated balance sheet.'

Rossi recalls one meeting with Calvi in which the banker claimed that it would take a year for the Bank of Italy to approve a certain change in Ambrosiano's by-laws that was a precondition to listing. In Calvi's presence, Rossi picked up the phone and called Governor Ciampi, who immediately contradicted Calvi, saying that approval of the change would take only a few weeks. The Governor then added: 'Be careful of Calvi, he's a liar.' Rossi replied: 'I know.'

Calvi finally gave in to CONSOB's pressure on 25 January. He agreed to apply for a listing on the Milan exchange and appoint the accountants

Coopers & Lybrand to prepare consolidated accounts and conduct an audit. Though the listing would take place in May, the shareholders would only reap the benefits of the tougher accounting and auditing standards the following year, since they would apply to the bank's 1982 accounts.

Calvi was also attracting the attention of several members of parliament. Since 1980, a parliamentary commission had been investigating the Sindona scandal, and some of the witnesses spoke of Calvi's dealings with the Sicilian banker. Another parliamentary commission was probing the P2 scandal, which threatened to uncover further damaging information about the Ambrosiano chairman. In characteristic fashion, Calvi responded to embarrassing questions with sweeping denials. When he testified before the Sindona panel in December 1981, he claimed he had never been 'a partner of Sindona'.

De Benedetti's hasty departure from Ambrosiano was followed by new disclosures about Calvi's dealings. The Olivetti chief told the press of some of the disturbing rumours he had picked up during his two months at the bank. De Benedetti's comments prompted two respected left-wing Members of Parliament, Gustavo Minervini and Luigi Spaventa, to pose questions to the government about Calvi from the floor of Parliament. Why, they asked, had the Bank of Italy not removed Calvi from the chairmanship of Banco Ambrosiano?

In February, the Bank of Italy decided to bypass Calvi and appeal to Ambrosiano's board of directors. A letter was sent demanding that each director 'declare that he is personally and fully aware of the foreign structure of the bank', and satisfied of his ability to supervise both the Italian and foreign subsidiaries.

When the letter was read to the board of Ambrosiano on 17 February many of the directors were shocked, not by the suggestion that Calvi had been engaging in questionable activities overseas, but by the insulting implication that the board was not doing its job. The minutes of the meeting record that one member, Giuseppe Prisco, said the Bank of Italy's letter caused him 'disconcertion and regret' since its requests 'appear unjustified, inopportune and offensive...' The minutes go on to say that every board member agreed with Prisco's remarks: 'The members of the board, for their part, declare that not only have no obstacles ever been put in their way... but, on the contrary, they have always received the maximum collaboration – at every level – in carrying out their functions.' A copy of the portion of the minutes containing these comments was then sent to the Bank of Italy – each page signed by every director present.

The annual general meeting of Banco Ambrosiano was held on 17 and 18 April. 'Calvi dominated it completely,' recalls union leader Gianni Bombacci. 'It's very difficult to criticise when the bank is always paying higher and higher dividends.' There were, to be sure, a few murmers of discontent because of the controversies surrounding Calvi. One woman shareholder stood up and said: 'As a Catholic, I'm worried about the image of Ambrosiano.' Another, more typical, shareholder commented: 'Forget it. Just look at the accounts – all the rest is gossip.'

Roberto Rosone was also worried about Ambrosiano and he was tempted to resign. But Calvi talked him out of it. Rosone said later that he stayed out of loyalty to the bank that had employed him since he was a teenager. Indeed, Rosone's whole life was bound up with Ambrosiano. He even lived in an apartment belonging to the bank, located above a branch he had once managed.

On Tuesday 27 April, Rosone was walking by that branch when he was approached by Danilo Abbruciati, a Roman gangster. Abbruciati pulled out a 6.35 calibre pistol and shot Rosone in the legs. Before he could fire again he was shot and killed by the 357 Magnum carried by the banker's bodyguard.

Rosone survived the attack and spent some weeks recuperating in a private clinic. Calvi visited him there and said he believed the gunman had been hired by 'enemies' of Ambrosiano. 'They want to intimidate us,' said Calvi, 'so they can take over the bank.' He later told the press: 'By striking at Rosone, they probably meant to strike at the bank, threatening its people.'

19

Billion-Dollar Deal

In the spring of 1982, Calvi showed that he fully deserved his nickname – 'the man with the eyes of ice'. In spite of the mounting pressures on him from the Bank of Italy, CONSOB and Parliament, he seemed as unflappable as ever. At the time of the annual meeting, one newspaper said: 'His self-control is remarkable. Today he seems as forceful and determined as ever to run things his way whatever the talk of his demise.'

But the banker's cool demeanour was every bit as misleading as his bank's image of solidity. Behind that stolid mask was an increasingly frightened and desperate man. His daughter recalls that in April and May he became 'more and more agitated and...very tired. He would arrive home very late, eat a mouthful and immediately go to bed, his face very tired.' Clara Calvi who had returned to Milan in March after several months abroad, says that his morale had deteriorated sharply: 'He would throw himself on the bed trembling and sweating, and say: "I feel that I'm in danger and I'm afraid for you, the children and for myself."'

Calvi's fears about his family's safety again prompted him to urge Clara and Anna to leave Italy. 'My father said that our presence put him in a state of anxiety because of the danger that he knew was around,' Anna says. Clara gave in to his pressures, but Anna resisted, arguing that she had to finish her university studies. Clara Calvi recalls that as she left Italy in mid-May, her husband told her: 'They're killing me. Perhaps we won't see each other again.'

In addition to his concerns about his family's safety, Calvi was still haunted by the financial plight of Ambrosiano and his own legal problems. Of the latter, Roberto Rosone has said: 'He had an insane fear of returning to prison.' Solutions to both had to be found within weeks. He had promised the head of Banco Andino that the ghost companies would repay their debts by 13 June and Marcinkus had told him that the patronage letters would expire around the same time. After several delays, the appeal against his conviction was scheduled for 21 June.

Since December, Flavio Carboni had been the almost constant companion of Calvi, acting as the banker's chief 'fixer'. Carboni, sometimes working with Francesco Pazienza, visited contacts in Rome and was involved in various schemes to rescue Ambrosiano. Among the people approached in the lobbying campaign were the following.

Giuseppe ('Beppe') Pisanu, Under Secretary of the Treasury was, like Carboni, a Sardinian. Carboni presumably hoped that Pisanu would use his influence to curb the Bank of Italy's pressures on Ambrosiano. One favour Pisanu performed for the banker was to reassure worried Members of Parliament about the government's supervision of the bank. In early June, Pisanu acted as the government's spokesman in answering parliamentary questions about Ambrosiano. He said that everything is under control.

Armando Corona was 'Grand Master' of Italian freemasonry and another Sardinian. In March 1982, he was elected Grand Master after promising to clean up the image of the masons in the wake of the P2 scandal. Nonetheless, he had five meetings with Calvi to discuss ways of helping the banker.

Wilfredo Vitalone was a leading Rome lawyer and brother of a prominent Christian Democratic politician. Vitalone has been accused of taking a three billion lire payment from Pazienza's partner, Maurizio Mazzotta, to be used to 'buy' magistrates.

Carlo Caracciolo was one of the most powerful publishers in Italy as part-owner of the weekly magazine *L'Espresso,* and the Rome daily *La Repubblica.* He was also a partner with Carboni in a daily newspaper in Sardinia. Carboni arranged a series of meeting between Calvi and Caracciolo, in the hope of curbing press attacks on the banker.

Carboni's lobbying campaign reached a high point on 4 May, when he held a reception at his Rome apartment, bringing together several of his contacts. The guests included publisher Caracciolo and masonic leader Corona, as well as Monsignor Hilary Franco, a Vatican official. The most prominent guest was Ciriaco De Mita, the newly elected leader of the Christian Democratic party. De Mita's presence in Carboni's home was just as ironic as Corona's. For he, like the masonic leader, had been elected to reform his organisation. De Mita's predecessor, Flaminio Piccoli, had been criticised for publicly defending Calvi during the banker's trial, and yet the new party leader was now being entertained by Calvi's lobbyist.

Carboni's and Pazienza's efforts to rally support for Calvi coincided with work on various schemes to rescue Ambrosiano. One such plan may have been conceived as early as the spring of 1981. Francesco Pazienza claims that, shortly after Calvi's arrest, the banker asked him to find buyers for about 12 per cent of Ambrosiano (owned by the ghost companies). The idea was that the money raised by selling the stock could be used to repay the ghost companies' debts.

If such a deal were to succeed, Calvi could not afford to let Ambrosiano's stock price drop. For years Calvi (and previous chairmen of Banco Ambrosiano) had been able to manipulate the bank's stock price because it was traded on the so-called 'restricted market'. This meant that the bank itself executed all buy and sell orders. At times when the stock price was dropping, Ambrosiano employees could simply tell potential sellers that they would have to wait a while for their orders to be processed. In January 1981, however, Calvi caved in to demands from CONSOB, the stock-market watchdog agency, that the bank apply for a full listing on the Milan stock exchange. Calvi knew that when the listing took place in May, he would lose much of his ability to manipulate the stock. And so, after agreeing to the listing, he secretly began to purchase Ambrosiano shares in the market in order to prop up the price. Between January and the spring, 53 billion lire (about $40 million) was spent this way.

Even if Calvi could prevent the stock from dropping in price, the kind of deal Pazienza has described, selling between 10 and 15 per cent of Ambrosiano's shares to repay the debts of the ghost companies, would be an extremely difficult, if not impossible, operation. The ghost companies owed more than $1 billion to Ambrosiano's foreign subsidiaries. Anyone who paid $1 billion for, say, 15 per cent of Ambrosiano would be spending about $133 per share – more than three times the highest price the stock had ever reached in the market (50,000 lire, or about $40 a share). A price of $133 a share would also imply that the whole bank was worth about $6.7 billion – a preposterous figure. To put that figure in perspective, the stock-market value of Bank of America was about $3 billion. Yet Bank of America was the largest bank in the world with total assets of $121 billion (about five times the combined assets of Ambrosiano and its two largest 'sister' banks in Italy). Michel Leemans says bluntly: 'I think anybody who wanted to buy 15 per cent of Ambrosiano for $1 billion would be nuts.'

But this did not stop Calvi from trying. Why he felt he could do such a deal is open to several interpretations. One possibility is that Calvi, in his desperation to rescue the bank, had simply lost touch with reality, convincing himself that it was worth far more than it actually was. Another possibility is that Calvi believed certain potential buyers would be willing to pay an exorbitant price from *non-economic motives*. For example, the Vatican, or individuals allied to the Vatican, might be willing to pay a steep price in order to curry favour with the Church by preventing it from being embroiled in another Sindona-type scandal. Another possible motive would be to gain control of the Rizzoli group, so as to use the newspapers and magazines that it owned as political tools.

Whatever was going on in Calvi's mind, there is no question that he tried a number of rescue schemes in 1981 and 1982, including the following – the Arab deal, the Pazienza deal, the Carboni deal, the 'superholding', the Fiorini plan and the Opus Dei deal.

The 'Arab' deal involved tapping Arab capital by merging Banco Ambrosiano Overseas with an Arab-backed bank, Artoc Bank and Trust, which also had its headquarters in the Bahamas. (The scheme was suggested by accountants Coopers & Lybrand, who audited the accounts of both banks.)

The founder and chairman of Artoc was Peter de Savary, a young British businessman with the reputation of a playboy. In October 1980 he had founded the St James's Club in the heart of fashionable London. One purpose of the club was to 'introduce his Arab financier friends into London high society', according to the magazine *Il Mondo*. Members were entitled to stay at the club, and Clara Calvi spent much of her time there in late 1981 and early 1982 – after her husband had sent her out of Italy because of his fears for her safety. De Savary's other claim to fame was that he had organised a British bid to win the America's Cup yacht race. (When the race was held in mid-1983, de Savary won considerable publicity, but not the cup.)

In early 1981, Banco Ambrosiano Overseas purchased 20 per cent of the stock of Artoc Bank. In 1981 a plan was conceived to boost BAO's stake to 50 per cent and then merge the two banks, forming a new institution to be called Artoc Ambrosiano. At the time, Calvi said: 'We are putting a foot in the Arab financial world.' Calvi may have felt that the rich Arab backers of Artoc could then be persuaded to help the Ambrosiano group out of its financial straits. One of the Arabs on the board of Artoc, Libyan banker Abdulla Saudi, already had considerable involvement in Italy. When Libyan strongman Muammar Qaddafi bought 10 per cent of the Fiat motor company in 1976, Abdulla Saudi joined the Fiat board as Qaddafi's representative.

In early 1982, however, the Bank of Italy vetoed the deal. And, when Artoc later increased its capital, BAO did not participate, letting its stake in Artoc drop to 10 per cent.

The Pazienza deal is based on his claims to have approached a wide range of potential buyers for the Ambrosiano stock owned by the ghost companies. In early 1982, he says, he was negotiating with a consortium of American, Saudi and (expatriate) Iranian investors. He says his partner was Robert Armao, formerly an aide to the Rockefellers and, later, to the Shah of Iran. (After the Shah left Iran in January 1979, Armao acted as his personal assistant.) 'Armao, Calvi and I met in February [1982] in Rome,' says Pazienza, adding that, by June, he was on the verge of closing the deal.

The details of the Carboni deal are not very clear; it may not even have been a rescue operation. About all that can be said is that Calvi and Carboni discussed a large financial transaction in early 1982 with several Swiss and South American businessmen.

One scheme, known as the 'superholding', envisaged merging the Ambrosiano group with the Pesenti group, the industrial and financial empire controlled by 'Catholic' businessman Carlo Pesenti. The two groups were already closely related: Pesenti was one of the largest shareholders in Ambrosiano, one of the largest borrowers from the bank, and sat on Ambrosiano's board.

The apparent rationale for the 'superholding' was that both Calvi and Pesenti would be seriously hurt if the other collapsed: the value of Pesenti's Ambrosiano shares would be wiped out and he would lose a prime source of credit. Ambrosiano would suffer if Pesenti could not service his debts. If the two groups were merged they could perhaps prop up each other.

The Fiorini plan was initiated not by Calvi, but by Florio Fiorini, finance director of ENI, the state-owned oil company. ENI had lent some $200 million to the Ambrosiano group and thus stood to suffer huge losses if the bank collapsed. In the spring of 1982 Fiorini conceived a plan to protect ENI's loans by taking over La Centrale in partnership with other interested parties (which reportedly included the Vatican and the Pesenti group). Fiorini later explained that he wanted to save the bank by turning its creditors into shareholders.

Since his arrest in May 1981, Calvi had put enormous pressure on the Vatican, seeking help with both his legal problems and the financial plight of Ambrosiano. While he was in prison, Calvi told his family that the questionable share dealings for which he was being tried had actually been done on behalf of IOR. Proof of the Vatican bank's involvement, he said, was in documents in the possession of Banca del Gottardo – which the bank would not release without IOR's permission because of Swiss bank secrecy laws. Calvi also claimed that IOR, as his main financial partner, was involved in his ghost company scheme and thus under an obligation to help the bank.

Whether or not these claims were true, Archbishop Marcinkus did help Calvi buy time by granting the 'patronage letters' in September 1981. But he apparently refused to go further than that. And so Calvi, with the help of Flavio Carboni, mounted an aggressive lobbying campaign with other Vatican officials.

In January 1982 Carboni approached attorney Luigi D'Agostini, said to be 'well-introduced' in Vatican circles. The lawyer contacted Cardinal Pietro Palazzini, a senior Vatican official. Palazzini said he would try to help. But he failed, saying that, even for him, IOR was 'impenetrable.'

An approach was then made to Monsignor Hilary Franco, a man said to be close to both Marcinkus and the Pope. Over a period of months, about ten meetings were held with him. Exactly what was discussed is a matter of some dispute. Calvi claimed to his family that he was working on a rescue plan that involved a secretive Catholic organisation called Opus Dei. Founded in Spain in 1928, Opus Dei's members now number more than 70,000 in eighty-seven countries. Though it claims to do nothing more than promote charitable works – universities, hospitals and the like – Spaniards say that it has enjoyed considerable economic and political clout in Spain, particularly before the death of General Franco. Critics claim that it uses its power to promote an authoritarian, right-wing ideology, prompting them to call it 'the holy Mafia'.

Calvi told his family that the Opus Dei deal would work as follows: the organisation would purchase the Ambrosiano stock owned by the ghost companies, thus saving the Holy See from the financial losses (and damage to its public image) it would suffer if the bank collapsed. In exchange Opus Dei would obtain various privileges within the Church. For example, it might take over the running of IOR, or perhaps move the Vatican's foreign policy more to the right.

There was, however, opposition to the plan inside the Vatican, Calvi said. One opponent was reportedly Cardinal Agostino Casaroli, the Vatican's Secretary of State – roughly equivalent to the Pope's prime minister.

Although Opus Dei and Archbishop Marcinkus have both denied that such a deal was discussed, it is widely known that Palazzini is an Opus Dei supporter and that Monsignor Franco is the Cardinal's protégé. Whatever the case, Calvi did spend months seeking help in the Vatican. And when help did not come, he began threatening to reveal damaging information about the Church. Anna Calvi says she eavesdropped on a conversation between her father and Carboni one weekend in May: 'I was curious to hear what my father and Carboni said during the long conversations they frequently had, so I hid myself behind the door. I heard my father and Carboni speaking in loud voices, discussing the Vatican. In particular I heard my father tell Carboni that he had to make the Vatican understand that the priests had to face their obligations, because otherwise he would tell everything he knew.' Her father said: 'Tell them if they don't do what I want, I'm going to tell everything about everybody.'

In late May, Calvi was almost always in Rome. 'He said he was meeting with Carboni and...continuously going to the Vatican,' says Anna. At one point her father said: 'I'm going to the Vatican tomorrow. I'll sit there and I won't move until they've decided to do what I want.'

Pope John Paul II went on a tour of Britain in late May and, as always, Marcinkus was the organiser and security chief for the trip. While Marcinkus was away, Carboni met the Archbishop's deputy at IOR, Luigi Mennini. 'The meeting with Mennini didn't settle anything,' according to Carboni. 'In the afternoon, I visited his [Calvi's] home. He was crying, almost delirious, and saying: "Everything's going badly, everything will collapse."'

When Marcinkus returned from the papal tour, he phoned Calvi and told him angrily to stop looking for help in the Vatican – that it was a waste of time.

The banker, however, refused to be deterred. Instead, he renewed his threats. According to Calvi, Marcinkus had provided money to Solidarity, the banned Polish trade union movement – information that if made public could provoke reprisals against the Vatican from the Soviet bloc. In a conversation with Carboni, Calvi said that he told Marcinkus: 'If it comes out that you are giving money to Solidarity, there won't be a stone left of St Peter's.' Calvi had said the same thing to Monsignor Pasquale Macchi, a Vatican official who had served as personal secretary to Pope Paul VI. 'I had a conversation with Father Macchi at home,' Calvi told Carboni. 'I had to kick him in the ass. "There won't be a stone left," I told him.'

At times, Calvi was tempted to give up hope. 'I'm against a gradual wasting away,' he once told Carboni. 'If we must, it's better to let Banco Ambrosiano crash.'

In some ways the lobbying campaign was making things worse, by draining more and more money from Ambrosiano's coffers. In the year following his arrest, Calvi is believed to have paid out tens of millions of dollars for 'protection' (on top of money he had previously paid to Gelli and others). Carboni's assistance apparently did not come cheaply. Anna Calvi remembers hearing the Sardinian middleman tell her father: 'I'm going to help you, but I want you to make me the richest man in Italy.'

'Everyone tried to extort money from him by saying that they were his friends,' says a businessman who knew Calvi. 'He was in a position where everyone could take a piece of him. He was a prisoner of the machine he had created.' Clara Calvi later described her husband as 'the most exploited, threatened and blackmailed man'.

One afternoon Anna Calvi saw her father take an old revolver from a closet and begin cleaning it. 'He put it together and he showed it to me,' she says. 'I asked him why he took it out, something I had never seen him do before, and he answered: "If they come, I'll shoot them", and he showed me how to grip the pistol.' When she asked who might try to kill him, he said that 'there are people who wanted to stop him from closing the deal, and he knew that these people were ready to kill in order to stop him.' He said: 'For that amount of money, people would kill.'

Calvi packed the pistol in his large black briefcase, the one containing confidential papers about his deals which was always with him. He told his daughter: 'I'm going to take the gun with me wherever I go.'

20

Rebellion

The lobbying and the negotiating, the pleading and threatening continued through the month of May. Only a few weeks remained before Calvi's appeal and the expiration of the patronage letters. But on the last day of the month, the deadline was abruptly pulled back.

Calvi had received many letters from the Bank of Italy, and he had usually managed to avoid complying with their demands for information. This one was different. It was dated 31 May 1982, on stationery headed 'Bank of Italy, Milan Branch', and it ran to four typed pages. Although it was addressed to Calvi, it demanded that the board of directors explain Ambrosiano's foreign activities. Specifically, the letter stated that the Bank of Italy wanted details of $1.4 billion in loans made by Ambrosiano's subsidiaries in Peru, Nicaragua and the Bahamas – most of which were loans to the ghost companies. The letter was to be read to the board of directors, the text of the letter was to be inserted in the minutes of the meeting and each director was to take personal responsibility for explaining the questionable loans.

Calvi is believed to have received the letter on Friday 4 June, and he immediately grasped its implications: the central bank had finally closed in on him. He would have to work faster than ever.

Calvi returned to his apartment in Milan that evening in 'a highly nervous state', his daughter recalls. He stayed up late that night, waiting for a phone call from Carboni.

On Saturday, Calvi woke Anna at about 5.00 or 6.00 a.m. and told her: 'The situation is coming to a head and I can't stay here any more. I'm going to have to continue my work outside Italy, in order to be safe.' He added that he would probably be sending her out of the country as well, and told her to pack her bags immediately. 'From his tone, I could tell it was useless to try to argue with him, so I packed my bags while he packed two suitcases for himself.' The luggage was loaded into Anna's car and the two set off for the country home in Drezzo.

On Sunday, Anna drove to the nearby Swiss town of Morcote, where she made a hotel reservation for herself, then drove to Milan with the luggage.

On Monday 7 June, fourteen directors of Banco Ambrosiano gathered in the fourth-floor boardroom. It was a rather distinguished group of men, including industrialists, property developers, and prominent lawyers. Some had only known the chairman for a short time. At least one, businessman Luigi Rotelli, had met Calvi during the war. If there was one important characteristic they shared, it was this: demonstrated loyalty to Calvi. For years, the board had ratified his decisions and stood by him in spite of the controversies that swirled around him. Their support did not waver even when he was sentenced to prison. When the Bank of Italy suggested in February that Calvi had failed to inform them of the bank's foreign operations, they reacted indignantly.

But on that Monday something was different. A change came over them, and the man most responsible was Orazio Bagnasco, who had expressed so much faith in Calvi when he joined the board in January, taking De Benedetti's place as a deputy chairman. When Calvi read the Bank of Italy's letter to the board, Bagnasco asked to see documents explaining the questionable loans – he would even like to take them out of the bank to study.

Calvi flatly refused. No documents, he said, would leave the bank. The question was put to a vote and, for the first time in his nearly seven years as chairman, Calvi was outvoted, by ten to four.

The meeting ended at about 6 p.m. Calvi left the bank and met Carboni. Over dinner at the banker's apartment the two men discussed Calvi's problems with the Vatican bank. Before Carboni left, Calvi said: 'Maybe I'll take a vacation with you in Sardinia.' He then asked his daughter to give Carboni the two bags that Calvi had packed on Saturday.

On Tuesday morning 8 June, Calvi told his daughter once again that she had to leave Italy. He added that he would probably leave as well. 'If things get better,' he said, 'I'll call you. Or else I'll go abroad and continue the operation in hiding. If things get worse, I'll start to tell everything I know.'

Calvi left his Milan apartment at 9 a.m. on Wednesday, telling her: 'If you don't hear from me for a while, don't worry, because I have to travel.' Anna then went to Varese, to the home of the parents of her boyfriend, Vittorio Senso. 'Vittorio and I [then] went to Switzerland, to the hotel in Morcote that I had reserved.' From the hotel, she phoned her father at the bank. 'He said there was a good possibility that he was going away from Italy, but he was not sure.'

That evening, Calvi dined with four financiers at the headquarters of Banco Ambrosiano. The meeting had been set up by Francesco Micheli, the adviser to Carlo De Benedetti who had been involved in the Olivetti chief's stormy 'marriage' to Calvi. The other dinner guests were Florio Fiorini, the finance director of ENI; Pierre Moussa, who had been chairman of Banque Paribas, until it was nationalised by French President François Mitterrand; and Karl Kahane, an Austrian businessman. The purpose of the meeting was to discuss a deal in which Moussa, Kahane and Fiorini would purchase Ambrosiano's foreign subsidiaries.

Calvi showed little interest in the proposal; he appeared distracted throughout the conversation. He said vaguely that his guests could meet with him again some time in the future. At around 11 p.m. Calvi suggested that Fiorini get in touch with executives of Ambrosiano's foreign department, said good evening, and disappeared. As Micheli has described the scene to the Milan newspaper *Il Giornale Nuovo:* 'He did it in such a rapid manner that he was already out of the hall when the others were still getting up to say goodbye to him. I managed to catch up with him in front of the elevator. In an instant, he had already vanished inside.' After witnessing Calvi's odd departure, Kahane turned to his dinner companions and said: 'Like the Devil, he's disappeared toward Hell.'

If Calvi was distracted during the dinner, it was probably because his mind was on the trip he had probably already decided to take.

On Thursday morning, 10 June, Calvi met his lawyers in Milan to discuss the appeal against his conviction. In the evening he flew to Rome, arriving at about 8 p.m. His chauffeur noticed that the banker appeared particularly tense during the ride from the airport; he was twisting his moustache, something he always did when he was concentrating. At about 9 p.m. the car arrived at Calvi's apartment, in Via Collegio Capranica, in what Romans call the 'historic centre' of the city. Calvi asked Tito to disconnect the alarm system, leaving on just the intercom. 'I'm waiting for friends,' he said. His last instruction to his driver was: 'Wake me up tomorrow morning at 6.30.' Tito left.

Calvi's driver returned on Friday morning; he found the apartment empty and reported that the banker was missing.

107

21

'A Worldwide Scandal'

Calvi had not told his wife or son of his plans to leave Italy, and they first learned of his disappearance from Francesco Pazienza, who phoned them in Washington at about 5 p.m. local time on Friday 11 June. 'Pazienza made an hysterical call to me,' says Clara Calvi, 'saying that Roberto was missing. "Clara," he said, "they can't find him."' Carlo Calvi said he feared 'something terrible' had happened.

Although the banker's wife and son did not hear from him, he did phone three people that Friday morning and his tone suggested that, wherever he was, he had not been kidnapped. He spoke to his secretary Graziella Corrocher, and asked her to buy him a round-trip Rome-Milan plane ticket. He rang Luigi Mennini of the Vatican bank to apologise for having missed the 8.30 a.m. appointment they had arranged for that day. And, around lunchtime, the banker phoned his deputy, Roberto Rosone. 'I told him,' says Rosone, 'that the Rome office was worried because they hadn't been able to contact him. They didn't know where he was. He told me to tell them to stay calm and not to worry, because he was involved in secret negotiations.'

Carlo Calvi woke up at about 3 or 4 a.m. Washington time on Saturday 12 June and phoned his father's lawyers in Rome for information. They said they had filed a statement with magistrates in Rome that Calvi was missing. Later that day Calvi contacted Anna and told her she should let the rest of the family know that he was safe.

The Bank of Italy was informed of Calvi's disappearance that Saturday. It decided to send inspectors to the bank on Monday and it ordered Ambrosiano's board of directors to hold a special meeting as soon as possible. On Sunday 13 June Roberto Rosone cut short a vacation in Sardinia and flew to Milan for the special board meeting. The bank's other deputy chairman, Orazio Bagnasco, came in from Venice.

Instead of coming to grips with the bank's problems – Calvi's disappearance and the questionable loans mentioned in the Bank of

Italy's letter – the two men squabbled over who would be 'acting chairman' during Calvi's absence. In a Milan half deserted during the hot Sunday afternoon, the battle raged for hours. Rosone had installed himself at Ambrosiano's headquarters in Via Clerici, while Bagnasco was at the luxury hotel he owned, the Principe e Savoia. Acting as a Kissinger-style intermediary, shuttling between the bank and the hotel, was publisher Giuseppe Ciarrapicco, a friend of Bagnasco. In the end Bagnasco was forced to concede defeat. The bank's statutes stated clearly that the acting chairman was to be the deputy chairman with the most seniority: in other words Rosone.

On Monday 14 June, six inspectors from the Bank of Italy arrived at Ambrosiano's headquarters, bearing a letter from Governor Ciampi demanding copies of various records. Calvi's disappearance caused some of the small depositors to panic and withdraw their savings from the bank. Most, however, were calm. The bank's shareholders were not so sanguine, and the share price dropped by 12 per cent that day. Shares of companies in the Pesenti group, which was closely related to Ambrosiano, suffered as well. In Rome, Archbishop Paul Marcinkus evidently decided it was a good time to distance himself from the fugitive banker, and resigned from the board of Banco Ambrosiano Overseas, the Bahamas subsidiary.

On Tuesday, Michel Leemans, head of La Centrale, felt that the top executives of Ambrosiano were confused and indecisive – a repetition of what had happened a year earlier when Calvi was arrested. So he decided to do what he could to help. Leemans contacted the international department of Ambrosiano and learned that the single largest debtor appeared to be the Vatican bank, since it had issued letters backing up more than $1 billion worth of loans to shadowy companies in Panama and Liechtenstein.

Leemans and Rosone contacted officials of Banco Andino in Peru and the Luxembourg holding company to obtain copies of the 'patronage letters'. Leemans then urged Rosone to go to Rome and demand that IOR repay the debts.

But the 'acting chairman' appeared to be immobilised by fear. 'I have no plane ticket,' Rosone said. When Leemans brushed aside that excuse, Rosone said he had no hotel reservation. By the afternoon Rosone finally agreed to make an appointment for the following morning with Luigi Mennini and Pellegrino De Strobel, Marcinkus's deputies. (The Archbishop would not be in the office, they had been told, since he had just returned from a foreign trip.)

On Wednesday morning, 16 June, Rosone and Leemans left the Grand Hotel in Rome for their appointment in the Vatican, when

Rosone again got cold feet. 'We were going out of the hotel at about 7 o'clock,' Leemans recalls, 'and Rosone said he wanted to go back to Milan.'

Ambrosiano's acting chairman had every reason to be frightened of the encounter, since it was to confirm his worst fears. When he and Leemans showed the patronage letters to Mennini and de Strobel, the Vatican bankers responded by showing them the secret letter from Calvi. It was, they said, a 'counter letter', which absolved IOR of any responsibility for the ghost companies' debts.

As Rosone later described the scene: 'They argued – as if they were talking about tram tickets – that none of it was true, that the patronage letters were only given to Calvi as a favour. "We have your counter letter," they said.'

Leemans then proposed a compromise solution. 'Let's find a way to resolve this situation because it will be a big scandal,' he says he told Mennini and de Strobel. He suggested that the Vatican bank take responsibility for the ghost companies' debts, adding that he would arrange for IOR to borrow an equivalent amount from international banks. 'They said they would think about it,' Leemans says.

Rosone, however, exploded at the IOR officials: 'Don't you realise that this is a fraud, that agreements like this are not admissible? Do you realise that in the future public opinion won't be able to – won't know how to – distinguish between IOR, the Vatican, the Pope?' He continued: 'There are hundreds of millions of Catholics in the world – how will they distinguish between IOR and the Vatican? This,' he told them, 'will be a worldwide scandal.'

Roberto Calvi, chairman and managing director, Banco Ambrosiano. His cold personality earned him the nickname 'The Man with the Eyes of Ice'.

The 30-year-old Calvi is a man on his way to the top. His superiors at Banco Ambrosiano are impressed by his drive and intelligence and reward him with a series of promotions.

Cavalry Lieutenant Calvi is ordered to report for duty in Verona on 28 July 1941.

F O N O G R A M M A A Mano

Verona li 28 Luglio 1941   ore 8

N 717

    DAL COMANDO DEPOSITO LANCIERI DI NOVARA

    AL COMANDO III GRUPPO CARRI "L"

        Pregasi disporre che il Sottotenente Calvi

Oggi alle ore 11 si trovi presso questo Comando per

prestare giuramento.

                IL COLONNELLO COMANDANTE
                   Luigo Scozia

EVE. . . . .   TRASMETTE. . . . .

Before Calvi became chairman, Banco Ambrosiano was regarded as an old-fashioned, provincial, Catholic bank. Calvi turned it into the centrepiece of an international financial empire.

A shy and isolated man, Calvi was only comfortable with his immediate family. In this photograph, taken by daughter Anna, he relaxes with his wife at their country home.

Calvi rose to the top with the help of Michele Sindona, a Sicilian banker who had close links with the Church and the Mafia.

Licio Gelli appeared to be nothing more than an obscure businessman. In reality, he was one of the most powerful men in Italy, leader of a secret masonic lodge called 'P2'. Calvi was just one of hundreds of members of an organisation that has been called a 'state within the state'.

'Villa Wanda', Gelli's home in Arezzo, was named after his wife. When Gelli's home and office were searched, he fled Italy and the P2 scandal exploded. Among his papers was information that proved highly damaging to Calvi.

Obsessed by secret societies and 'hidden power', Calvi often turned to mysterious 'fixers' for help. One of them was Francesco Pazienza, who boasted of connections with intelligence agencies.

Flavio Carboni was Calvi's frequent companion during the last six months of the banker's life. He reportedly told Calvi: 'I'll help you, but I want you to make me the richest man in Italy.' Carboni organised Calvi's journey to London – the last trip the banker was to make.

Calvi enters the courtroom for his 1981 trial on charges of illegally exporting more than $20 million from Italy. While in prison, Calvi attempted – or pretended to attempt – suicide by slashing a wrist and taking an overdose of pills.

Right: 17 June 1982 – an ambulance carries the lifeless body of Calvi's secretary, Graziella Corrocher, from the headquarters of Banco Ambrosiano. She had plunged to her death from a fourth-floor window of the bank, leaving behind a note denouncing Calvi.

The following morning Calvi's body was found hanging by the neck from scaffolding under Blackfriars Bridge in the City of London. His pockets contained 12 lb of bricks and concrete, and nearly $15,000 in assorted currencies.

Above: Calvi's family successfully appealed for the suicide verdict to be quashed and for a new coroner's inquest to be held. At the new inquest, in June 1983, Clara Calvi and her children all testified.

Right: Two of the last people known to have seen Calvi alive were Silvano Vittor, a smuggler from Trieste, and Michaela Kleinszig, Vittor's Austrian girlfriend.

Left: Archbishop Paul Marcinkus ran the Vatican's bank in addition to his duties as organiser of papal trips. He is shown here with Pope John Paul II. Though Marcinkus was one of Calvi's closest business partners, he refused to rescue Banco Ambrosiano from collapse.

The police photograph of Calvi's corpse appeared in The Sunday Times *and* L'Espresso. *Professor Keith Simpson, who performed the autopsy, said Calvi appeared to have committed suicide. In July 1982, the jury in a coroner's inquest agreed.*

22

Final Trip

Michele Sindona has often complained that Calvi created his financial empire by copying Sindona's techniques. It also appears that Calvi imitated his one-time mentor when he made his final attempt to save himself and his bank.

Sindona vanished from New York on 2 August 1979 just before he was to stand trial on charges stemming from the collapse of the Franklin National Bank. Calvi disappeared from Rome on 10 June 1982, shortly before he was to appear in the appeals court. The purpose of Sindona's trip was to acquire material that he could use in his defence. That also appears to have been one of the purposes of Calvi's trip. The parallels do not end there. Carlo Calvi's remark that he feared 'something terrible has happened' is reminiscent of what Sindona's son Nino said after his father disappeared: 'I fear my father is already dead.'

Whatever his reasons for leaving Italy, Calvi made a long and complicated journey. Many of his movements have been confirmed by the police, some of them are in dispute – since the credibility of certain witnesses has been questioned. The following reconstruction is based on sources identified in the text or in notes at the end of the book.

Thursday 10 June
After arriving at his Rome apartment and sending away his chauffeur, Calvi has a snack and makes some phone calls. One call is to his wife and son in Washington, to confirm that Carlo will attend a banking conference in Los Angeles. 'He was glad I would be able to participate', Carlo recalls, 'and even happier that my mother would be coming with me.'

He then calls Flavio Carboni. He says he isn't feeling well and doesn't want to stay alone in his apartment. Carboni borrows the keys to a friend's home and takes Calvi there. Calvi then tells him: 'I need to stay alone for a while' and asks Carboni to find him a house in a quiet place, where no one will be able to find him.

111

Friday 11 June

Silvano Vittor is a 37-year-old man living in the Adriatic port of Trieste who earns his living by smuggling coffee into Yugoslavia in exchange for blue jeans to be sold in Italy. He has known Carboni for about two years. Vittor's girlfriend is Austrian, an attractive blonde in her early twenties named Michaela Kleinszig. About two years ago, Michaela's sister, a brunette named Manuela, became a mistress of Carboni. (The girls' first names are Italian because their mother is from Italy.)

When Vittor learned that Carboni knew Calvi, he asked his friend if the banker could give him a job, perhaps as a driver. 'I wanted to better myself,' Vittor later explained. Carboni helped him get in touch with Calvi, but nothing has come of it – until this morning.

At about 8 or 9 a.m. Calvi phones Vittor and asks the smuggler to meet him in Trieste later in the day. Calvi then gets into a Volkswagen Golf driven by Emilio Pellicani, one of Carboni's aides, and the two men head for Rome's Fiumicino Airport. Around mid-day, they board Alitalia flight 154 for Tessera Airport, just outside Venice. Calvi, wearing dark glasses, is unnoticed by another 'celebrity' on the plane: Tina Anselmi, chairman of the parliamentary commission probing the P2 scandal. Upon arrival, Pellicani rents a car and drives Calvi to Trieste. At about 6.15 p.m. they meet Silvano Vittor at the Hotel Savoy Excelsior there.

Shortly after the banker's arrival, Carboni's private plane (piloted by Paolo Uberti, a man whose name had appeared on Gelli's P2 lists) lands at Triestes's Ronchi dei Legionari airport. The three passengers are Carboni; an unidentified man with blond hair; and Ernesto Diotallevi, a reputed 'boss' of the Roman underworld. Diotallevi is carrying a small 'gift' for Calvi: a forged passport in the name of Gian Roberto Calvini, procured at a cost of several million lire. (Calvi's real passport is in the hands of the magistrates, since he is not permitted to leave the country while awaiting trial.)

Saturday 12 June

After travelling all night, Calvi arrives in Klagenfurt, Austria. There are two conflicting versions of how he made the trip. Vittor claims that he left Calvi at Trieste railway station the night before, with instructions on how to reach the Austrian town. Pellicani gives this version: Calvi was taken at night by motorboat to Yugoslavia and then driven through Yugoslavia to Austria.

Calvi arrives at a house near the airport, at number 40 Herzoghof Strasse, the home of the Kleinszig sisters and their father Stephan, a wealthy timber merchant. Calvi knocks on the door and Michaela answers. In what she has described as 'good German', the banker asks her if Carboni is in. No, she answers, but she thinks he is coming later in the day. Calvi asks if he can wait in the house for Carboni. 'I offered to find him a hotel,' Michaela says, 'but he insisted on staying here.'

Michaela finds the banker a comfortable chair where he can make some phone calls. One call is to his daughter Anna, who is in Switzerland with her boyfriend. 'At about 6 or 7 o'clock,' says Anna, 'I got a call from my father. He told me: "I'm in Austria, with a family, and I'm dead tired because I've travelled all night."' He instructs her to 'call Washington and tell Mamma and Carlo that all is well. If they want to know my whereabouts, tell them I'm in the home of friends. Don't tell anybody I'm in Austria.'

The conversation lasts about a half-hour and Anna notices that her father's mood seems much better than it did in Italy. 'Before leaving Italy, he was nervous,' she says. In that phone call, however, 'he spoke in a secure manner, unusual for him in those times.' Calvi mentioned the deal he was working on, and gave the impression that he was optimistic about its outcome. He used expressions like 'I think we can straighten everything out' and 'You'll see that things will work out.'

Anna soon phones her mother and brother to pass on the message that Calvi is safe. They tell her that they had learned of his disappearance the day before, when Pazienza phoned.

Michaela suggests that the banker take a nap in her sister's room since Manuela is in Italy with Carboni. Calvi accepts and sleeps until mid-day.

After his nap, Calvi eats some würstel, then a roast Michaela had bought at the airport restaurant. He then phones his daughter again. When Anna tells him that Pazienza has phoned the family he reacts angrily, saying he wants Pazienza to stop contacting his wife.

In the late afternoon, Carboni and Manuela Kleinszig arrive in Klagenfurt in Carboni's plane. In the evening, Calvi, Carboni, the Kleinszig sisters and their father dine at home.

Calvi appears unusually relaxed and sociable at dinner and starts to reminisce about the war. 'After a few glasses of wine,' says Michaela, 'Calvi began to tell us in German some stories about his war experiences in Russia. He said he had been lucky to survive, remembering the bitter cold. He also said that he never shot or killed anyone, that he detested wars and violence in general.'

Around midnight, Silvano Vittor arrives at the Kleinszig home.

Sunday 13 June

Calvi calls his wife and daughter, then goes out for lunch. He knows that his disappearance has been reported in Italy, and when he sees a car with

Italian licence plates he refuses to enter the restaurant.

After dinner in the Kleinszig home, Calvi is ready for the next leg of his trip. He asks Vittor to drive him to Innsbruck. They leave at about 10.15 p.m., in a cream-coloured Alfa Romeo belonging to Michaela.

Monday 14 June

It is a long drive – 450 kilometres, only 200 of them by motorway – and it lasts all night. During the journey they stop several times so that Calvi can make phone calls. Three or four are to his wife. At least one is to Carboni, to arrange a meeting for later in the day. At about 4 or 5 a.m. Calvi and Vittor arrive at Innsbruck and check into the Hotel Europa-Tyrol.

Later in the day Carboni and the Kleinszig sisters fly to Zurich, where they are met at the airport by Swiss businessman Hans Kunz.

Kunz is the latest of the long series of shadowy characters in Calvi's life. Described by a lawyer who knows him as a professional 'fixer', Kunz is reputedly involved in the oil trade and arms trafficking. He says he met Carboni in 1981 through 'personalities employed by Italian state companies' – possibly ENI, the state-owned oil company.

Carboni and the two girls check into the Hôtel Bar au Lac in Zurich. The girls go out shopping while Carboni stays in the room making dozens of phone calls. Hotel records show that, in the course of a one-day stay, calls are made to Austria, Italy, London, the United States, the Vatican and, curiously, Czechoslovakia. One local call made from the room is to the nearby hotel room of Ernesto Diotallevi, the reputed gangster who supplied Calvi with a forged passport on the previous Friday.

After sleeping until about 10 or 11 a.m. Calvi makes some more phone calls. He then tells Vittor that they will not be going to Switzerland as had originally been planned, but will instead be meeting Carboni and Kunz at the Austrian town of Bregenz, near the Swiss border.

Calvi and Vittor reach Bregenz at about 7 or 8 o'clock in the evening, and register at the Hotel Central. Calvi then phones his daughter and tells her she will be contacted by Hans Kunz, who should be able to find a place where she and her boyfriend Vittorio can stay in Switzerland. He adds that although Kunz will be able to help her, she should not trust him too much.

Calvi tells Vittor he is surprised that Carboni and Kunz have not yet reached Bregenz. They leave a message at the hotel and then go to a nearby pizzeria for dinner. Toward the end of the meal, Carboni and Kunz arrive at the restaurant. It's about 10 p.m. The meeting is brief, just

114

long enough for Kunz to agree to make arrangements for Calvi and Vittor to go to London.

Tuesday 15 June

In the morning, Kunz's business partner, Lovatt McDonald, phones his London solicitor, Robert Clarke of the firm of Wood Nash and Winters, for advice on finding a place for Calvi and Vittor to stay. McDonald does not say it is for a fugitive banker and his travelling companion, but rather for two directors of Fiat. 'The little apartment,' a lawyer at the firm later said, 'was to serve two Italian industrialists, well known, who wanted a discreet lodging for a discreet weekend.' Clarke suggests the Chelsea Cloisters, and McDonald phones the hotel to book a room. He also arranges for a private plane to fly from London to Innsbruck to pick up Calvi and Vittor in Innsbruck. The passengers are identified as 'Mr Vittor plus one'.

While Calvi waits in the hotel in Bregenz for information about the arrangements for the trip, Carboni and the Kleinszig sisters fly by private plane to Amsterdam and check into the Amstel Hotel.

At about 1.30 p.m. Calvi receives a phone call, presumably from Kunz, and learns of the arrangements for the trip. 'He wrote some numbers on a piece of paper,' says Vittor, 'then told me that I had to accompany him to Innsbruck again, to the airport.' They arrive at about 4.30 p.m., and are met by a British pilot, Reginald Mulligan, who hands an envelope to Vittor, containing the address where they will be staying.

Calvi loosens up a bit during the two-hour flight, and begins to chat with Vittor about his daughter and her studies at Bocconi University. 'Perhaps he felt a bit more relaxed,' says Vittor.

The plane lands at Gatwick at about 8 p.m., but the car that was to take them into London has not appeared. After waiting for about half an hour, they decide to take a taxi to the hotel. They register in the names of Silvano Vittor and 'G.R. Calvini' – from the name in Calvi's bogus passport (Gian Roberto Calvini) – and are given room 881.

As soon as they arrive in the room the house phone rings – it's the driver who was supposed to have picked them up at the airport. Vittor goes downstairs and pays him.

The Chelsea Cloisters is a large and crowded residential hotel in Sloane Avenue, Chelsea. There are 748 flats on nine floors, and many of the rooms are occupied by students. For the chairman of an international bank – someone used to staying at the finest hotels – it is, to say the least, a step down. Calvi, says Vittor, 'had been expecting an isolated house, a place where he could be tranquil,' and he describes the Chelsea Cloisters as a 'horrible place'.

115

If the hotel is disappointing, the room is even more so. It is a small flat with a bedroom and sitting room (plus a kitchenette), each measuring about 10 feet by 16 feet. Calvi, says Vittor, 'said it was a squalid environment: two poorly furnished little rooms with small windows that didn't give much ventilation. He didn't feel comfortable any more.'

After taking a quick look around the room Calvi picks up the phone and calls Kunz to complain about the accommodation. 'He said it wasn't any good at all, that he wasn't happy about it, and that he couldn't stay there.' The banker tells Kunz to send Carboni to London immediately to find him another place to stay.

In the evening, says Vittor, 'we didn't go out. I stayed in the sitting room watching television, while Calvi rested in the other room.'

Wednesday 16 June

In the morning, Vittor gives the signed lease agreement to the manager of the Chelsea Cloisters and then goes out with Calvi to eat at a nearby restaurant called The Brasserie. 'Calvi gave the impression of knowing the city well,' says Vittor, 'while I had never been there before.' At a certain point, Calvi buys a pink-coloured English newspaper – presumably the *Financial Times* which, the day before, had carried an article about his disappearance.

After returning to the hotel, Calvi sends Vittor out on some errands: first to get some timetables from British Airways and then to bring back some food. Calvi told Vittor that when he went out he was to phone every fifteen to twenty minutes. On returning, he was to knock three times and identify himself as 'Silvano'.

Calvi spends the afternoon resting, while Vittor watches television. 'Every now and then,' says Vittor, 'he would say: "Enough television. Come here, let's talk for a while, keep each other company."'

Carboni and the Kleinszig sisters arrive at Heathrow Airport in the late afternoon and take a taxi to the Hilton Hotel near Hyde Park. At 5.45 p.m. they register in Michaela's name. About half an hour later, Carboni phones Calvi and arranges a meeting in front of the Hilton. Calvi and Vittor go there by taxi, but the banker refuses to go into the Hilton, saying he's afraid he'll be recognised there. Carboni and the girls get into the taxi and ask the driver to drop everyone off a short distance away. They get out and take a walk through Hyde Park.

During the walk, Calvi complains about his accommodation. 'He swore against Hans Kunz for the choice of the Chelsea Cloisters,' Carboni later said. Since Carboni speaks little English he says he will contact some friends of his in London for help in finding another place for the banker to stay.

116

Calvi and Vittor return to the Chelsea Cloisters by taxi, while Carboni and the girls go back to the Hilton. Carboni then phones his friends: Alma and William Morris, a middle-aged couple who live in Heston, Middlesex, a suburb of London not far from Heathrow Airport. Carboni met them through one of his mistresses, Laura Scanu-Concas. Miss Scanu-Concas, a woman in her thirties who has been supported by Carboni for more than a decade, is the niece of Mrs Morris. The Morrises say they will help Carboni and agree to meet him at their flat the following morning.

Calvi may have been thinking about changing his residence – at least according to Carboni and Carboni's friends. But, in his phone calls to his family, the banker expressed other preoccupations. He was worried about his daughter's safety and ordered her to leave Switzerland and join the rest of the family in Washington. 'You must immediately join your mother in America,' he said. He told his wife and son not to leave Carlo's home: 'In that house,' he said, 'you will be protected.'

Calvi's final call that Wednesday was to his wife. In it, he spoke of the deal he was working on. Although he did not explain the nature of the deal, he said that he was on the verge of completing it – and that it could solve all his problems.

'Things are going ahead slowly,' he said, 'but they're moving. It's a question of very little. A crazy, marvellous thing is about to explode which could even help me in my appeal. It could solve everything.' But the conversation also contained an ominous note: 'I don't trust the people I'm with any more.' It was the last time Clara Calvi heard her husband's voice.

23

'Twice-Damned'

Ten members of Banco Ambrosiano's board of directors entered the boardroom a little after 12.30 p.m. on Thursday 17 June 1982. Five members were absent and, the minutes record drily, all but Roberto Calvi had justified their absences. Also present at the meeting were four senior executives of the bank who were not directors and all five members of the 'board of auditors' – employees responsible for checking Ambrosiano's financial statements.

After the ritual reading and approval of the minutes of the last two meetings, the board considered a resolution relating to Calvi's disappearance. Calvi, the resolution noted, had been 'absent since the twelfth of this month' and there was a risk that he could be forced to sign papers against his will – since he could have been abducted. And so it was proposed that Calvi be stripped of 'all powers that he has or that have been conferred upon him' and that he be suspended 'from his duties as chairman and managing director'. The resolution was passed unanimously and Calvi's powers were given to Roberto Rosone, the senior of the two deputy chairmen.

The price of Ambrosiano shares had been declining rapidly since Monday because of Calvi's disappearance. There was now the danger of a full-scale collapse of the stock price – perhaps even a run on deposits – touched off by new disclosures in the press. A copy of the Bank of Italy's letter of 31 May to Ambrosiano had been leaked to the business daily *Il Sole-24 Ore*, and the paper had just published lengthy extracts. It was now public knowledge that the Bank of Italy was worried about more than $1 billion in questionable loans.

The faces of the directors were drawn, the tone of the meeting sombre, as Rosone moved on to the main topic of discussion: Banco Ambrosiano's financial plight. Rosone began by proposing that the board of Ambrosiano be dissolved, with power handed over to the Bank of Italy. Rosone's resolution was followed by a detailed explanation of

118

the loans to the ghost companies, of the patronage letters from the Vatican bank, and of IOR's refusal to honour the ghost companies' debts because of the counter letter it had received from Calvi.

As this extraordinary tale unfolded, the board members expressed amazement that they had not been told about all this before, and they pressed Rosone and international chief Filippo Leoni for explanations. For the most part, the directors' questions were put in soft, controlled voices. One man, however, exploded angrily. Orazio Bagnasco shouted at Rosone: 'You knew everything that was happening at the bank and you never said anything!' Rosone answered that as soon as he knew about the questionable loans he went to the Vatican bank and tried to get the loans repaid.

Giuseppe Prisco, the director who had expressed so much confidence in Calvi after the chairman's release from prison and at the board meeting on 17 February, asked if there were any other matters the board did not know about. Bagnasco said that there were: only a few days before, Bagnasco said, he had learned that Calvi had ordered secret purchases of Ambrosiano shares in order to prop up the price.

The questions, accusations, explanations and denials continued for hours. A member of the board of auditors said that he and his colleagues had tried to get details of the loans to the ghost companies when the 1981 accounts of Ambrosiano were being closed in December. But, he said, the auditors received no co-operation from Calvi, Rosone, or the executives in charge of the foreign department. It was, they were told, a question of foreign 'bank secrecy' laws. Calvi had also pointed out that the accounts of Banco Andino and the other foreign subsidiaries had been approved by independent auditing firms. Rosone then defended himself by saying that Calvi had given him such strong assurances about the loans that anyone would have been satisfied. Rosone then turned his fire on the board. He reminded them that they never questioned Calvi, had expressed the greatest faith and esteem in his leadership – and had even reconfirmed him as chairman after his release from prison. 'What do I know?' he asked. 'I know that you have always approved and ratified [Calvi's decisions] without ever making the slightest objections.'

During a recess, Rosone went into another room to take a phone call from Michel Leemans, who had made a last-ditch appeal to Archbishop Marcinkus. Leemans had repeated the proposal he had made to Marcinkus's deputies the day before: that IOR repay the ghost companies' debts by raising the funds from international banks. As Leemans later described his meeting, Marcinkus said 'he was under no obligation whatsoever and, second, there was no room in [IOR's] balance sheet for such an obligation.' Leemans then told him:

'*Monsignore,* I know it's a difficult deal. But if you don't do it, the bank [Ambrosiano] will go bankrupt. Your letters will become public. It will be the scandal of the 1980s.' Marcinkus said, 'I know. I gave the letters of patronage for one reason: I wanted to give assistance to a friend. I'm going to pay personally for that mistake' – by which he meant, says Leemans, that 'there would be damage to his personal reputation, and he might lose his responsibility in the Vatican.'

When Leemans conveyed the bad news to Rosone, they agreed that the only remaining alternative was to call in the Bank of Italy.

When the board meeting resumed, Rosone described Leemans' meeting with Marcinkus. The board then debated Rosone's motion to call in the Bank of Italy. If adopted, the following announcement would be made:

'The Board of Banco Ambrosiano, after having examined the exceptional situation caused by recent events . . . has decided [in the interests of] the bank, its shareholders, its depositors, its clientele and its employees . . . [to dissolve] the administrative organs in order for there to be the nomination of a commissioner. This important decision was taken in the awareness that, given the exceptional nature of the situation, [there was the need for] the presence at the top level of the bank of a person designated by the competent authorities to dissipate uncertainties and perplexities generated by uncontrolled and contradictory news of recent events.'

After some further discussion, the resolution was adopted by a vote of nine to zero, with Bagnasco abstaining.

At 5 p.m. the meeting was dissolved.

As they walked out of the board room, Bagnasco took a parting shot at Rosone. 'It's a dirty political manoeuvre,' he said. Rosone countered: 'It's the only serious thing to do at this moment.' The board's decision was immediately transmitted to the authorities in Rome and a meeting was held between Treasury Minister Andreatta, Governor Ciampi of the Bank of Italy, and CONSOB Chairman Guido Rossi. Andreatta signed the appropriate decree that evening and Ciampi appointed a temporary commissioner to take the place of Ambrosiano's board of directors. Ambrosiano's stock – which had plunged to 26,000 lire that day – was suspended from trading.

At about 7.15 p.m. Rosone was in his office, giving a telephone interview to a reporter from the weekly magazine *L'Espresso*. The reporter heard background noises, gradually getting louder, and asked what was going on. 'I don't know,' said Rosone. 'People are coming in. Wait a second . . . Oh my God! Calvi's secretary has killed herself . . . She threw herself out the window!'

Fifty-five-year-old Graziella Teresa Corrocher, an employee of Ambrosiano for three decades and Calvi's secretary for many years, had plunged to her death from an office window – an apparent suicide. On her desk was a note in which she apologised 'for the disturbance I give'. The note then went on to denounce Calvi bitterly. She described her relationship with her boss as 'so much coldness and so much dissatisfaction'. She ended with a curse: 'He should be twice-damned for the damage he did to the group and to all of us, who were at one time so proud of it.'

Late that night, or early the following morning, Roberto Calvi died in London.

24

Il Dopo Calvi

Roberto Calvi's death in London was not the end of 'the Calvi affair'. In some ways, it was just the beginning. Like an earthquake, it was followed by a series of aftershocks, which rocked the financial world, the political world and the Roman Catholic Church. The banker's death also left unanswered a series of disturbing questions, including: How did Calvi die? What was the role of the Vatican? What really caused the financial crisis of Ambrosiano?

Before dealing with these and other questions, it makes sense to record what happened, and what was revealed, during '*il dopo Calvi*' – the immediate aftermath of the banker's death.

Friday 18 June
London

Anthony Huntley is a young man who works as a postal clerk at the *Daily Express* newspaper. Early in the morning he leaves his home in the south London district of Streatham. At about 7.30 a.m., he walks across Blackfriars Bridge on his way to the *Daily Express* building in Fleet Street.

On recent walks Huntley has noticed some scaffolding, which had been erected in April by workmen repainting the bridge. Today Huntley glances down at the scaffolding and sees a man's head. Startled, he moves closer for a better look, and sees a body hanging by an orange-coloured rope from a scaffolding pole.

Huntley can hardly believe his eyes, and decides to tell a friend rather than report the body. 'He came in and said, "You'll never believe what I've just seen,"' recalls Stephen Pullen, a postal clerk at the London *Evening Standard*. Pullen phones the police, then he and Huntley walk back to the bridge and find that the police have already arrived.

The City of London Police contact the Thames River police, who bring a boat to the scaffolding. They photograph the body, remove it from the scaffolding and take it by boat to Waterloo Pier.

It is the body of a man of about sixty, overweight, of medium height, clad in a light-weight grey suit. The man's pockets contain four pieces of brick and concrete; a fifth piece, about half a house brick, is down the front of the trousers. The total weight of the bricks and rocks is just under 12 pounds. The police also find nearly $15,000 worth of currency and coins: Italian lire, Austrian Schillings, Swiss francs, pounds sterling, and US dollars. There are two expensive Patek Philippe watches (a wrist watch and a pocket watch); a ring; cufflinks; four pairs of spectacles; three spectacle cases; two wallets; papers; correspondence; photographs; and a pencil. To the police, the most useful item is an Italian passport in the name of Gian Roberto Calvini.

At 9.35 a.m., a doctor arrives at Waterloo Pier and certifies death.

Zurich

Anna Calvi last spoke to her father yesterday about noon. He wanted to make sure that she would be leaving Switzerland today to join her mother and brother in Washington. He said he would phone her today at about 8 a.m. to confirm that she has made a plane reservation.

Her father does not call. Instead, at about 8 a.m. Hans Kunz phones 'telling me that his wife would come to the hotel to bring me money,' says Anna. 'I asked him if he had news and if he had seen my father, and he answered: "I'm seeing him today."'

Between 10 a.m. and 10.30 a.m. a woman identifying herself as Mrs Kunz arrives at the hotel where Anna and her boyfriend are staying. She hands them an envelope containing 50,000 Swiss francs, then stops to chat for a few minutes with Anna and Vittorio. In the course of the conversation they tell Mrs Kunz that they had just learned of the death of Calvi's secretary. 'The news really frightened Mrs Kunz,' Anna says, adding that the woman, whose English was 'rather poor', apparently thought they were referring to someone else's death.

Before leaving, Mrs Kunz tells them that Calvi is in London. 'She said that the bookings were in the name of somebody else, "but your father is living there, so the people who own the apartment want to know who is living there."' Anna adds: 'She thought I knew where he was, so she was surprised that I was looking for news from her.'

At about noon, Anna boards a plane for the United States at Zurich airport. Vittorio returns to the hotel, to wait for a phone call he is to receive from Calvi at 3 p.m. – a call which does not come.

Milan

The decision by Ambrosiano's board last night to call in the Bank of

Italy has produced 'an atmosphere of desperation' at Via Clerici, according to a Bank of Italy official who was there. 'Banco Ambrosiano,' he says, 'was an old bank with good employees who were very proud of working there. And what happened was really something traumatic. All the officers felt as if they had been betrayed by Calvi.' The arrival of the Bank of Italy's temporary commissioner helps to allay some of their concerns. 'He sent a telex to all the branches, saying that all business should be carried on normally, and that he hoped all the officers would do their duty as usual.'

In an effort to calm depositors, the Bank of Italy tells reporters that Ambrosiano is solid and is functioning normally. Based on these reassurances a *Financial Times* correspondent files a story for Saturday's paper, saying in part:

'Despite the implication that Signor Calvi may have involved Banco Ambrosiano in questionable or illegal dealings, the bank is considered financially sound...Had the Bank of Italy considered Banco Ambrosiano unsound, it could have appointed a commissioner on its own initiative.'

Other reporters are more sceptical, because of yesterday's revelation that Ambrosiano's foreign subsidiaries had made some $1.4 billion in questionable loans. One paper describes the loans as 'a possible "hole" of enormous proportions', and goes on to theorise – correctly, as it later turns out – that much of the money Calvi borrowed was used to buy Ambrosiano shares.

London

After recovering the passport from Calvi's body, the City of London Police send a telex to Rome, hoping to identify the corpse. The reply is not long in coming. The Italian authorities think it is Calvi, says Detective Inspector John White of the City police. 'We heard he could be an Italian financier who was missing.' He adds: 'And things took off from there.'

At 2 p.m., the post-mortem examination is begun by Professor Keith Simpson, probably the most respected forensic pathologist in Britain. In his autobiography, *Forty Years of Murder*, Simpson wrote engagingly of his macabre speciality: '...it isn't everyone who would choose to spend so much of his professional life with the dead. For me it is the spice of life...' Simpson has been told that the body is that of a Mr Calvini, and that it was found hanging from scaffolding that would have been accessible to the victim. From rigor mortis, he estimates that death occurred at around 2 a.m. – give or take three or four hours. The cause of death, he writes in his report, is asphyxia due to hanging. The most important point he must answer, however, is whether Calvi killed himself or was killed by others. To answer that question, Simpson looks for marks of violence on the body or signs that the victim was immobilised by drugs or alcohol. As he explains in his book:

'Strangling is usually murder; hanging, almost never. Mostly hanging is suicidal; much less commonly, accidental. In the recorded cases of murder by hanging, the victim has always been rendered physically incapable of resistance. In lynchings he was overpowered by several persons acting in concert; in the few other known cases he was either old or infirm, enfeebled by alcohol or drugs, or severely injured.'

Simpson's examination reveals no marks of violence and no traces of drugs or alcohol. He later says: 'I formed the view that this group of findings was consistent with...what I commonly see in deliberate self-suspension,' in other words: suicide. He writes in his notes: 'Crime?'

Milan

In the afternoon Roberto Rosone sees Alfonso Marra, the magistrate investigating the attempt on his life on 27 April. Marra asks the banker whether he knows a certain Flavio Carboni. 'Well, yes,' says Rosone. 'For the past few months he's always been phoning Calvi.' What about Domenico Balducci, a reputed gangster who, he says, had been employed by Carboni. 'Never heard of him,' answers Rosone. The magistrate then tells him that Balducci was a friend of Danilo Abbruciati – the gangster who was killed by Rosone's bodyguard while attempting to murder Rosone.

Gradually Rosone begins to realise what the magistrate is trying to tell him: that the man who had tried to kill him in April was connected with Flavio Carboni, the almost constant companion of Calvi. Could it mean that Calvi was involved? The magistrate realises that Rosone cannot accept the possible implications of what he has heard, so he turns to his secretary and, in Rosone's presence, tells her: 'Prepare a warrant for the arrest of Roberto Calvi for the attempted murder of Roberto Rosone.'

Rosone is overwhelmed by what he has just heard. 'I feel as if I'm dying,' Rosone says, and he walks out of the judge's office in a daze.

At 11.30 p.m., Italian television broadcasts a report that a body found under a bridge in London may be Calvi's.

Washington, DC

Anna Calvi arrives at her brother's home in Washington, and tells Carlo and her mother that her father is apparently in London.

Clara Calvi has not heard from her husband for two days, although he was supposed to have phoned. When the phone finally rings early the following morning, Clara later said, 'I literally flew down the stairs, hoping that it was him.' Instead, it is her brother Luciano. 'They've found a body in the Thames,' he whispers. The news of her husband's death is a devastating blow. 'I dragged myself up the stairs like a wild beast,' she says. 'I screamed and beat my fists against the wall until they bled.' For days afterwards she is virtually paralysed with shock.

Not long after the news of Calvi's death, his wife and children, mindful of his warnings about their safety, move to more secure lodgings: an apartment in the Watergate complex, put at their disposal by friends. Five bodyguards protect them.

Saturday 19 June

Detective Inspector White of the City of London Police drives to Heathrow Airport at 3.30 a.m. to meet five Italian officials – magistrates and police officers who have been investigating Calvi's disappearance and are now concerned with the banker's death.

The Italian investigators learned from Calvi's chauffeur that the banker had met with Flavio Carboni shortly before his disappearance. From Carboni's assistant, Emilio Pellicani, they have been able to piece together the first leg of Calvi's trip – from Rome to Trieste. But they have not been able to locate Carboni.

The Italians have brought with them a set of Calvi's fingerprints, which are soon compared with ones taken from the corpse. At about midday the City of London Police issue the following press release:

'Shortly before 8 a.m. on Friday 18th June, 1982, the body of Mr. Roberto Calvi was found hanging by the neck from scaffolding beneath the northern arch of Blackfriars Bridge.

A post-mortem examination has been completed, the full results of which are not yet known.

Mr. Calvi had been missing from his home in Italy for seven days and his movements during that time are at present unknown. It is not yet known how long he had been in England or where he had been staying. Any information concerning these matters would be welcomed by the City of London Police (telephone 01-601 2222).

There is at this time no evidence to suggest that Mr. Calvi's death was the result of anything other than suicide, but the circumstances surrounding his disappearance and subsequent death are being investigated by members of the City of London Police who are co-operating with the Police in Rome.'

In the City of London violent deaths are extremely rare, since that

126

square mile of metropolitan London has only a few thousand residents. As one police detective puts it: 'We don't get many bodies in the City.'

But it did not take the police long to realise that this body was in a class by itself – not only for the bizarre manner of the death, but because of the world-wide attention it is attracting. Dozens of local reporters and foreign correspondents, including an Italian press corps supplemented by 'special' writers flown in from Italy, begin bombarding the police with questions.

Sunday 20 June

Robert Clarke, the London solicitor who had assisted Kunz in finding the room for Calvi at the Chelsea Cloisters, has received an urgent message to phone Bill Power, an associate of Kunz. Clarke returns the call at 2 a.m. Power tells him to look at the Sunday newspapers, because one of the men who stayed at the Chelsea Cloisters is mentioned in them. When Clarke sees the articles about Calvi, he phones Power and tells him: 'We ought to inform the police.'

Snow Hill Police Station is in a nondescript little building in a side street near St Paul's Cathedral. Today it is filled with reporters attending a press conference given by Commander Hugh Moore, the man in charge of the Calvi case. Commander Moore soon finds himself the target of barbed questions from some of the Italian journalists, who find it hard to believe that Calvi committed suicide. Why would the banker come all the way to London to kill himself? Why would he put rocks in his pockets first? Why under a bridge? Could a man of Calvi's age and weight make the 'acrobatic' manoeuvres necessary to hang himself from the scaffolding? The police officer, however, stands his ground – perhaps because of Professor Simpson's belief that it was probably suicide. 'I am keeping an open mind,' says Moore. 'We have not decided one way or the other.' But, he adds: 'There are no indications at this stage that it was not suicide.'

The scepticism of much of the Italian press is reflected in the stories that appear on Monday and Tuesday, in which tough questions about the rocks, the 'acrobatic' manoeuvres, and so on, are raised. A typical headline appears in Turin's *La Stampa:* 'Calvi, suicide or "suicided". How many wanted his silence?'

Monday 21 June
London

Robert Clarke contacts the police and tells them about Calvi's flight to London and the banker's room at the Chelsea Cloisters. On the basis of

127

this information, John White of the City Police locates several witnesses, such as the pilot who brought Calvi and Vittor to London, and employees of the Chelsea Cloisters. White visits the room where Calvi stayed, and finds the banker's belongings neatly packed in two suitcases in a cupboard. But there is no trace of the black briefcase stuffed with secret papers that Calvi always carried with him.

Milan

When Banco Ambrosiano opens its doors for business, a number of nervous depositors withdraw their savings. This prompts a columnist for Milan's *Il Giornale Nuovo* to write a reassuring piece for Tuesday's paper:

'Now, the reaction, comprehensible but illogical, of both depositors and shareholders, respectively, is to run to the tellers' windows and pull out deposits and dump at any price the shares of Ambrosiano, as if Ambrosiano were on the brink of insolvency.... There's no reason to believe that this will be a replay of Sindona...'

What the writer did not realise was that Ambrosiano was *already* insolvent and that its collapse would be even greater than that of Sindona's banks. Most small depositors do remain calm, but the same cannot be said for *banks* that have placed funds with Ambosiano. Figures released later show that a 'run on the bank' has been in progress for months. It is not the classic sort of run – with depositors stampeding into branches demanding their money back – but rather a 'silent run', confined mostly to the interbank market. Banks that had money on deposit with Ambrosiano would simply wait for the deposits to mature, and then refuse to renew them. The effect was just as damaging.

Over the weekend, the Bank of Italy replaced the temporary commissioner running Ambrosiano with three commissioners, all of them respected by the financial community: Giovanni Arduino, Alberto Bertoni and Antonio Occhiuto. In an attempt to bolster confidence in Ambrosiano, the Bank of Italy contacts international banks through phone calls, telexes and personal visits. Italy's central bank insists that it will stand behind Ambrosiano. But when it is asked whether these assurances apply to Ambrosiano's foreign subsidiaries – where most of the problems are concentrated – the Bank of Italy is non-commital.

Seeking an historical parallel for the Ambrosiano crisis, the newspaper *La Stampa* reaches back to the Banca Romana affair of the 1890s, which turned into a major political scandal. The paper then sends reporters to Ambrosiano branches for a 'reaction' story, and finds that some of the customers are responding to Calvi's death with graveyard humour. Addressing Ambrosiano tellers, customers refer to 'Your chairman, sorry, your ex-chairman, pardon, ex-everything...' Even film director Federico Fellini contributes an observation. 'A thriller like this,' he muses, sounding as if he's visualising a new film. 'The Thames, the noose, the black monks, an old-fashioned bloodthirsty story...'

Tuesday 22 June

The Italian Bankers' Association holds its annual meeting in Rome. In a speech to the bankers, Treasury Minister Andreatta urges the passage of legislation that would require banks to publish consolidated accounts and reveal who their shareholders are. If these laws had been in effect, says Andreatta, the Ambrosiano affair might have been prevented.

Rumours about the Vatican's patronage letters have been circulating since the weekend, prompting reporters to submit written questions to Archbishop Marcinkus. Is it true, they ask, that IOR gave letters guaranteeing the questionable loans? It is also true that Marcinkus himself refused to honour those letters? The Archbishop declines to answer.

The parliamentary commission investigating the P2 scandal decides to ask judicial and government authorities to supply it with all relevant information on the Calvi case. They believe Calvi's death could be connected to the P2 Lodge.

At about 3 p.m., Roberto Rosone leaves Milan's Palace of Justice, after a meeting with the magistrate investigating the attempt on his life. Reporters approach him and ask whether it is true that Rosone believes Calvi sent the hired killer. At first, he refuses to answer. The reporters persist, and Rosone finally blurts out: 'There's no doubt it was him. It was Calvi who had me shot.' He adds that he feels he is still in danger.

In the evening magistrate Domenico Sica spends more than four hours interrogating Emilio Pellicani, Carboni's aide who took Calvi from Rome to Trieste. Pellicani leads investigators to documents relating to Calvi. On examination, they prove to contain potentially explosive material: including information on Carboni's lobbying with politicians and magistrates on Calvi's behalf.

Wednesday 23 June

The political fallout from the Calvi case includes a question in Parliament from the Communists. MPs ask why Calvi was permitted to remain chairman of Ambrosiano after his conviction. The day before, the party newspaper *L'Unità* had described the case as an example of 'the entanglement of political and financial criminality' in an article headlined 'Calvi overthrown by the same world that had made him powerful'.

The business daily *Il Sole-24 Ore* had taken a very different slant a few days earlier under the headline: 'The second Sindona has fallen. Who will be the third?'

Tomorrow, the paper will carry a letter from a man identifying himself as an ordinary shareholder of Banco Ambrosiano. Under the title 'But who controls the controllers?' the letter-writer asks:

'Where was the Bank of Italy when CONSOB authorised the stock-market listing of Ambrosiano? What controls did CONSOB exercise when it received and then allowed to be distributed the prospectus with Ambrosiano's financial statements? Why didn't the Bank of Italy intervene then instead of now? On what basis did CONSOB say that Ambrosiano had made adequate disclosure? What faith can the small investor now have in the stock-market?'

In London Leone Calvi, the banker's brother, and Luciano Canetti, his brother-in-law, visit the City of London Mortuary to identify the body officially. It is definitely Calvi's, although it does not have the moustache that the banker always wore. He presumably shaved it off during his trip so he wouldn't be recognised.

Upon leaving the building, they tell reporters they are certain that Calvi was murdered. That view is echoed by the banker's Rome lawyers who are with them. Attorney Pietro Moscato says: 'I imagined the scene. But how, I thought, is it possible that Calvi would go there at night, with masonry and concrete in his pockets, with a rope, under a bridge to hang himself making leaps like an acrobat?' His colleague, Giorgio Gregori, adds that Calvi suffered from vertigo. 'When I used to tell him I was going mountain climbing, he would smile and confide to me: "I could never do that."'

It is now more than a week since Italian investigators began searching for Flavio Carboni. At first they wanted to question him about Calvi's disappearance. Now, they want to know about the banker's death. On Sunday Carboni telephoned Domenico Sica, an investigating magistrate in Rome, and said: 'I'm coming. I'll clarify everything.' But he did not come. Sica issues a warrant for Carboni's arrest.

Thursday 24 June

Silvano Vittor is in custody in Rome, charged with helping Calvi jump bail. He gave himself up to police near Trieste yesterday morning, after crossing the border from Austria. At about midnight, magistrate Sica begins a six-hour interrogation.

Friday 25 June

Florio Fioroni, finance director of ENI, is suspended from his job for having devised a plan to rescue Banco Ambrosiano without informing his superiors.

Calvi's wife and children say publicly that they believe the banker was murdered, adding that they are ready to tell everything they know to investigators.

Sunday 27 June

On the basis of the Carboni papers found through Pellicani, police arrest Roman lawyer Wilfredo Vitalone, on charges that he took a three billion lire payment from one of Calvi's middlemen, part of which was to be used to 'buy' magistrates.

Wednesday 30 June

London

Midland Bank, which arranged a $40 million loan to Ambrosiano's Luxembourg holding company in 1980, has contacted the sixteen other lenders about what to do if the borrower fails to make the payment due on 8 July – $5.7 million in principal and $3 million in interest. The lenders agree unanimously that, if the payment is not made, they should declare that the borrower is in default. An official of one of the creditor banks expresses his amazement at the Vatican's role in the affair. 'The rumour is that most of the loans made by Banco Andino were to Vatican-related companies,' he says. *'What on earth are Vatican related companies?'*

Milan

The Milan stock exchange has suffered a huge decline almost entirely due to the effects of the Ambrosiano crisis. One stock-market operator is quoted as saying that the market 'seems to be under that bridge on the Thames'. As of the end of June, the market as a whole has lost four trillion lire, more than $3 billion, because of 'the Calvi effect'.

Friday 2 July

The Bank of Italy commissioners running Ambrosiano meet top officials of IOR. According to the commissioners' calculations, the Vatican bank owes $1.275 billion – the loans covered by the patronage

131

letters. IOR officials reply by showing them Calvi's 'counter letter'. The meeting does not last very long. According to one report, Archbishop Marcinkus 'showed the officials to the door, saying that he was not required to answer questions by Italian authorities, who have no jurisdiction over the bank because it is located in Vatican City'.

IOR's flat refusal to honour the patronage letters means that Ambrosiano's foreign subsidiaries cannot service *their* debts. The commissioners instruct the foreign subsidiaries to ask their creditors to grant a delay, a 'moratorium', on debt service.

The commissioners are not the only officials displeased by the Vatican's refusal to pay. That feeling is shared by Beniamino Andreatta, Italy's Treasury Minister. Andreatta, a pipe-smoking, Oxford-educated economist, sometimes gives the impression of being a rumpled academic. But when he feels strongly about an issue, he speaks in blunt, unequivocal terms. A parliamentary colleague says of Andreatta's undiplomatic style: 'We're lucky he isn't foreign minister; he would have involved us in some war – even with Switzerland.'

In the afternoon, Andreatta faces sharp questioning from several Members of Parliament, and he replies in forceful language. He calls the Ambrosiano affair one of the worst banking scandals in a major industrialised country since the 1940s. Banco Ambrosiano, he says, was 'entangled by a series of abnormal and reckless transactions, beyond any banking logic, attributable to a highly centralised and personalised management'. At the same time, however, the Treasury Minister freely admits that not all the blame can be placed on Ambrosiano's executives. The scandal, he says, 'is also the product of confusion of powers, of influences, of environments that characterise such aspects of Italian life in this decade'. Andreatta continues: 'At the bottom of the Ambrosiano affair is the usual mixture that has characterised all the other scandals in Italian banking history: administrative improprieties, political friendships, hidden relationships.

He then turns his wrath on the Vatican bank, which, he says, appears to have been a *'de facto* partner of Ambrosiano' in numerous business deals. 'The government,' he says, 'is waiting for a clear assumption of responsibility by IOR.'

Monday 5 July to Saturday 10 July

The Calvi and P2 scandals may be connected to international arms traffic and right-wing terrorism, according to a series of rumours.

Ezio Giunchiglia, a former Defence Ministry employee and member of the P2 Lodge, tells the parliamentary commission investigating P2 about a 'super lodge' in Monte Carlo. The lodge, he says, includes members from several countries and was engaged in secret international arms deals. This lodge is also said to be linked to the August 1980 terrorist bombing of the Bologna railway station.

A rumour circulates that Ambrosiano may have helped to finance Argentine imports of Exocet missiles during the country's war with Britain last spring over the Falkland Islands. This rumour reportedly brings the Calvi case to the attention of British Prime Minister Margaret Thatcher and Foreign Secretary Francis Pym. At a summit meeting in Rome Virginio Rognoni, Italy's Interior Minister, reportedly tells Pym that the Calvi case should not be treated as an ordinary crime, but as 'a political affair'. During a press conference, reports the *Observer,* Thatcher denies that she had discussed the Calvi case, but the paper adds, 'It was certainly discussed informally by British and Italian officials.'

Reports that Ambrosiano and/or the Vatican bank provided funds for Solidarity, the banned Polish trade union movement, prompt speculation that East European intelligence agencies may somehow have been involved in the Calvi case.

Sunday 11 July

At the request of the Bank of Italy, six Italian banks – three from the public sector and three from the private sector – form a 'rescue pool' to provide liquidity to Banco Ambrosiano. But, as the creditors of Ambrosiano's foreign subsidiaries have feared, the rescue operation will only apply to the parent bank in Milan.

Monday 12 July

Banco Ambrosiano Holding (Luxembourg) is declared to be in default on the $40 million loan arranged by Midland Bank. This soon triggers the 'cross-default' clause on the $75 million loan put together by National Westminster.

The default of BAH marks the official beginning of the biggest bank failure in years and sends shockwaves through the Euromarket. Confidence in Luxembourg, a major offshore banking centre, is seriously eroded. As *The Economist* is to report later: 'West German banks, who are the Grand Duchy's mainstay, suddenly found themselves short of liquidity as depositors withdrew their cash. West Germany's Bundesbank [the central bank] stepped in. People got the message: take care not only with whom you place your money but where.'

133

Tuesday 13 July

The Vatican finally breaks the almost total silence it has maintained about the Calvi affair, by announcing that a team of three experts will be appointed to study 'the known events concerning the relationship of the IOR with the Banco Ambrosiano'. The panel, appointed by the Vatican Secretary of State, Cardinal Agostino Casaroli, consists of Joseph Brennan, former chairman of the Emigrant Savings Bank of New York; Carlo Cerutti, deputy chairman of STET, Italy's state-owned telecommunications holding company; and Philippe De Weck, former chairman of Union Bank of Switzerland, one of the 'big three' Swiss banks.

Several Vatican-watchers interpret the move as a major setback for Archbishop Marcinkus who, it is rumoured, has long been at odds with Cardinal Casaroli.

An inquest to determine the cause of Calvi's death will be held on 23 July, according to an announcement by Dr David Paul, coroner for the City of London.

Wednesday 14 July

The Italian press reports that Licio Gelli may have been planning to stage a 'civil coup' in Italy, a bloodless takeover of power by a centrist government led by a strong president. The plan included suppression of trade unions, the press, and the Italian Communist Party. These reports are based on papers found in the possession of the P2 leader's daughter.

Sunday 18 July

Carlo Calvi is quoted in the press as saying that his father was not acting on his own but 'was in the service of others', although the banker's son says he does not know who those 'others' were. He adds that his father told the family that secret payments were made to Solidarity.

Tuesday 20 July

Central bankers throughout Europe are becoming increasingly disturbed by the Bank of Italy's handling of the Ambrosiano affair, according to a report in today's edition of *The Times* of London. Italy's failure to stand behind Ambrosiano's foreign subsidiaries is said to be undermining confidence in the international banking system.

Thursday 22 July

Michele Sindona and twenty-five others are indicted on charges of 'fraudulent bankruptcy', violation of Italian banking laws, and falsification of company accounts in connection with the collapse of

Sindona's Banca Privata. Among the accused are three Vatican financiers, including Marcinkus's deputy, Luigi Mennini. In a public statement, Prime Minister Spadolini implies that the government's refusal to bail out Ambrosiano's foreign subsidiaries is based on the fear that such a move would let the Vatican off the hook. A full-scale rescue operation, the Prime Minister says, would carry 'the risk of favouring persons or institutions involved in the responsibility for the financial difficulty'.

Relations between the Vatican and the Italian Republic are said to be at their lowest ebb for decades.

It is now just over a month since Calvi's body was discovered under Blackfriars Bridge, and the revelations and events since then have been astounding – even to Italians, who are largely inured to major scandals. Looking back on that period, one of Calvi's closest colleagues, Michel Leemans, says: 'If someone put in a novel the billion-dollar loss, the Vatican, the big banker found dead, the death of his secretary – people would say it's impossible. They wouldn't accept it from a serious writer. But this is real life!'

25

The Inquest

How did Roberto Calvi die? Did he kill himself, or was he killed by others? In the weeks following the discovery of his body under Blackfriars Bridge, British and Italian police searched for clues to explain what happened on the night of 17–18 June 1982. By late July the mystery was still unsolved. There was persuasive evidence to support either hypothesis: that he was murdered or that he had committed suicide. Before reviewing the evidence for each hypothesis, it makes sense to summarise Calvi's trip.

1. Calvi travelled from Rome to London with the help of Flavio Carboni and three of Carboni's friends: Emilio Pellicani, Silvano Vittor and Hans Kunz. His stops were Rome, Venice and Trieste in Italy; Klagenfurt, Innsbruck, Bregenz, and Innsbruck again, in Austria. He then flew to London.

2. Calvi arrived in London on Tuesday 15 June with Vittor. They spent the next two days in a small apartment at the Chelsea Cloisters, a large residential hotel.

3. Carboni met Calvi in Klagenfurt on Saturday 12 June. On Monday he went to Zurich with his girlfriend Manuela Kleinszig and her sister Michaela (Vittor's girlfriend). That evening, Carboni and Kunz met Calvi in Bregenz to discuss arrangements for Calvi's trip to London. Carboni then travelled to Amsterdam with the Kleinszig sisters. On Wednesday 16 June, Carboni and the girls arrived in London and checked into the Hilton Hotel near Hyde Park. That evening, according to Carboni, he met Calvi to discuss finding the banker new accommodation.

4. Thursday 17 June was the last day of Calvi's life. Carboni's version is that he spent most of the day travelling around London with his English friends, Alma and William Morris, looking for new accommodation for Calvi. Late that evening he took a taxi to the Chelsea Cloisters and talked to Vittor in the lobby. They went to a

nearby restaurant, where the Kleinszig sisters had been waiting for several hours. Carboni and the girls then checked into the Sheraton Hotel near Heathrow Airport (and also not very far away from the Morrises' flat).

5. Vittor's version of 17 June is that he last saw Calvi at about 11 p.m. After going to the restaurant with Carboni, Vittor returned and found that Calvi had disappeared. The following morning, having heard nothing from Calvi or Carboni, he flew to Austria. On 23 June he gave himself up to Italian police in Trieste.

6. Carboni says he tried to phone Calvi's room at the Chelsea Cloisters several times on 18 June, but there was no reply. He then took a taxi to a nearby hotel, checked in, and tried phoning from there. He then sent the Morrises' daughter, Odette, to the Chelsea Cloisters to knock on the door and leave notes for Vittor. Later in the day he talked to Vittor on the phone and learned of Calvi's disappearance the night before. Late that evening he spoke on the phone to a friend in Italy, who told him of Calvi's death – which had just been broadcast on Italian television.

7. Carboni and Odette Morris went to Gatwick Airport on Saturday 19 June, where they took a plane to Edinburgh and checked into a hotel. On Sunday, Odette returned to London while Carboni took a private plane (supplied by Hans Kunz) to Switzerland. He then went into hiding, although he released statements claiming he had nothing to do with Calvi's death.

The murder-versus-suicide debate has been conducted on the basis of two types of evidence: the physical details of the banker's death (the post-mortem examination and so on) and the circumstances surrounding it.

As far as the 'physical evidence' was concerned, there were essentially two possibilities. If it was murder, Calvi was taken to Blackfriars Bridge by physical force, threats or trickery. He was then lowered down a ladder to the scaffolding or else lifted to the scaffolding from the deck of a boat. He was then hanged. If it was suicide, Calvi went to the bridge, climbed down the ladder and then jumped a few feet to the scaffolding. He then attached a rope (already around his neck) to a scaffolding pole or else tied a rope (already attached to the scaffolding) around his neck. He then hanged himself.

Those who believe it was murder make the following points:

1. Why would Calvi choose such a bizarre and complicated way to die? Why not jump out of a window at the Chelsea Cloisters or take drugs (from the ample supply in his luggage)? This particular point has been made persuasively by Jeremy Paxman, a BBC reporter, in the

course of a television documentary:

'To believe that [Calvi] committed suicide we must accept that he travelled over four miles to Blackfriars Bridge, and once there discovered scaffolding which was not visible from the road. We have to accept, too, that he happened to find several lumps of brick which he then put down his trousers and in his pockets. We have to believe that he happened to find some convenient rope. And all the time, back in the flat, he had enough sleeping pills to kill himself easily and painlessly. All that would have been missing is the element of theatricality.'

Or, as an Italian politician put it: 'Calvi puts stones in his pockets, goes down to the bridge, does acrobatics – these things could be true, but they are not true to life.'

2. Could Calvi, an overweight man of sixty-two, have manoeuvred himself into the position to hang himself from the scaffolding? His family claims that he was unathletic and suffered from vertigo.

3. The choice of Blackfriars Bridge could be evidence of a ritual killing. It has been reported in the Italian press that members of the P2 Lodge wore black robes in some of their ceremonies and addressed each other as *'frate'* – 'friar'. In some old masonic initiation ceremonies the new member is told that if he tells the secrets of the lodge he will be hanged and his body will be washed by the ebb and flow of the tide. Many executions carried out by the Mafia are done in a symbolic way, to indicate the 'crime' that led to the victim's death sentence. Gaia Servadio writes in her book *Mafioso*:

'...a Mafia killing must be publicised as well as untraceable. Everybody must know why it was done and on whose behalf. Consequently grim signs on the corpse explain the reason for punishment...if the dead man was guilty of talking too much (to the police) his tongue would be severed, or a stone inserted in the corpse's mouth as a sign of *'nfamità*. A severed hand placed on the chest: the victim was a *scassapaggiari*, a small thief operating against the wishes of the local boss.'

Could the stones in Calvi's pockets be symbols of the Masons or the Mafia?

Among the points made by those who believe it was suicide are that:

1. While it would have been awkward for Calvi to hang himself from the scaffolding, it would also have been difficult for other people to kill him that way.

2. Killers would have been far more likely to be caught if they took Calvi to the bridge than if they killed him in, say, his hotel room or even a dark alley.

3. The post-mortem examination revealed none of the classic signs of murder by hanging. There were no signs of struggle, nor were any traces of drugs or alcohol found.

Lawyers for the Calvi family and others have cited the following points to support the idea of murder:

1. The banker had made countless enemies over the years, some of whom may have been willing – and able – to have him 'eliminated'. The elaborate security arrangements at his homes and office may well have been justified. Calvi made more enemies in 1981 when he bought the Rizzoli group and when he began giving magistrates information about his P2 activities and his secret payments to politicians. Before leaving Italy in June 1982, Calvi told his family that if his appeal went badly he was prepared to 'name names' – that is, reveal what he knew about the questionable dealings of politicians and the Vatican.

2. Carboni's movements before and after Calvi's death: in the space of six days he went from Klagenfurt to Zurich to Bregenz to Amsterdam to London (where he slept in three different places). After Calvi's death Carboni went into hiding.

3. Several of the shadowy characters Calvi was involved with had friends in the criminal underworld – including Sindona, Gelli and Carboni. Calvi's deputy, Roberto Rosone, was wounded in an attempt on his life by a reputed gangster.

4. In his last phone call to his wife, on Wednesday 16 June, Calvi said: 'I no longer trust the people I'm with.'

The proponents of the suicide hypothesis, however, have these points in their favour:

1. Calvi attempted suicide in July 1981 during his trial and the attempt may have been genuine.

2. His bank was on the verge of collapse and he stood a real risk of returning to prison.

3. During the afternoon and early evening before Calvi's death three events occurred that would have been a major shock to him. The board of Banco Ambrosiano stripped him of his powers as chairman, management of the bank was handed over to the Bank of Italy, and his secretary plunged to her death in an apparent suicide. Though no one knows whether Calvi knew of these events, they had been broadcast on Italian radio and television hours before he died.

4. Silvano Vittor, though a potential suspect, voluntarily surrendered to the police just days after Calvi's death.

To a certain extent, the murder-versus-suicide debate was an argument between the British police and perhaps most Italians who have followed the case. Each side stressed different aspects of the evidence. The police in London put a great deal of weight on the findings of the pathologist, whose post-mortem report pointed to suicide. As Detective Inspector John White later said: 'We treated it as suicide from the word go.' The Italians, however, tended to put more emphasis on what they knew of Calvi's background. In late July, for example, the London correspondent of *La Repubblica* wrote of the forthcoming coroner's inquest: 'In this case, it is important to realise that the jury is comprised of people who know very little about "God's Banker" and are completely unaware of Italian power games.'

There was some harsh criticism of the British police, even allegations of a 'cover-up'. As one British paper reported:

'Some Italian newspapers are even suggesting that instructions have been given to police investigators in London and Rome from the highest political levels to record a verdict of suicide and close the Calvi file because of the uncomfortable associations about arms trading with Argentina and the involvement of the Vatican bank in the case.'

It was thus in an atmosphere of tremendous anticipation that the coroner's inquest into Calvi's death began.

Milton Court is a drab building in the City of London, housing a fire station, a mortuary and several other local government offices. On the second floor is the coroner's court, a small room furnished with wooden benches. On the wall behind the coroner's raised desk are the arms of the City of London, bearing the motto *'Domine Dirige Nos'* ('O Lord, Guide Us') and the cross of Saint George.

The inquest was presided over by Dr David Paul, Her Majesty's Coroner for the City of London. The Calvi family was represented by Sir David Napley, a well-known solicitor often involved in 'celebrity' cases. Napley's clients have included Princess Anne (fighting a speeding ticket) and Jeremy Thorpe, former leader of the Liberal Party (acquitted of conspiring to murder his homosexual lover).

Flavio Carboni was represented in court by barrister John Blofeld, instructed by solicitor Eric Leigh Howard.

The spectators included two members of the Calvi family (the banker's younger brothers Lorenzo and Leone) and dozens of journalists.

The jury of nine, six men and three women, were to hear from nearly forty witnesses, most of them testifying in person, the rest through written statements. At the end, they would be asked to choose one of three possible verdicts: murder, suicide, or 'open verdict'.

The inquest began at 10 a.m. The first five witnesses were police constables and detectives, testifying about the position of the corpse on the scaffolding and the official identification of it by Calvi's relatives. The police witnesses were followed by Sidney Hall, a foreman who worked on the scaffolding, Anthony Huntley, who found the body, and then Huntley's workmate, who phoned the police. After testimony by two more police officers, Sidney Hall was recalled to the witness box. He testified that it would be difficult to carry a heavy weight down the ladder leading to the scaffolding – a point in favour of suicide. But when Sir David Napley examined him, Hall said it would also be difficult for a man to walk on the scaffolding. Napley asked:

Q: So that anyone without experience would have very great difficulty both in getting on to the scaffold and then perhaps remaining on it, if it was slippery and he didn't realise it?
A: That is correct, sir.

Three officers of the Thames River police were then asked to describe how they removed the body from the scaffolding. In examining one of these witnesses, Blofeld tried to establish that it would have been hard for killers to take Calvi to the scaffolding by boat.

Q: How difficult would it be to place any boat in position near the scaffolding so that a body could be suspended in this way?
A: You would need a boat crew with considerable experience and knowledge of the River Thames to place a boat alongside there, to enable the body to be secured in this way.

The jury then heard from perhaps the most important witness: Professor Keith Simpson. Asked by the coroner to summarise his post-mortem report, Simpson testified:

'I found this man heavily built, sir. Although only 5 foot 9 in height, he weighed 13 stones 2 pounds [184 pounds]. He was a little obese, heavily built, but in every other respect in the course of my full examination after death, I found him to be a healthy person. The only organ for which I cannot speak, as regard its ordinary function, is the brain. I am unable to say what processes of thought were going through his mind, but I can say there was no disease of the brain and there was no disease elsewhere to cause him pain or distress, or to give rise to any anxiety from his physical point of view.'

Simpson went on to say that the corpse showed 'characterisic features of asphyxia by constriction of the neck'. Under examination, he said:

'My conclusions were, sir, that death was due without question in my view to asphyxiation by hanging.'

141

In other words, Calvi was not strangled and *then* hanged from the scaffolding and he did not drown.

On the crucial question – homicide versus suicide – Simpson was too experienced a witness to state his opinion explicitly, which could prejudice the jury. But he left little doubt about what he believed. He said he found 'no marks of violence or pinning' and no signs that Calvi had been 'under the influence of drink or drugs or both'. Choosing his words with great care, Simpson said 'there was no evidence to suggest that the hanging was other than a self-suspension…'

Simpson was followed by Dr William Wilson, a scientist from Scotland Yard, who had examined the contents of Calvi's stomach and samples of his urine, liver and blood. He said he had found no alcohol and no significant traces of drugs. Blofeld asked him:

Q: So you certainly have found…no drug in your investigations that could account for anything more than a possibility of drowsiness?
A: That is my conclusion.

In the afternoon, attention focused on the movements of Calvi, Carboni and Vittor. The witnesses included Robert Clarke, the London solicitor involved in the booking of the accommodation at the Chelsea Cloisters; Reginald Mulligan, the pilot who flew to Innsbruck to pick up Calvi and Vittor and brought them to London; and employees of the Chelsea Cloisters. The most important witnesses in this part of the inquest were Carboni's friend, William Morris, and Morris's daughter, Odette. Morris said that he had received a phone call from Carboni on Wednesday 16 June, asking for his help in renting a flat in London. Morris said he spent most of Thursday with Carboni visiting estate agents. The coroner, Dr Paul, then asked Morris what Carboni's mood was like on Friday morning, since this was shortly after Calvi's death.

Q: Did you notice anything about his demeanour?
A: Well in a sense, sir, he might have been a bit pensive and thoughtful.

The coroner then pointed out that Morris had once given a different reply (when he was asked this question by the police).

Q: Now today you are describing his behaviour as pensive? Have you ever described it in any other way?
A: I described it once as agitated, sir.

Odette Morris entered the witness box and recounted the events of Friday 18 June. She said that she and Carboni checked into the Chelsea Hotel, near the Chelsea Cloisters, so that Carboni could make some phone calls. While they were in the room, he asked her to phone Room 881 at the Chelsea Cloisters, but there was no reply. At about 5.30

p.m., she and Carboni went to the Chelsea Cloisters to find Carboni's friend – the name 'Calvi', she said, was never mentioned. While Carboni waited outside, Odette Morris knocked on the door of Room 881, but there was no answer. Carboni then asked her to leave two notes at the hotel, addressed to Silvano Vittor and requesting him to telephone a certain 'Elda'.

Miss Morris then described her curious trip with Carboni to Edinburgh. Carboni had offered her a job in Italy, and yet on Saturday 19 June they flew to Scotland. Sir David Napley asked her:

Q: Did your father ask you to accompany him [Carboni] wherever he went?
A: Yes. My father said to me to go...with him to Italy.
Q: Well, Edinburgh isn't Italy.

Throughout their testimony, the Morrises appeared very obtuse. They ran around London with Carboni, watched him make countless telephone calls, and never once asked him to explain his frantic activity. Miss Morris, who speaks Italian (her mother is Italian), did not overhear what Carboni said in any of his telephone calls.

Two of the people who knew the most about Calvi's stay in London, Flavio Carboni and Silvano Vittor, did not attend the inquest. Vittor was still in custody in Rome (charged with having helped Calvi jump bail), while Carboni was still hiding. Nonetheless, their versions of the trip were given to the jury – Vittor's in the form of a statement taken by an Italian magistrate, Carboni's in the form of a letter sent to a magistrate from his hiding place. Both statements were read by Detective Chief Superintendent Barry Tarbun of the City of London Police. During his reading of the statements, Tarbun was interrupted repeatedly by the coroner who wanted to exclude material he deemed to be irrelevant.

In one portion of his statement, Vittor described the last day of Calvi's life:

'[On] Thursday 17th June, I woke as usual and went to find Calvi. I found him in shorts and vest on the bed; I noticed he had shaved off his moustache. He said to me that it was the first time in his life that he had ever cut his moustache. A little while later Carboni telephoned and I took the occasion of making an appointment with the two girls [the Kleinszig sisters] for half-an-hour later, in order to go and buy a change of clothing. Calvi gave me £200–£300. After shopping I returned home, it was midday, I heard that Carboni had not yet telephoned. We ate food left over from the previous day. Carboni's call arrived in the early afternoon. He said that so far he had not been able to find anything but the prospects were very good. He phoned again about 5 p.m. to say he would be with us within forty minutes since he was on the side of the city. After about two hours Carboni called on the house phone to tell us to go down and

143

join him. Calvi did not want to go and told me to tell him [Carboni] to come up. I went down and found Carboni [next to] a taxi. I explained to him that Calvi did not want to go out and after having let the taxi go I went by foot to collect the girls who were in a nearby restaurant. The girls wanted to eat something…We returned in the direction of the residence by foot…I wish to point out that Carboni had told me that he had left the Hilton and had not yet taken other accommodation…

'I remember that the two girls had very small bags with them but no suitcases like Carboni. I explained to Carboni before going that I was fed up with Calvi's company since he was continually complaining. Carboni assured me that as soon as he arrived at his hotel he would phone Calvi. I returned to the residence about half-an-hour to three-quarters of an hour after I had left it. I had gone out about 11.30 p.m. or perhaps midnight, probably therefore I got there about 1 a.m. London time. I went up to the apartment and knocked as usual. Nobody answered. After having insisted I went down to the hall and asked a clerk, rather two staff members, to phone the apartment. They did so and no one answered. I did not ask the two if my friend had gone out since I was not able to express myself in English. After phoning I went back and knocked again. I remember having heard the phone ring [inside the flat]…

'Then I went back down and after much difficulty and talking with the switchboard operator, who spoke Italian well, I was able to get the apartment door open with a duplicate key. I asked them to leave me the key but the staff did not want to. During my attempts to get the door open I had gone to the nearby restaurants in the hope that Calvi had gone out to eat something, though I was not at all convinced of this possibility…When I returned to the room I found the television on but no programmes were being transmitted.

'The reception desk was situated in such a way that they could see who went out. Staff are present at the desk both day and night. The door is always open. In the room I found Calvi's suitcase, which was closed with a combination lock. I lay down on the bed and spent the night in a state of apprehension. I did not receive any phone calls and was not able to call Carboni to tell him since I did not know which hotel he had moved to. After a sleepless night, at about 8 a.m. English time, I left the residence. I left the suitcases in the residence. I took a taxi to the principal London airport. I took a plane to Vienna, paying with the money Calvi had given me, the same money I mentioned above. I paid £142. I left at 10.10 a.m. with a British Airways flight.'

After answering questions about the police investigation of the Calvi case, Tarbun read Carboni's letter. It began with a grandiloquent statement about Carboni's desire to make 'a dutiful contribution to the work of justice with regard to the tragic events culminating in the death of the banker, Roberto Calvi…' He added that he had written the letter in the hope of clearing his name.

Carboni said he spent most of Thursday 17 June with William Morris and his wife Alma, making the rounds of estate agents. 'But the search,' he said, 'turned out to be much more difficult and laborious than foreseen.' They returned to the Morrises' flat at about 9 p.m., then received a call from an agency, saying that one of the apartments they had seen might be available the next day. At 9.30 p.m. Carboni 'hurried to telephone the news to Calvi, whom I had last talked to in the late morning. Vittor answered, I told him the news and said I was on my way over.'

When Carboni arrived at the Chelsea Cloisters by taxi late that night, he saw Vittor in the lobby of the hotel, the statement continued. Vittor suggested that they go over to the nearby restaurant where the Kleinszig sisters had been waiting for several hours. The restaurant was about to close, so they stayed for only about fifteen to twenty minutes. Carboni told Vittor that he would 'let Calvi know the latest news on the apartment' the next morning. In the meantime, Vittor should tell Calvi to stay calm.

Carboni spent the night at the Sheraton Hotel near Heathrow Airport. The following morning, Friday 18 June, he and Odette Morris took a taxi to Chelsea where Miss Morris tried to contact Calvi and Vittor in their room. In the afternoon, Carboni spoke by phone to Vittor – who was by then in Austria. Vittor, he said, 'was very alarmed and told me that the evening before…he had not found Calvi in the apartment. He waited a long time for Calvi and then, taken by panic at the thought that the threats that Calvi himself had feared had actually come about, he was terrified and had run off…' Carboni's statement continued:

'At that moment I was also taken by fear, not knowing if the danger that had been realised for Calvi would not also come to me. I returned to the Morrises with Miss Morris…I told them of the news and of the pointlessness of busying themselves with the matter of the apartment. Then, from a call made to Rome about midnight, I got the news given on television that the English police had found what they presumed to be Calvi's body in the Thames, carrying the passport of Roberto Calvini. I spent a very agitated night at the Morrises' apartment. The next day, Saturday, I feared for my safety, not knowing the cause of the tragedy and remembering Calvi's fears. I asked Miss Morris to accompany me, due to my ignorance of English, to some place as far away from London as possible; we left London for Edinburgh where at the Hotel George we took two rooms and rested the night. The next morning I called Hans Kunz so that he could come and get me with a private plane…

'For my part, I can only add that I believed I was helping a desperate man who feared great danger, without saying from where, and for whom I felt great compassion. What I have said here represents a true reconstruction of my doings during the last days in the life of Roberto Calvi.'

The final witness was Barry Tarbun of the City Police. Under

145

questioning from Blofeld, Tarbun indicated that the police had found little or no evidence of murder.

When Tarbun completed his testimony, it was after 7 p.m. – more than nine hours since the inquest had begun. In fact, Dr Paul commented on the amount of time that had gone by – remarks for which he was later to be criticised. He said:

'I could say my summing-up is going to take all of two hours, I assure you it will take considerably less and if you do require an adjournment you may have one until, good heavens, a quarter to eight at night. This is breaking almost every record in the law courts. We will reassemble at a quarter to eight. I will then sum up to you and send you out and with any luck, we should be away from here soon after.'

At 7.50 p.m., Dr Paul began his half-hour summing-up. He told the jury they would have to answer four questions, the first three of which were not in dispute: who had died, where and when was the fact of death certified, and what was the medical cause of death. The fourth question was: what were the circumstances under which this man met his death in this way?

Dr Paul summarised the evidence the jury had heard about Calvi's trip to London and the movements of Carboni and Vittor. He then reminded them of different ways Calvi, if he had killed himself, could have gained access to the scaffolding. 'You either go down the ladder and swing over the eighteen inches onto the scaffold board or the two feet eight inches onto the tubes of the scaffolding, and then go along the scaffold board to the edge, or you approach it from the river, standing on the fairly high part of the boat.'

The coroner then explained – in somewhat less neutral language – how murderers would have had to manoeuvre:

'Could a man of Mr Calvi's weight, unconscious, as has been suggested, be carried down that ladder, across this gap of eighteen inches or two feet eight inches onto the planks, be carried to the end and then be suspended in such a way without sustaining some marks upon his body of carriage across that rather awkward scaffolding?

'Could a boat be handled with sufficient skill so that it could maintain its position beneath the scaffolding while a heavy man such as Mr Calvi was supported upright and then suspended from a rope when, if that theory is to hold water, he was unconscious and unable to resist? Because there were no marks of resistance.'

In the next part of his summation, the coroner made some remarks which seemed to imply that Calvi had committed suicide. (The italics are the author's.) 'Why did *Mr Calvi decide* to make this journey from

146

Chelsea Cloisters, some four miles, and why did *he* then *choose* Blackfriars Bridge?...But *he did choose* Blackfriars.'

Dr Paul summarised the evidence of Professor Simpson, then explained the three verdicts that were available to the jury: murder, suicide or an open verdict. He was later criticised for his description of the open verdict, which seemed to imply that there was something wrong with such a verdict (emphasis added):

'What this means is that if, on the evidence you have heard, there is not enough evidence to say that he killed himself...and equally if, on the evidence, there is not enough proof so that you are sure that he was unlawfully killed by other people, then *the open verdict may seem like a super open door to scuttle through* if you are in any difficulty about returning another verdict.

Let me tell you that this was not, never has been, and I hope will never be a convenient, comfortable way out.'

The jury withdrew at 8.20 p.m. – 10 hours and 20 minutes after the inquest began. After a few minutes the jury foreman came in and said the jury was having trouble reaching a unanimous verdict. Dr Paul told them a majority verdict was acceptable, as long as the majority was at least seven of the nine jurors. At 9 p.m. the foreman said there were still problems in reaching a verdict. The jurors continued their deliberations and returned at 10 p.m. There was then the following exchange:

Coroner: Mr Foreman, has the jury reached a verdict?
Foreman: Yes, we have, sir.
Coroner: Would you please tell us what that verdict is?
Foreman: Yes. By a majority verdict the jury has decided that the deceased killed himself.
Coroner: Is the minority of your number two or less?
Foreman: Yes.
Coroner: I therefore record that the jury find that Roberto Calvi, a male of 62 years, of Via Frua 9, Milan, Italy, was certified dead at Waterloo Pier, London, on Friday 18th June 1982, the cause of death being asphyxia due to hanging, and that he killed himself.'

After the verdict was delivered Sir David Napley left Milton Court to return home in his Rolls Royce. Outside the building, he stopped for a moment to talk to Dr Paul. 'I'm sorry, David,' Napley said, 'but I'm going to appeal.'

Many reactions were far less polite than that. A number of Italians regarded the verdict as preposterous – or even as proof of a cover-up. Magistrate Domenico Sica, who had been investigating Calvi's disappearance from Italy, referred sarcastically to the banker's death as 'that car accident Calvi had'.

147

Yet when one considers what the jurors were told during the inquest, the verdict is not that surprising. They heard persuasive testimony from Professor Simpson and the police supporting the suicide hypothesis. Most of the evidence about Calvi's trip to London came from the statements of Carboni, Vittor and the Morrises. Carboni's portrayal of himself as a sort of 'good Samaritan' was largely unchallenged. After the inquest too many questions still remained unanswered. Why did Calvi come to London? What was his relationship with Carboni? What really happened on the night of 17–18 June?

Carlo Calvi has said he spends hours trying to solve the mystery of his father's death. 'Every night,' he said, 'I think about all the possibilities, racking my brain to find the right trail.' When the inquest was over, Clara Calvi said simply: 'My husband was murdered. I won't have peace until the killers are brought to justice.'

The Calvi family soon applied to Britain's Attorney General, Sir Michael Havers, for permission to file an appeal against the suicide verdict. Among the grounds for their application, they cited some of the questionable remarks made by the coroner in his summing-up and the long time that the jury had sat before retiring to consider their verdict. Their request was granted on 13 January 1983.

Asked in an interview about the Calvi case, former Italian Prime Minister Giulio Andreotti said: 'Perhaps it would be a good idea to dig a bit into [Calvi's] connections and the people who accompanied the banker in his last period.' He noted that in mystery novels 'you find the murderer on the last page. In the Calvi story, we haven't arrived there yet.'

26

Death of a Bank

In recent banking history, one year stands out as particularly traumatic: 1974. That year, confidence in the international banking system was shaken by a series of major jolts, including the failure of Bankhaus Herstatt in West Germany and the collapse of Michele Sindona's banks in New York and Milan. British bankers associate 1974 with the so-called 'secondary banking crisis', which forced the Bank of England to organise a massive 'lifeboat' operation to rescue banks that had lent too much to property speculators. American bankers recall the collapse of real estate investment trusts and the near bankruptcy of New York City.

In early 1982, the banking world began to experience an eerie sense of *déjà vu*. Just as bankers were absorbing the shock of Poland's debt crisis, Argentina was forced to reschedule its foreign debts and Drysdale Securities, an obscure Wall Street firm, suddenly collapsed, causing huge losses to its biggest creditor, Chase Manhattan Bank.

By the spring, leading bankers were obviously nervous and defensive. The chairman of Chase Manhattan, Willard Butcher, visited London in the spring, and was asked at a press conference whether 1982 would be as bad for the major banks as 1974. Butcher snapped at the reporter: 'Have we got problems? Yes! But I do not see signs of basic collapse, catastrophe, a menacing series of accidents. Sometimes we tend to say, "Oh my God, all hell will break loose, everything will collapse!" Yet the facts are that the sun will rise tomorrow and set tomorrow night.' What the Chase Manhattan chairman did not realise was that, as he was speaking, the world banking system was about to be hit by another major shock: the Ambrosiano crisis, one of the biggest bank failures in the post-war era.

Few people had ever doubted the health of Banco Ambrosiano, because Calvi had kept his ghost company scheme so well hidden. As far as most people could tell, it was a solid and profitable bank. After

Calvi's arrest in May 1981, an Italian weekly wrote reassuringly: 'There won't be – as there was during the time of Sindona – a financial *crack*. The balance sheet of the Ambrosiano-Centrale group is strong and so there is no reason to fear a collapse...'

In fact for a long time Ambrosiano was, at least in theory, relatively protected from the debt problems of the ghost companies. All the loans to the ghost companies were extended by foreign-based subsidiaries (such as Banco Andino in Peru) which, in turn, had raised the money from international banks. If Andino and the others were to declare bankruptcy, Ambrosiano's direct loss would be limited to the money it had invested in their parent company – Banco Ambrosiano Holding in Luxembourg.

But after Calvi's arrest in May 1981 many foreign banks became reluctant to provide money to the Ambrosiano group. Many of those that would lend began to insist that the borrower be the parent bank in Milan. So Ambrosiano (Milan) began borrowing hundreds of millions of dollars, to be re-lent to Banco Andino and the other foreign subsidiaries. By the end of June 1982 Ambrosiano was owed $743 million by its own subsidiaries – most of which it would lose if the ghost companies could not repay their debts. To conceal the fact that he was recycling the money this way, Calvi resorted to a favourite device of Michele Sindona, the 'fiduciary deposit'. A fiduciary deposit enables a customer of a bank to move money around anonymously by using a bank as his 'front'. The bank simply acts as an intermediary between the depositor and the institution where the funds are placed, collecting a commission. Ambrosiano made a total of about $400 million in fiduciary deposits with a number of international banks, and then instructed those banks to transmit the money to Ambrosiano's foreign subsidiaries. The Milan bank's records showed these as deposits with banks 'not affiliated' to Ambrosiano, and it thus managed to dupe inspectors from the Bank of Italy.

When Ambrosiano's foreign subsidiaries could not repay the money the Milan bank had deposited with them (since they could not collect from the ghost companies), Ambrosiano was unable to repay *its* depositors and creditors. Eventually, Ambrosiano's liabilities (the money it owed to others) exceeded its assets (the money it could collect from others). In short, it was insolvent – bankrupt.

In addition to this 'insolvency' crisis, Ambrosiano was suffering from what bankers call a 'liquidity crisis' – it was short of ready cash. Between 1 January and 17 June 1982, deposits to Ambrosiano from other banks plunged by nearly two-thirds, from 1,232 billion lire (about $1 billion) to 484 billion lire.

Ambrosiano's board of directors apparently only learned of the dubious loans on 7 June, when Calvi read them the Bank of Italy's letter of 31 May. After Calvi disappeared from Italy, his subordinates visited the Vatican bank, demanding that the loans be repaid – since IOR's 'patronage letters' implied responsibility for the debts. For their part, IOR officials claimed that the letters had only been issued as a 'favour' to Calvi, and that, in any event, they were nullified by the 'counter letter' from Calvi.

IOR's refusal to pay forced the board of Ambrosiano to hand over management of the bank to a special commissioner from the Bank of Italy on 17 June. He was soon replaced by a panel of three commissioners.

The Bank of Italy and other government entities followed a three-pronged strategy to deal with the Ambrosiano crisis:

1. Pumping cash into the Milan bank – to allay the liquidity crisis – through a 'rescue pool' of six, later increased to seven, Italian banks. (The press dubbed these banks 'the magnificent seven'.)

2. Honouring the debts and deposits of Ambrosiano (Milan), while refusing to do the same for the foreign subsidiaries.

3. Demanding that IOR repay the debts of the ghost companies.

What this 'solution' meant was that depositors and creditors of Ambrosiano (Milan) were protected. But the bank's shareholders, and the creditors and depositors of the foreign subsidiaries, faced potential losses of hundreds of millions of dollars. Not surprisingly, there were immediate howls of protest. Nearly 40,000 Italians owned stock in Ambrosiano – and they now feared that their share certificates were worthless pieces of paper. The Italian press was soon filled with stories of widows and pensioners who had been induced by the bank's branch managers to part with their savings. One of the more pathetic examples was an eighty-year-old man, nearly blind, who had lost much of his savings. 'I am not a speculator,' he said. 'I have never speculated in the stock market.' But a branch manager 'convinced me to buy Banco Ambrosiano shares... investing in a bank seemed safe.'

Groups of disgruntled shareholders formed protest groups and filed lawsuits. Letters were written to the press demanding to know why the Bank of Italy had not acted sooner, and why CONSOB had permitted Ambrosiano to list its shares on the Milan exchange since. They argued that the listing seemed to imply that CONSOB was satisfied that Ambrosiano had made adequate financial disclosure. CONSOB officials responded that the Bank of Italy had not informed the agency that it was worried about Ambrosiano.

About 700 of Ambrosiano's 4,200 employees owned shares in the bank and they were now worried not only about their job security, but about their savings. Referring to two of the bank's biggest shareholders, one employee said: 'They can't treat us as if we were Bagnasco or Pesenti.'

In fact Carlo Pesenti was seriously wounded by the Ambrosiano crisis. His industrial and financial empire was already in trouble, and when the value of his Ambrosiano shares was wiped out he was forced to dispose of one of his most valuable holdings. In late July he agreed to sell one of his banks, Istituto Bancario Italiano, to Italy's largest savings bank, Cassa di Risparmio delle Provincie Lombarde (CARIPLO).

As Ambrosiano's shareholders squabbled with the Italian authorities, hundreds of foreign bankers who had lent money to Calvi's foreign subsidiaries watched helplessly as their customers collapsed one by one. (The only major exception was Banca del Gottardo, the Swiss bank in which Ambrosiano had a 45 per cent stake.) On 19 June Banco Andino 'effectively suspended operations', according to one press report, and began 'passing copies of all incoming telexes to the Bank of Italy commissioners running Banco Ambrosiano in Milan'. On 12 July Banco Ambrosiano Holding (Luxembourg) was declared in default by Britain's Midland Bank, which had arranged a $40 million loan. Two days later another British bank, National Westminster, declared BAH to be in default on a $75 million loan. On 15 July the Luxembourg authorities put BAH under *gestion contrôllée* (controlled administration). On 19 July the Bahamas authorities suspended the licence of Banco Ambrosiano Overseas, in the wake of a declaration of default by BAO's creditors. In late July the business daily, *Il Sole-24 Ore,* noted: 'Now, all the nerve centres through which Roberto Calvi operated for years – weaving his financial web – are under the control of commissioners.'

The Bank of Italy's refusal to bail out Calvi's foreign subsidiaries outraged foreign bankers. Many of them argued that Italy's central bank was seriously undermining confidence in the international banking system. At the centre of the controversy was the Euromarket, where the Ambrosiano group had raised most of the funds for the ghost company scheme. Also called the 'Eurodollar market', since most transactions are in dollars, this pool of capital has grown enormously since the 1960s to a total of more than $2,000 billion, according to some estimates. It began as a market in which banks could deal with each other in US dollars without the funds flowing through the United States. A French bank with a surplus of dollars would, for example, deposit the funds with the London branch of a German bank. The rapid growth of the Euromarket in the 1960s and early 1970s was fuelled by, for example, huge deposits from oil-rich countries and massive borrowing by oil-importing nations.

The growth of the market made banks far more interdependent than in the past. The collapse of, say, a German bank was no longer a matter of little concern to Canadian bankers; the German bank may have collected millions of dollars in Euromarket deposits from Canadian banks. This point was made dramatically by the bank failures of 1974, which had international repercussions. As Margaret Reid has written of the Herstatt failure: 'The collapse sent more powerful currents of shock through the international banking system than at any time since the early 1930s.'

Bank regulators reacted by taking a more 'global' view of their job. Central bankers from major countries made a number of agreements to tighten supervision of banks and to act in concert to prevent panics from spreading. Two major agreements were the 'Basle Declaration' of 1974 and the 'Basle Concordat' of 1975. (Basle in Switzerland is the home of the central bankers' 'club': the Bank for International Settlements.)

These understandings seemed adequate – until the Ambrosiano crisis. One agreement was that a central bank would be responsible for supervising the foreign branches of a bank with headquarters in its country. In other words, if Ambrosiano had a branch in London the Bank of Italy was supposed to know what that branch was doing. But Calvi did not operate overseas through branches, he used a majority-owned subsidiary in Luxembourg, which, in turn, controlled banks incorporated in other countries. The Basle Concordat tried to foresee the problem of foreign subsidiaries, by saying that there was to be *dual responsibility* in such cases – the regulator of the parent bank and the regulator in the country where the subsidiary was incorporated. That sounded fine on paper, but there were several flaws in practice. The most serious flaw was that the Bank of Italy lacked the legal power to inspect Calvi's foreign subsidiaries. Another flaw, which no one seems to have noticed until the crisis, was that the Luxembourg holding company was not in fact a bank, even though it had the word 'banco' in its name. Thus the Luxembourg banking authorities never inspected it.

Another weakness of the central bankers' agreements concerned rescue operations. Many of Ambrosiano's creditors read the agreements to mean that the Bank of Italy was obliged to intervene to prop up Ambrosiano's foreign subsidiaries in the event of a crisis. The Bank of Italy, however, said that the agreements applied to temporary *liquidity crises* and not to *solvency crises*.

It would be misleading to imply that the default of Calvi's foreign subsidiaries was followed by nothing more than academic debates about banking supervision. Many of the creditors reacted with shock and anger. 'I am twenty-two years in international banking,' a German banker was quoted as saying, 'and in my personal view the actions of the Italians are totally unacceptable.' A columnist for the *Wall Street Journal* wrote of 'an intensifying howl of outrage from European financial centres'. An American banker took his anger out on Alessandro Mennini, an Ambrosiano official who had been involved in the international borrowing of the Luxembourg holding company (and whose father was the number two man at the Vatican bank). Said this banker: 'I'd like to spit in his face or punch him out. He was one of Calvi's biggest defenders.'

There have been no reports of fist fights between bankers, but the creditors did resort to other tactics. In 'not-for-attribution' interviews with journalists, some bankers threatened to boycott Italian borrowers in the Euromarket unless the Bank of Italy agreed to bail out Ambrosiano. The Euromarket newsletter *AGEFI* later conducted a survey of its readers and found that 64 per cent of those responding said that Italy's creditworthiness had been damaged by the Ambrosiano affair. Ambrosiano's creditors asked central bankers in their own countries to put pressure on the Bank of Italy, apparently with some success, at least on the propaganda front. By late July, there were press reports that officials of the Bank of England, the Swiss National Bank and West Germany's Bundesbank were critical of the Bank of Italy's conduct. One notable omission was the US Federal Reserve which, according to a report in *Business Week*, appeared to be tacitly supporting the Italians. Banking expert Richard Dale contrasted the attitudes of the Fed and the Bank of England: 'The US doesn't like the Euromarkets...[and] doesn't like offshore banking, whereas London lives off it.'

The Italians, however, refused to alter their position, insisting that the agreements among central bankers did not apply to the Ambrosiano crisis. Perhaps the most persuasive statement of the Italians' point of view appeared in the *Wall Street Journal*, in an interview with Treasury Minister Andreatta.

'"I am ready to change my position. But only if the following happens," [Andreatta] declares, smiling broadly. "The Federal Reserve, the Bank of England and the Bundesbank will all agree that banking isn't a business anymore. Banking is now an administrative branch of the national government." Central banks will be the lender of last resort not only in cases of banks having a temporary liquidity crisis, he continues, "but also in cases of mismanagement and insolvency. So it will be the end of a free market in banking activity."'

Ambrosiano's disgruntled creditors were given their first real chance to air their complaints when creditors' meetings were scheduled for Thursday 29 July. The setting was the Tower Hotel, beside the River Thames in the City of London. The first meeting was for creditors of the Bahamas subsidiary, the second for lenders to the Luxembourg holding company.

At about 9.30 a.m. some fifty bankers gathered in a small conference room to meet Pierre Siegenthaler, President of Banco Ambrosiano Overseas. Some reporters tried to pass themselves off as bankers and sneak into the room, and the police had to be called. It turned out to be a wasted call, because someone had forgotten to switch off the sound system. As the *Financial Times* reported the next day: 'The few journalists that managed to get up early enough were able to hear everything that went on through the hotel loudspeaker system.'

What the bankers and reporters heard was an account of the incredibly tangled finances of Calvi's Bahamas bank. Figures released by Siegenthaler seemed to suggest that BAO's main activity was shuttling money among Ambrosiano affiliates and the Vatican bank. The liability side of its (roughly $500 million) balance sheet included $110.2 million owed to Ambrosiano in Milan, $40.4 million owed to Banca del Gottardo, $8.9 million owed to 'other affiliates' and $72.9 million owed to IOR. The asset side included $155 million owed to BAO by the Luxembourg holding company (its parent) and $89.8 million owed by IOR. Another peculiar feature of the balance sheet was that it included $14 million in loans made in February at Calvi's request to what Siegenthaler described as four unknown clients.

In the afternoon, 200 to 300 bankers crowded into the hotel's York Room. They represented an estimated 250 banks that had lent money to Calvi's foreign subsidiaries – about $400 million of it to Banco Ambrosiano Holding (Luxembourg). As the room became progressively more crowded, new arrivals were turned away with comments like 'There's already somebody here from your bank.' The size of the crowd could perhaps be explained by the excitement of the Calvi case – something to which even sober and conservative bankers were not immune.

It was a hot, sunny day, the conference room was overflowing, the air conditioning was far from adequate. The uncomfortable conditions only exacerbated the ugly mood of the creditors. The borrower was represented by Giovanni Arduino, one of the three Bank of Italy commissioners running the parent bank in Milan. He opened the meeting by explaining why the Italian authorities were refusing to bail out the Luxembourg holding company. He then took questions that

155

were put to him from the floor.

It was not a pleasant spectacle, according to a number of participants. The bankers were angry and Arduino was made a scapegoat. 'We felt betrayed by Banco Ambrosiano and by the Bank of Italy,' says an American banker who was present. 'The tone of the questions was very belligerent. There were even personal attacks on this poor guy Arduino.'

One of the first questions was from a representative of West Germany's Stuttgart Landesbank, which had made a large loan to BAH just a few months before the Ambrosiano crisis. He accused the Bank of Italy of undermining confidence in the Euromarkets. The German banker was followed by a man from Swiss Bank Corporation, who argued that it was absurd to separate the Luxembourg holding company from the parent bank in Milan. Brandishing a copy of a Banco Ambrosiano brochure, he pointed out the similarities in the names and logos of the two. The Swiss banker then read aloud a telex he said his bank had sent to Governor Ciampi, of the Bank of Italy, which warned of the possible consequences for other Italian borrowers if the Bank of Italy did not change its attitude.

Other speakers pointed out that the loans to BAH had been negotiated in Milan by executives of the parent bank – a French banker referred to them in his halting, less than perfect English as 'people wearing two caps'.

While the bankers pointed their fingers at Arduino – as a representative of the Italian government – he placed the blame on certain Ambrosiano officials who, he said, had engaged in 'tragic corruption'. He also criticised the Vatican bank, pointing out that much of the money in question had been lent to companies 'stated to be controlled by IOR'.

The meetings at the Tower Hotel did nothing to satisfy Ambrosiano's creditors. Indeed, several of them complained that Arduino had wasted their time by calling them together simply to say that he wasn't going to give them any money. And as they spoke, the condition of the parent bank in Milan continued to deteriorate. In spite of the efforts of the Bank of Italy to bolster confidence in Ambrosiano by honouring all of its debts and deposits, the run on the bank continued. Between 17 June and early August, it lost more than 700 billion lire (about $500 million) in deposits. And that cash had to be replaced by money from the seven-bank rescue pool. As far as solvency was concerned, it was later determined that as of early August Ambrosiano's liabilities exceeded its assets by 480 billion lire.

The authorities soon decided that Ambrosiano could only be kept alive if it received a massive injection of new capital – estimated at 1,000 billion lire (about $700 million). But no one – not the rescue banks, not the bank's shareholders – was willing to put up that money. And so the three commissioners recommended that the bank be put into what is known as 'compulsory liquidation'. The old corporation, Banco Ambrosiano SpA, would be dissolved, and its business would be taken over by a new corporation, to be called Nuovo Banco Ambrosiano SpA. The share capital for the new bank would be provided by the seven banks in the rescue pool.

On Friday 6 August Treasury Minister Andreatta signed the liquidation decree, thus signifying what one news agency called 'the most spectacular financial collapse in the country's post-war history'.

By any standard the Ambrosiano crash was large, by the standards of Italy's relatively small stock-market it was enormous. It has been estimated that, at about 2,500 billion lire (the value of Ambrosiano based on its highest share price), the Ambrosiano failure exceeded all the money raised in the Italian stock-market during the previous three to four years by Italy's largest companies, including Fiat, Montedison, Olivetti and Pirelli. Andreatta spoke of the failure of Calvi's bank in historical terms. It represented, he said, 'the destruction of an important institution laden with history; a good history, until the deviations of the past ten years'.

One thing that was clear was that Roberto Calvi's fate and that of Banco Ambrosiano could not be separated. Less than two months after the banker's death his bank was formally pronounced dead.

If a new bank was to rise from the ashes of Ambrosiano, the employees knew they had to work quickly. The liquidation decree was signed on a Friday and if the new bank did not open its doors on the following Monday, customers might panic, destroying any chance the new bank might have of surviving. 'The situation was desperate,' says Giovanni Bazoli, the man appointed chairman of Nuovo Banco Ambrosiano. 'If we did not re-open on Monday, who knows what would have happened? There could have been a run on the bank. We could have had buildings and employees, but no customers.'

Like many Italian cities, Milan is virtually deserted during August for the 'ferragosto' holidays. Even Milanese who are not on holiday tend to go away at week-ends to the countryside or the beach. But on the week-end of 7–8 August 1982 the headquarters of what was now Nuovo Banco Ambrosiano was a hive of activity.

That week-end will undoubtedly remain one of the most memorable in Giovanni Bazoli's life. 'I had never been here,' he says, 'and to come here for the first time as chairman – it's something that would affect

157

anyone.' He remembers arriving at the building at night: 'It was an eerie atmosphere. The rest of Milan was dark and empty, the bank was all lit up. It was like a surrealistic painting by De Chirico.' He walked into the chairman's office and immediately noticed the security apparatus Calvi had installed. This, coupled with what he knew about Calvi's life and death, made him very uncomfortable. 'I immediately moved to another office,' he says, adding: 'I was tempted to move to another floor.' Later, he found it 'a bit of a shock to see myself described in the newspapers – not as the chairman of Nuovo Banco Ambrosiano, but as Calvi's successor.'

On Sunday night Bazoli chatted with Ambrosiano officers and tried to strike the right balance between the old and the new. 'I asked for their collaboration,' he says, 'without expressing any judgment on the recent past. I referred to the old bank, to its traditions, and said that the bank should not forget its traditions.'

On Monday morning, 9 August, Nuovo Banco Ambrosiano opened for business. Much to the relief of the executives and other employees it appeared to be just an ordinary working day. Still, there were uncomfortable reminders of the trauma the bank had gone through. An old man outside one of the branches was approached by a reporter and identified himself as an Ambrosiano shareholder. 'My father was one of the founders of this bank,' he said. 'It used to be "the priests' bank". My father was twenty years old then. I'm retired now. My money? Who knows if I'll ever see it again…'

The new executives of the bank took a number of steps to reassure depositors that their money was safe. A full-page advertisement placed in national newspapers stressed that Nuovo Banco Ambrosiano, unlike its predecessor, was a solid institution. It read in part:

'Friday 6 August 1982: seven banks give life to Nuovo Banco Ambrosiano. And so one of the major financial crises of the post-war era is quickly resolved: the savings of more than 300,000 depositors are guaranteed, the continuity of relationships with innumerable business customers is assured, the jobs of thousands of employees are safeguarded…
'New ownership…
'New management…
'Nuovo Banco Ambrosiano is trying to return to its healthier roots…'

Another early step was to dismiss several senior officials who were regarded as too closely identified with the 'Calvi era'. (Even before Nuovo Banco was established, the Bank of Italy commissioners had sacked Roberto Rosone, the deputy chairman, and Filippo Leoni, the head of the international department. Leoni went quietly, while Rosone

158

protested that he was being made a scapegoat.)

Bazoli and his colleagues also tried, in symbolic ways, to dissociate the new bank from Calvi. The special lock in the lift that had restricted access to the fourth floor was replaced with an ordinary button and the bullet-proof doors were flung open. The electronic security devices were removed from Calvi's old office, which was converted into a conference room.

Although these and other moves helped to restore confidence in Ambrosiano, there was a difficult job ahead. The flight of deposits meant that the new bank was less than half the size of the 'old' Ambrosiano. Between May and August deposits plunged from 5,000 billion lire (about $4 billion) to 2,000 billion lire. Yet, because employees had been promised job security, the work-force could not be reduced proportionately. This meant that the bank was grossly overstaffed in relation to its volume of business.

Another problem was the ghost company scheme, even allowing for the fact that Nuovo Ambrosiano refused to recognise the debts of the foreign subsidiaries. This was because the new bank *did* agree to honour deposits and loans made directly to the parent bank – and much of that money had been recycled to the now defunct ghost companies.

Finally, Nuovo Ambrosiano executives found that the bank had made a large number of dubious loans and investments, on Calvi's instructions, apparently aimed at buying 'protection' or helping P2 'brothers'. The most egregious example was the 40 per cent stake in Rizzoli, purchased through La Centrale at a vastly inflated price. The Rizzoli deal, says Bazoli, seemed to have had no business logic at all, and has cost La Centrale an enormous amount of money. The only apparent motive, he says, was to expand the 'power' of the Ambrosiano group.

It was a new bank with a new name and new management, but it will take years for it to exorcise the ghost of Roberto Calvi.

27

The Trail of Gold

The liquidation of Banco Ambrosiano was as much of an anti-climax as the coroner's inquest. For just as the inquest failed to clarify how Calvi died, the liquidation of Ambrosiano left unresolved the mystery of how the bank 'died'. Although it was clear that Ambrosiano had collapsed because the ghost companies could not repay more than $1 billion in debts, it was not clear where that money had gone.

The puzzle of the missing money can be outlined fairly simply. Ambrosiano's foreign subsidiaries had made loans totalling some $1.2 billion to companies Calvi had set up in Panama and other 'fiscal paradises'. A large chunk of that money had been used to buy Ambrosiano shares. But even using very high estimates of the prices paid for the shares, no more than $600 million could have vanished this way. Another portion of the money, perhaps as much as $200 million, disappeared because of the strengthening of the dollar against the lira and because some of the interest on the loans was not paid. But that still left at least $400 million unaccounted for. Where did it go?

These two mysteries – how Calvi died and where the money went – may have been intertwined. For example, he may have been killed by people who had siphoned cash out of the ghost companies. Indeed, it was largely because he was dealing with vast amounts of money that Calvi felt he was in danger. As he told his daughter shortly before his death: 'For that amount of money, people would kill.' These puzzles could, in turn, be connected to others, including the following:

Who owned the ghost companies? Whoever owned them, or some of them, may have received some of the borrowed money and may have been not too unhappy at Calvi's death. Calvi had said that the ghost companies were owned by the Vatican bank, while Marcinkus claimed that IOR had nothing to do with them. The patronage letters, he said, had only been granted to Calvi as a 'favour'. There were also theories that Gelli and Ortolani, the P2 leaders, may have been owners, or part-owners, of the ghost companies.

What was Calvi's relationship with Flavio Carboni? Was Carboni a lobbyist working purely in Calvi's interests? Or was he playing the role of a new Gelli – manipulating the banker? If Carboni really *was* a new 'puppetmaster', was he operating on his own, or on behalf of others?

How was Calvi linked to the various 'underworlds' that have appeared so frequently in the story? A long series of major and minor characters in the banker's life have been connected to organised crime, intelligence agencies, right-wing politics and arms trafficking. Is this simply a coincidence or is it perhaps evidence of some sort of plot or conspiracy?

In the weeks following Calvi's disappearance and death investigators in Italy, Britain and other countries searched for clues that could help them solve these and other mysteries. One of their first priorities was to find Flavio Carboni.

Italian police began investigating Calvi's disappearance soon after the banker vanished from Rome on Friday 11 June. When his body was found under Blackfriars Bridge a week later the British police joined the case. On Tuesday 22 June an Italian magistrate interrogated Carboni's aide, Emilio Pellicani, who had taken Calvi on the first leg of his trip. After his arrest in late June, Pellicani led police to a treasure trove of documents on Carboni's and Calvi's affairs, which had been stored in the Rome office of Carboni's notary and in the Volkswagen Golf in which Pellicani and Calvi had travelled to Rome's Fiumicino Airport. Still more papers were reportedly discovered buried in a cornfield near Italy's border with Yugoslavia.

When these documents were examined, they put a new light on Carboni's relationship with the banker. They contained evidence of Carboni's extensive lobbying campaign on Calvi's behalf. It soon became clear that Carboni, although an obscure businessman, had a very large number of powerful friends. He seemed like another Gelli – albeit on a smaller scale. But the similarities with the P2 leader may not have ended there. Some of the material Carboni had collected was extremely sensitive, and could have been used to blackmail Calvi. For example, there were fourteen cassette tapes containing eight hours of Carboni's conversations – mostly with Calvi. Commenting on the tapes, one newspaper said: 'The image of a disinterested friend of Calvi has changed into the image of a dangerous person, a character who travels around with a hidden microphone to record everything people say – people who trust him blindly.'

While Italian investigators pored over Carboni's secret archives, the

'Sardinian businessman' was nowhere to be found, having vanished shortly after Calvi's death. From his hiding place he released several statements claiming he had nothing to do with the banker's death. In some of these statements he implied that Calvi may have committed suicide because of Ambrosiano's financial plight and his fears about returning to prison. Carboni said he was in hiding because he feared that he would be falsely accused of having murdered the banker. There had, for example, been press reports that the suit jacket on Calvi's body had been buttoned incorrectly – suggesting that it had been buttoned not by Calvi, but by his presumed killers. (It emerged at the inquest that the jacket may have been buttoned by a British policeman.) Said Carboni: 'I don't want to be convicted of murder because a jacket is buttoned wrong.'

As Carboni protested his innocence, the police continued their hunt. They obtained telephone records from some of the hotels where he had stayed around the time of Calvi's death, and put some of the recipients of these calls under surveillance. In late July Carboni was traced to Lugano, Switzerland, the largest city in the Italian-speaking canton of Ticino. It seems he was leading a life of luxury there with at least six cars, including two Rolls Royces, at his disposal. He could not have been too comfortable, though, since he had changed his residence five times since Calvi's death.

On the morning of Friday 30 July Carboni was driving through Lugano in one of his cars (a Volkswagen, not a Rolls) with his girlfriend Manuela Kleinszig and his brother Andrea. The car was suddenly stopped by the police and, in what appeared to one passer-by to be an anti-terrorist raid, Carboni was seized and pinned to the ground.

While the Italian authorities prepared a request for Carboni's extradition (on the charge of helping Calvi jump bail), the Swiss authorities discovered still more documents relating to Calvi – in the back of Carboni's Volkswagen. These papers provided new details of Carboni's lobbying campaign, and something even more exciting: evidence that Carboni had received some $20 million from Ambrosiano. Early in 1982 Calvi had transferred the money from foreign subsidiaries of Ambrosiano into Swiss bank accounts controlled by Carboni and three of his friends. What was the reason for making these payments?

Carboni claimed that the money was a 'commission' for his role in a deal he was working on with Calvi – presumably to rescue Ambrosiano. Since the deal was not concluded, this explanation was greeted with some scepticism. One possibility is that Calvi paid him part of the commission in advance, with the rest to come on completion of the deal. In fact a comment by Carboni to one of his associates lends support to that possibility. In one of Carboni's taped conversations, he said: 'Calvi has checked with the Union Bank [of Switzerland] and confirmed that $20 million has been deposited. In a short time, another $50 million can be deposited there.'

This deal may have been the same one Calvi told his family he was working on, and could therefore explain why Carboni joined him in London. What kind of deal was it? Calvi had told his wife that it 'could even help me in my appeal', which means it could not have been simply a scheme to bail out Ambrosiano – since Calvi's trial was on charges of illegally exporting capital from Italy. It is more likely that the deal involved obtaining documents he could use to put pressure on the Vatican bank to rescue Ambrosiano *and* help him in his legal case. In fact, several months after Carboni's arrest Pellicani said that Calvi had '[gone] abroad to get some documents to force Marcinkus to do his duty'.

In his last telephone conversations with his family, Calvi said he was on the verge of completing this deal. On Wednesday 16 June he told his wife that 'a crazy, marvellous thing is about to explode'. On Thursday morning, he told his daughter that 'something very important will happen between today and tomorrow…' By early Friday morning the banker was dead.

The fact that Calvi died when he believed he was on the verge of completing this deal suggests a number of possibilities.

1. The deal fell through at the last minute, destroying Calvi's last hope of saving himself, thus driving him to suicide.

2. Calvi was killed by people who wanted to prevent him from completing the deal.

3. Calvi had been lured to London with tales of a non-existent deal and then murdered.

Among those who subscribe to the third possibility is Michel Leemans, Calvi's long-standing colleague. 'My theory,' he says, 'is that [Calvi] may have been running after one of those [rescue] deals – "a billion-dollar Arab deposit" or what have you. He probably discovered in London that it was a joke… and they killed him.'

None of the evidence that came out after Carboni's arrest connected him to Calvi's death, but it further undermined his claim that his only concern was finding Calvi a new apartment.

Other information that emerged after Carboni's arrest suggested that, if he was a new 'puppetmaster', he may have been working on behalf of the old 'puppetmaster', Licio Gelli. The parliamentary commission investigating the P2 scandal found evidence that Carboni may have known Licio Gelli and Umberto Ortolani for years. Could it be that the P2 leader was continuing to manipulate Calvi – by working through Carboni?

The evidence that came to light after Carboni's arrest helped to clarify two of the mysteries: the fate of some of the missing money and the relationship between Calvi and Carboni.

There were still many unanswered questions and still hundreds of millions of dollars unaccounted for. Italian investigators had a hunch that there was one fugitive from justice who might be able to solve some of those mysteries: Licio Gelli.

Gelli had fled Italy in March 1981, when Italian investigators had stumbled upon his secret archives. In the months following his disappearance, there was constant speculation about where he was hiding. Carlo De Benedetti said that during his stormy 'marriage' to Calvi, he heard a rumour that the P2 leader had undergone plastic surgery and was hiding in South America.

Early in 1982 Italian intelligence agents traced Gelli to the south of France, where he was staying with friends in a series of villas along the Côte d'Azur. After several days of surveillance two Italian agents were ready to intercept the P2 leader when, they later said, they were obstructed by the French secret service. Once again, Gelli vanished from sight.

Italian investigators then followed a new path in their hunt for Gelli – what could be called 'the trail of gold'. There had long been rumours that Gelli and his partner Umberto Ortolani had secreted vast sums of money in Swiss bank accounts, and it seemed likely that they would try to put their hands on the money before the funds could be blocked. On 16 July 1982 Tina Anselmi, chairman of the parliamentary P2 commission, asked the Swiss authorities to try to locate bank acounts belonging to Gelli. After Carboni was arrested, the Swiss police found that his papers contained records of a large number of bank accounts that had received funds from Ambrosiano (besides the ones controlled by Carboni), and these accounts were put under surveillance.

Confirmation that the police were on the right trail came in August, when Michele Sindona granted an interview to the American television network ABC. Sindona said: 'There is a P2 treasure – millions of dollars, scattered among numbered Swiss accounts', much of it having been transferred by Calvi from 'South American affiliates of the Milanese bank'. Sindona also seemed to imply that Gelli and Ortolani would soon try to put their hands on the money. 'The war to possess [the treasure],' said Sindona, 'is at the culmination.'

When the Sindona interview was later broadcast in Italy, one of the people who saw it was Paolo Bernasconi, a Swiss magistrate who had been investigating Carboni. Bernasconi sent a telex to every bank in Switzerland, ordering them to freeze dubious bank accounts belonging to South Americans.

The magistrate's instincts were right. Using an assumed name, Licio Gelli reportedly had some $100 million on deposit with two Swiss banks, and he decided to move the money to other accounts before it could be traced. In late August Gelli made the first of a series of phone calls to the bank, requesting that the funds be transferred. But the bank refused – the amount was too large to be moved on the strength of a simple phone call. The customer, they said, would have to come to the bank personally.

On Sunday 12 September, Gelli landed at Madrid airport on a flight from Argentina, then boarded a connecting flight to Geneva. He checked into the Noga Hilton Hotel, just across the street from the main Geneva office of Union Bank of Switzerland. Contrary to the rumour De Benedetti had heard, the P2 leader had not had plastic surgery. His disguise consisted of dying his hair brown, growing a moustache and not wearing his glasses.

On Monday afternoon, at about 3 p.m., Gelli entered the bank accompanied by a lawyer, Augusto Sinagra, whose name had appeared on the list of presumed P2 members. Gelli and Sinagra asked one of the managers to effect the transfer he had earlier requested by telephone. The banker asked the two gentlemen to wait in an office. A few minutes later there was a knock on the door. Two policemen entered and asked for identification. Gelli produced an Argentine passport with his photograph, but with a different name. He was then taken to police headquarters. Within minutes he soon admitted his true identity. The man at the centre of the biggest scandal in recent Italian history was now behind bars. That evening the Swiss police announced his capture in a terse press release: 'This afternoon in Geneva, Italian citizen Gelli Licio, born 21 April 1919, was arrested...at the request of Italian authorities.'

Licio Gelli has been linked to espionage, terrorism, conspiracies to overthrow the Italian government, extortion – the list is overwhelming. But when it was found that he had nearly $100 million from the coffers of Banco Ambrosiano, another charge was added to the list: 'fraudulent bankruptcy'. This charge, as one newspaper noted, was 'the first official accusation by Italian investigators that links the P2 scandal and the Ambrosiano collapse'.

There were probably five people who knew more than anyone where the 'missing millions' went. One of them, Roberto Calvi, was dead.

Two of the five, Licio Gelli and Flavio Carboni, were in prison. The fourth, Umberto Ortolani, was still a fugitive. Only one of the five was alive and free: Archbishop Paul Marcinkus. In other words the 'trail of gold' appeared to lead to Vatican City.

28

The Pope and the Money-Changers

In the heart of the world's smallest sovereign state, Vatican City, is what may be the world's strangest bank: l'Istituto per le Opere di Religione, 'the Institute for Religious Works'. A visitor to IOR will typically enter Vatican City through the Porta Sant'Anna, to the right of St Peter's Square, walk down Via Sant'Anna, and then turn left into a large tower, or *torrione*, built in the sixteenth century by Pope Sixtus V. Through a courtyard and up some stairs is the one and only office of the Vatican bank.

It doesn't look very different from banks on Italian soil. The walls are pale yellow, set off by green marble pilasters. Customers queue up to make deposits and withdrawals. Bank clerks shuffle papers and tap figures into desk calculators. On closer inspection, a visitor will notice some unusual features: a crucifix on the wall, a picture of the current Pope, and a disproportionate number of priests and nuns among the customers. If anything, the religious flavour of the bank and its clientele gives it an almost quaint, other-worldly atmosphere.

Appearances can be misleading. This quiet little religious bank has been at the centre of two of the biggest financial scandals in recent history: the collapse of Michele Sindona and the Calvi affair. IOR's involvement in the Calvi affair has made it more than just a financial scandal: it has turned it into a Vatican scandal as well, causing grave concern to many of the world's more than 700 million Roman Catholics.

An understanding of IOR's involvement with Banco Ambrosiano is crucial to explaining the collapse of the bank and the fall of Calvi. The essential questions are these:

1. Was IOR the owner, or part-owner, of the ghost companies Calvi had created to gain control of Banco Ambrosiano?

2. How much did IOR know about the ghost company scheme?

3. If IOR owned the ghost companies and was aware of the scheme,

did this mean that it received some of the millions of dollars that were unaccounted for when Ambrosiano collapsed?

4. In the light of the interesting evidence of Archbishop Marcinkus's conduct, how did he manage to keep his job as head of IOR for so many years?

Speculation about who owned the ghost companies began at least as far back as 1978, when the Bank of Italy conducted a major investigation of Banco Ambrosiano. At the time, the inspectors wrote that 'behind [the ghost companies] could be concealed direct interests of the [Ambrosiano] group itself or of the Istituto per le Opere di Religione – I.O.R. – Vatican City...' The inspectors presumably based this speculation on the fact that IOR had long been a partner of Ambrosiano in a number of banks and companies, often with a Vatican representative on the board of directors. For example, IOR owned shares in Ambrosiano, Banca del Gottardo, Banco Ambrosiano Overseas and Banco Cattolica del Veneto, all of them major components of Calvi's empire. As noted earlier, there was evidence that it was the owner, or part-owner, of Suprafin, the firm of stockbrokers used by Calvi to acquire the Ambrosiano shares that were sold to the ghost companies. What this all suggests is that it would have been perfectly *in character* for IOR also to be a partner in the ghost company scheme.

Further evidence of IOR's possible involvement in the scheme is Calvi's – and Marcinkus's – behaviour after Calvi's arrest in May 1981. Calvi conducted a major lobbying campaign to enlist IOR's support in his trial. He argued that Marcinkus, as his main 'partner', could show the court that it was involved in his questionable share dealings, and thus remove some of the onus from him. In August 1981 Marcinkus agreed to issue the notorious 'patronage letters', affirming IOR's support for the ghost companies' debts – although the Archbishop did obtain a secret letter from Calvi nullifying the patronage letters.

During the first half of 1982 Calvi and Carboni spent a tremendous amount of time lobbying with Vatican officials to, as Calvi often put it, force IOR to 'do its duty'. Calvi told his family that he was working on a deal that involved selling the Ambrosiano shares to Opus Dei, a secretive Catholic organisation, as a way of repaying the ghost companies' debts. Finally, Calvi's trip to London was apparently aimed – at least in part – at acquiring documents he felt would enable him to force IOR to rescue him and his bank.

The Ambrosiano scandal exploded on 17 June 1982. The proximate cause was a meeting at IOR. Michel Leemans, the head of La Centrale, called on Marcinkus and asked him to honour the debts backed by the patronage letters. Marcinkus refused, on the basis of Calvi's 'counter letter' and because, he said, IOR did not really own the ghost companies. As has been seen, the Archbishop said the letters had only been granted to Calvi as 'a favour'. Marcinkus's refusal to pay forced Ambrosiano's board of directors to hand over management of the bank to the Bank of Italy. Ultimately, Marcinkus's refusal caused Ambrosiano to collapse. Was Marcinkus correct when he claimed IOR had no responsibility for the debts?

In the weeks following Calvi's death, Vatican spokesmen stuck to Marcinkus's version of the IOR/Ambrosiano relationship. On 21 June the Vatican newspaper, *L'Osservatore Romano*, denounced 'media lies' in reporting of the Calvi affair. On 2 July Marcinkus was visited by the Bank of Italy commissioners running Ambrosiano, and he reiterated his refusal to repay the ghost companies' debts. A few days later he was quoted in the press as saying 'I've never done anything that could be considered fraudulent.'

The Italian authorities kept up their pressure on the Vatican. On 13 July that pressure, coupled with the weight of public opinion, forced Cardinal Agostino Casaroli, the Vatican Secretary of State, to appoint the panel of 'three wise men' to investigate relations between IOR and Ambrosiano. At the same time, though, the Vatican continued to insist on its innocence. For example, when on 22 July the *Financial Times* published a report saying that IOR may have owned seven of the ghost companies, Vatican spokesmen issued a fierce denial.

By then, the conflict between Italy and the Holy See had reached a point that would have been unimaginable just a few years before, when the Church-backed Christian Democratic Party dominated Italian politics. The Italian press reported on 28 July that Milanese magistrates were conducting a criminal investigation of IOR officials. This news was so sensitive that when magistrate Bruno Siclari was asked to comment, he told a reporter: 'Don't even write that I don't deny and I don't confirm. You can only write that I don't respond.' The following day, however, it was more than just a rumour: the press was able to confirm that the magistrates had sent 'judicial communications' – documents that inform a person he is under investigation – to IOR's top three officials: Marcinkus, Luigi Mennini and Pellegrino de Strobel. The Vatican, however, rejected the documents – reportedly unopened – on the grounds that they should have been sent through diplomatic channels.

By early the following week, the Italy-Vatican row had reached the highest political level. Prime Minister Giovanni Spadolini held meetings with Justice Minister Clelio Darida and Bank of Italy Governor Carlo

Azeglio Ciampi. Soon after that, Treasury Minister Andreatta reportedly had a meeting with Cardinal Casaroli.

Still the Vatican resisted. In August it was reported that in his talks with Andreatta Cardinal Casaroli said the Vatican would resist demands to pay the ghost companies' debts.

The Vatican's case suffered a major blow in early October, when the results of an investigation into the Ambrosiano affair were leaked to the press. Investigators for CONSOB, the stock market regulatory agency had found evidence that IOR owned a Luxembourg company called Manic, which in turn controlled six of the ghost companies that owed money to Ambrosiano's foreign subsidiaries and whose debts had been backed up by IOR's patronage letters. What is more, the collateral for the loans included 10 per cent of the shares of Banco Ambrosiano – apparently confirming that much of the borrowed money had been used to buy shares in the Milan bank.

Within days of this disclosure, there was a noticeable change in the Vatican's public posture. For observers who had followed the Watergate scandal in America, it was an event reminiscent of the discovery of President Nixon's secret tape recordings of his conversations. And just as Nixon's press secretary was forced to change his line of defence – declaring that his previous denials were now 'inoperative' – Vatican spokesmen now retreated. There were no more flat denials, no more attacks on 'media lies'.

But they did not surrender. Instead, IOR adopted a fallback position. The Vatican bank began to purvey a new version of its role in the Ambrosiano affair. 'Reliable sources' were quoted in the Italian press as saying that the 'three wise men' had completed a preliminary report, giving it more credence than if it had been described as IOR's version. (A correction appeared in the Vatican newspaper on 16 October.) The new version published was this: IOR may have owned *some* of the ghost companies after all, but it was still not responsible for their debts – because it didn't manage the companies!

In November the Vatican was forced to retreat still further from its original position. The 'three wise men' appointed by Cardinal Casaroli delivered their report, which now concluded that IOR owned even more of the ghost companies. Specifically, the report said that the Vatican bank controlled two companies – which in turn controlled another eight, making a grand total of ten.

In spite of this startling admission of ownership, the three financial experts concluded that IOR still did not owe any money. They supported that case with a piece of reasoning so tortured that many people were beginning to question whether 'wise men' was an

170

appropriate appellation for the panel. The Vatican bank, they said, became the owner of the ghost companies *without even realising it* – through a tricky manoeuvre of Calvi's. IOR only discovered that it owned the companies in July 1981 – after the money had been borrowed. The report added that IOR never managed the companies. *Ipso facto,* the Vatican didn't owe a lira.

This, at least, was the official position. In private, though, the Vatican soon acknowledged to the Italian government that it bore a share of the responsibility for the Ambrosiano collapse, and began negotiating a partial financial settlement. On Christmas Eve 1982 it was officially announced that a joint Italy-Vatican commission with six members would look into the Ambrosiano affair, and, presumably, work out how much money the Vatican should pay. An official at one of the banks owed money by Ambrosiano grumbled: 'Maybe we'll get 50 cents in the dollar.'

Even though the Vatican finally admitted that it owned the ghost companies and accepted the idea of a partial repayment of the ghost companies' debts, its official statements on the Ambrosiano affair were far from satisfactory. Both before and after the report of the 'wise men' was released, considerable evidence emerged suggesting strongly that the Vatican was still less than candid about its relationship with Calvi.

For example, it is hard to believe that it only learned of the ghost companies and their debts in July 1981. The report by CONSOB, leaked in October, showed that the collateral for the ghost companies' loans included two million shares in Vianini, a Rome-based construction company which is controlled by IOR and whose deputy chairman is Pellegrino de Strobel, one of IOR's top officials. CONSOB also uncovered a letter from IOR – writen in November 1981 – in which it asked Calvi to manage the ghost companies.

Further indications that the Vatican was continuing to play down its role in the scheme emerged the following month. On 23 November two of Calvi's key subordinates – Roberto Rosone, his deputy chairman, and Filippo Leoni, the head of the international department – testified before the P2 parliamentary commission. Leoni revealed that when Calvi was in prison in the summer of 1981 Ambrosiano officials had two meetings with Marcinkus, at which the Archbishop said he would 'straighten out' the ghost companies' debts.

Additional evidence about the Vatican's role was uncovered by Carlo Calvi, the banker's son. After his father's death Carlo began collecting and examining Ambrosiano documents, some of which he found in the vaults of a Bahamas bank. In late 1982 he began to share his findings with the press. One point Carlo made was that the

171

Vatican's claim that it knew nothing about the ghost companies until July 1981 was a blatant lie. He said he had evidence that some of the ghost companies – such as Manic – had been owned by IOR as far back as the early 1970s. 'They bought and sold [shares] through these companies,' he said. 'In some cases, the companies belonged directly to IOR. In other cases, there were companies nominally owned by IOR but the assets in the companies were not owned by them.'

Carlo Calvi's boldest assertion was that the Vatican bank, and not his father, had always been the real *padrone* – owner – of Banco Ambrosiano, through a 16 per cent block of shares controlled via a network of ghost companies. He added that Marcinkus was under pressure to earn money for the Church, and 'began to pump money from Ambrosiano and continued to do so until the death of my father'.

At first Carlo Calvi's statements were greeted with widespread scepticism. It seemed as if he was constructing wild theories in a desperate attempt to clear his father's name. During the next several months, though, independent confirmation for most of his statements began to emerge, as liquidators of Ambrosiano and others uncovered new evidence. In February 1983, for example, the *Sunday Times* reported that it had obtained a document dated 21 November 1974, in which IOR instructed Banca del Gottardo to form one of the ghost companies, United Trading Corporation. As for another ghost company, Manic, the newspaper quoted a Luxembourg banker, whom it identified as a director of Manic throughout its existence. This man 'told us...that he had always understood that Manic existed for the benefit of IOR, "although they deny it now". In March 1983 the British newspaper uncovered still more evidence that Marcinkus had been lying about his knowledge of the ghost companies' debts. Among other things, it reported that Coopers & Lybrand, the accounting firm, had raised questions about loans to the ghost companies extended by Calvi's Bahamas bank, and that their concerns were allayed after a meeting with Marcinkus. This encounter occurred in 1978 – three years before, according to the 'three wise men', IOR learned that it owned the ghost companies.

The full story of the relationship between Banco Ambrosiano and IOR may never be known. There were evidently secret understandings between Calvi and Marcinkus known only to those two men. But the evidence that has emerged since Calvi's death seems to provide ample support for the following conclusions:

1. IOR was a partner in the ghost company scheme and fully aware of that fact.

2. By issuing the patronage letters in exchange for Calvi's secret

'counter letter', IOR enabled Calvi to mislead Ambrosiano's depositors, creditors and shareholders about the true financial condition of the bank. Thousands of individual investors were thus duped into buying stock in the bank, while international banks were induced to lend millions of dollars.

3. IOR officials played down to a minimum their relationship with Calvi before and after the Ambrosiano crisis exploded, in what appears to have been a systematic cover-up.

4. Since IOR owned – and knew it owned – many of the ghost companies, and since it has been willing to make a partial settlement, it is probably safe to assume that it received much of the money borrowed by the ghost companies. In other words, another chunk of the 'missing millions' may be accounted for.

5. Since Calvi was threatening to expose IOR's role in the ghost company scheme, it cannot have been unhappy at his death.

The Vatican's involvement in the Ambrosiano scandal would be disturbing enough if it were an isolated incident. Unfortunately, it was just the latest in a long series of financial scandals involving the Vatican.

The first major scandal in the post-war era involved Monsignor Edoardo Cippico, an official of the Vatican's Secretariat of State. During the Allied occupation of Italy, Cippico used Vatican channels to help wealthy Italians smuggle vast amounts of lire out of the country, in violation of the country's exchange control laws. Although Italian courts ruled that he was acting on his own – and not with the approval of his superiors – there is no question that IOR has made a speciality out of helping Italians export capital. Italians with Church connections have long been able to open foreign currency accounts at the Vatican bank, and then instruct IOR to move the funds to other countries. In exchange, customers were expected to make a contribution to the Church. In addition to earning commissions by helping Italians break the laws of their country, IOR has acquired potentially valuable information. As *Newsweek* magazine has pointed out: 'It is commonly believed that many powerful members of Italy's Christian Democratic Party have had secret accounts with IOR – and Marcinkus presumably has their names.'

IOR's role as a funnel for flight capital dates back to its founding in 1942. But since Marcinkus became head of the bank in 1971 it has engaged in other questionable activities. In February 1973, for example, it was accused by the US Securities and Exchange Commission of acquiring a large stake in a company called Vetco Industries without having filed the proper disclosure statements. The case was settled when IOR agreed to pay a fine and sign a 'consent

173

decree' stating that it would not violate US securities laws in the future. In April that year US officials investigating organised crime flew to Rome to question Marcinkus about reports that IOR was involved in an underworld racket to dispose of $1 billion worth of counterfeit securities. The allegations were never substantiated.

One of the most curious episodes occurred in 1975, and involved an obscure American bank, Security National in Newark, New Jersey. The founder and President of the bank, Joseph P. Dunn, thought up a scheme to build up the bank's personal loan portfolio by offering unsecured loans at favourable interest rates to agents of the Federal Bureau of Investigation. His reasoning was that FBI men would be fine credit risks, since the agency runs thorough background investigations on all its agents. Eventually, some 300 G-men became customers of the bank.

The client base of FBI men suddenly gave the bank a potential allure that it lacked before — at least to gangsters who might want to gain influence with the crime-fighters. But in every other respect it was an insignificant institution, indistinguishable from thousands of others in the United States.

A takeover bid was launched in 1975, and the bidder was not a Mafioso but a Swiss bank, 51 per cent owned by IOR, Banco di Roma per la Svizzera. When Security Bank went to court to block the bid, it presented persuasive evidence that the Swiss bank was actually a screen for IOR. The takeover bid was withdrawn, but the question remained: why would IOR choose Security National, whose only apparent distinction was a long list of FBI agents as customers?

Finally, there was the matter of IOR's involvement with Michele Sindona, a man who has for a long time been linked with the criminal underworld and who has been accused of hiring Mafia thugs to threaten his enemies.

In the light of IOR's checkered past, Vatican-watchers have long been baffled by Archbishop Marcinkus's longevity at the top of IOR. The Archbishop does have a long list of enemies in the Vatican, but managed to survive because he had the support of two men who counted: Pope Paul VI and Pope John Paul II. When Sindona collapsed in 1974 Marcinkus had been at Pope Paul's side for a decade as manager of papal tours, bodyguard and occasional interpreter. He had even been credited with saving the pontiff's life – which certainly did not hurt their relationship. Another reason offered for Paul's decision to keep Marcinkus on after the Sindona débâcle was that the Pope himself is believed to have introduced the Sicilian banker to the Vatican bank, and thus bore some of the responsibility. As Nino Lo Bello puts it in his book *The Vatican Papers:* 'Curia officials raised a cry for Marcinkus's head to put on the chopping block, but Pope Paul came to his rescue and took the blame by admitting he gave the final appproval on the misguided deals with Sindona.'

Marcinkus's protector died on 6 August 1978, and on 26 August Cardinal Albino Luciani, the Patriarch of Venice, was elected to take his place, choosing the name John Paul I. Within days of his election the new Pope met Cardinal Pericle Felici, a curia official, and Cardinal Giovanni Benelli, Archbishop of Florence, who had compiled a thick dossier on IOR's involvement in the Sindona affair, and urged the Pope to oust Marcinkus. Before he could act on their suggestion – and it is believed that he would have – he died on 29 September, just thirty-four days into his pontificate.

He was succeeded on 16 October by Cardinal Karol Wojtyla, Archbishop of Cracow, in Poland, who selected the name John Paul II. It would be hard to imagine a more fortunate choice from Marcinkus's point of view, for the two men had a great deal in common. For one thing, neither of them fit the Italian stereotype of a priest – a somewhat effeminate character with a pallid complexion and a gentle manner. On the contrary, they seemed tough and manly and engaged in vigorous sports. They also had similar roots. Marcinkus's parents came from Lithuania, and the dialect he learned from them was so close to Polish that he was able to converse comfortably in the new pontiff's native tongue. It also didn't hurt matters that Marcinkus hailed from Chicago, which has more Poles than any city outside Warsaw, and that a large part of his job as head of IOR involved channelling funds from Polish-Americans to the Catholic Church in Poland.

Shortly after his election Pope John Paul II was shown the IOR file prepared by Cardinals Felici and Benelli, and he apparently took no action. Instead, he prepared for a papal tour of Mexico in December 1978, the first major foreign trip since his election, and one of fifteen trips he was to take during the first four years of his pontificate. The new Pope's taste for travel meant that Marcinkus would spend countless hours by his side, in his long-standing role as tour organiser and security chief, enabling him to strengthen his friendship with the pontiff. The heavy travelling proved beneficial to Marcinkus in another way; it kept the Pope distracted from the internal workings of the Vatican – including its bank. It appears that about all he knew – or cared – about IOR was that whenever the Vatican had a financial crunch (which was often) Marcinkus somehow managed to tide it over with profits from his banking operations.

If papal tours were the hallmark of the first phase of John Paul's pontificate, the Polish crisis overshadowed the next phase of it. And this, too, seems to have redounded to Marcinkus's advantage. In their book *Pontiff*, Gordon Thomas and Max Morgan-Witts provide details of a startling incident that was rumoured to have occurred in 1980. Pope John Paul, they write, conducted two months of secret diplomacy to help secure recognition for the Solidarity trade union movement and dissuade the Soviets from invading his native land. In August 1980, according to Thomas and Morgan-Witts, the Pope wrote a personal note to Soviet President Leonid Brezhnev, containing the following threat: 'John Paul warned Brezhnev that if [the Soviets invaded Poland] he would relinquish the throne of St Peter and return to stand at the barricades beside his fellow Poles.' It is a mark of his trust in Marcinkus that he chose the American Archbishop to deliver the note.

In 1981 other events occurred which must have pushed IOR far from the Pontiff's mind. On 13 May 1981 the Pope was seriously wounded in an assassination attempt, and spent months recuperating. On 13 December of that year martial law was declared in Poland, undoing the reforms that had earlier been achieved. Once again, Marcinkus reportedly assisted the Pope in his work on the Polish crisis, and, it has been rumoured, transmitted money from IOR to Poland. The affairs of IOR and its relationship with Banco Ambrosiano were probably the farthest thing from the pontiff's mind. Indeed, he was so pleased with Marcinkus that in late 1981 he appointed the Vatican banker to the important post of Pro-President of the Pontifical Commission for the Vatican City State – making him, in effect, 'mayor' of Vatican City.

Considering all this, it is not hard to understand why the Pope was apparently slow to heed Marcinkus's critics – even after the Ambrosiano crisis exploded in June 1982. Marcinkus remained on the job for months, even as the disturbing revelations mounted. But eventually there were signs that his position had eroded. When the Pope travelled to Spain in October 1982 Marcinkus was not at his side. When eighteen new cardinals were announced in January 1983, Marcinkus – who had long been expecting to receive the 'red hat' – was not on the list. Two months before, the Pope had delivered what was widely interpreted as a rebuke to Marcinkus, in the Pope's first public reference to the Ambrosiano scandal. He said that those who manage the money of the Church – which he called 'a widow's money' in an allusion to the Gospel of Luke – should exercise 'great and meticulous responsibility'.

The Vatican's willingness to discuss a financial settlement for the Ambrosiano crisis could cause new financial strain on the Church, and there were several indications that it was trying hard to raise the necessary money. It entered into negotiations with American Express to sell its stake in Banca del Gottardo, but Amex broke off the talks in October 1982 because of Gottardo's involvement in the Ambrosiano affair. There have been reports of Vatican negotiations with American banks to raise money. If so, there would be ample precedent for a bailout loan. In the sixteenth century Pope Leo X borrowed large sums from Florentine bankers. In 1870 the Vatican was rescued by a $200,000 loan from the House of Rothschild.

The Church, because of its special character, does have other means available for raising cash. In November 1982 – just at the time when the Vatican acknowledged that it would pay some of the ghost companies' debts – the Pope declared that an extraordinary Holy Year would begin on Ash Wednesday, 16 February 1983, in the hopes of attracting millions of Catholic pilgrims to Rome. For more than six centuries, Holy Years have almost always been held every twenty-five years – 1925, 1950, 1975, etc. The pattern is generally only broken when the Church has a special need for cash.

Yet another money-making scheme was an American tour of Vatican art treasures, replete with sales of film and television rights, souvenirs, and a club for 'friends of the Vatican Museums'. The three-city tour began in early 1983 in New York, and then progressed to Chicago and San Francisco. Marcinkus was said to be involved in the plans.

There is no doubt that Holy Year and the art exhibition were aimed at raising funds for the Church. But there was another event, also announced in November, which could conceivably have a financial aspect to it. Roberto Calvi insisted to his family that the scheme he was working on with the Vatican to bail out Ambrosiano involved Opus Dei, a controversial Catholic organisation. He told his family that, in exchange for this help, Opus Dei would obtain certain privileges in the Vatican.

For twenty years it was the goal of Opus Dei to have its status upgraded from that of a secular institute – under the supervision of the Vatican bureaucracy – to a 'personal prelature', which would mean it would report directly to the Pope. On 26 November 1982 Pope John Paul II announced that he would grant Opus Dei this special status, with effect the following day. His action just happened to occur as Vatican officials were negotiating with Italy to repay part of the debts of the ghost companies. It may, of course, just be a coincidence.

The financial cost to the Holy See of the Ambrosiano scandal and the other misdeeds of IOR may really be trivial compared with the cost in terms of moral authority. For it suggests that, in its financial affairs, the Church ignores the moral values its clergymen preach from their pulpits. Catholic scholar Malachy Martin has said that the Vatican's involvement in the Ambrosiano scandal 'makes the Roman Catholic Church, its clerics, its pope, its cardinals, the entire institutions, just some more members of the human race clawing in the jungle. And that was not the will of Christ.' That sentiment was echoed by another observer. 'The Pope, like Christ, must remove the money changers from the temple,' said Clara Calvi.

29

Potere Occulto

Roberto Calvi was a great believer in what Italians call *potere occulto* – hidden power. His fascination with secret societies and the like helps explain his involvement with Gelli, Carboni and Pazienza, all of whom boasted of strong connections with shadowy and powerful organisations.

At times Calvi was ridiculed for his beliefs; it was said that he was naive and gullible, perhaps even mentally unbalanced. But when the P2 scandal exploded Calvi's ideas no longer seemed so foolish: there really *was* a powerful cabal that had infiltrated the country's establishment and seemed to wield enormous power. After Calvi died, and his connections with Pazienza and Carboni came to light, there was a similar reaction. Like Gelli, these were obscure men with no obvious power bases – Carboni was a property developer in Sardinia, Pazienza a self-styled business consultant – yet they knew a surprising number of important people.

Calvi's relationships with these and other shadowy characters have spawned a number of conspiracy theories to explain his life and death. Some are plausible, others far-fetched. Perhaps even more important is the fact that the P2 and Ambrosiano scandals have helped to expose how the 'hidden world' operates, and how elements within it work together. Gelli, for example, has been involved with spies and right-wing terrorists, some of whom plotted coups d'état in Italy. Sindona and Carboni have both been linked to the Mafia and intelligence agencies.

A number of Italian officials have noted these relationships and tried hard to find coherent patterns. Massimo Teodori, a Radical Member of Parliament who has spent years tracing Sindona's career, speaks of an overlap between 'financial criminality and common criminality'. Former Prime Minister Giovanni Spadolini calls it 'a new Mafia', which he describes as 'a multinational of crime'. A Communist MP, Giuseppe

D'Alema, has characterised the P2 Lodge as 'a political-military-business complex with strong ties and international connections, in which fascists and various other forces co-exist'. Before examining some of these theories, it probably makes sense to review some of the strange social and business contacts of the people closest to Calvi towards the end of his life.

Carboni has been linked to the criminal underworld. A friend of his was Domenico Balducci, a member of the Sicilian Mafia clan of the Inzerillo, Spatola and Gambino families – the same clan that worked with Sindona by, for example, helping him during his phoney kidnapping in 1979. Balducci in turn was a friend of Danilo Abbruciati, the hired assassin who was killed during the April 1982 attempt on the life of Calvi's deputy, Roberto Rosone. Another member of that circle was Ernesto Diotallevi, the Mafioso who provided Calvi with a fake passport for his trip to London, and is believed to have met Carboni in Zurich after Calvi left Italy.

After Carboni was arrested on 30 July 1982 the Swiss police found records of his banking transactions, which showed that he had made a large payment to Diotallevi two days after the attempt on Rosone. On 30 October Carboni was extradited to Italy and was imprisoned at Lodi – the same place in which Calvi was held during his 1981 trial. In February 1983 Carboni and nine others were charged with a long list of offences, including fraud, and laundering money from kidnap ransoms, robberies and drug trafficking. Some of the robberies were allegedly carried out by neo-fascist terrorists.

On 16 April 1983 Carboni and Diotallevi were officially charged with involvement in the attempted murder of Rosone. Diotallevi was implicated directly; Carboni was charged with criminal association with the killers.

Pazienza and Carboni are also believed to have worked with Italian intelligence agencies. Pazienza was a relative of General Giuseppe Santovito, who headed SISMI, Italy's military intelligence agency, until he was forced out of office when his name appeared on the P2 lists. Pazienza has said openly that he worked for SISMI under Santovito's direction. Pazienza also introduced Carboni to Santovito, who asked Carboni to arrange an introduction to masonic leader Armando Corona. A member of the parliamentary P2 commission cites this as one of many indications that Carboni also worked for intelligence agencies. 'Carboni was a small businessman in Sardinia,' says this MP, 'and yet the boss of the secret services asked him for an introduction to Corona!' He says he also finds it odd that Carboni seemed to have friends all over the world – judging from, for example, the records of his phone calls during Calvi's trip – even though he was a 'small businessman' and spoke no English.

Another possibility is that Pazienza and Carboni may have known the leaders of the P2 Lodge. One common link is General Santovito, since he was on the presumed membership list of the lodge. More solid evidence emerged after Carboni's secret tape recordings were found; on one of them Carboni says, 'I've known Ortolani since 1955.' The P2 commission also found a copy of a letter sent by Gelli to Carboni in 1975. Carboni denied knowing Gelli, but reportedly said that Pazienza did know the P2 leader – which Pazienza has denied.

Calvi's 'fixers' not only knew spies and Mafiosi, they also had friends in more respectable circles. Gelli's political contacts have reached as high as the Italian cabinet and the presidential palace. Ortolani had important friends in the Catholic Church. In 1963 he was made a Vatican nobleman. In 1979 he was appointed ambassador to Uruguay by the Grand Military Order of the Knights of Malta, a Catholic organisation that is recognised as a sovereign state by several (mainly Latin American) countries. Similarly, Pazienza and Carboni were able to arrange appointments with senior politicians when they were lobbying on Calvi's behalf.

The banker's son has expressed amazement that his father's 'fixers' moved freely in both dubious and more respectable circles. As noted in Chapter 13 of this book, Pazienza visited Carlo Calvi in the United States during his father's trial. Accompanied by a priest and a Mafioso, they called on Archbishop Giovanni Cheli, the Vatican's observer at the United Nations. The wide-ranging contacts of Carboni have suggested to many people that when he was lobbying for Calvi he may easily have been acting on behalf of someone else. And that 'someone else' may, in turn, have taken orders from above. There is, for example, a widespread belief in Italy – held by many members of the parliamentary P2 commission – that Gelli was not the real leader of the P2; that the 'puppetmaster' was himself the puppet of someone higher up. It is an interesting example of the 'peeling an onion' analogy adopted by conspiracy theorists.

Several theories have been advanced as to who might have given an order to kill Calvi. Carlo Calvi has said that many Italian and Swiss investigators believe it was 'a family matter within the P2'. Asked what the British police believe, he says: 'I don't think they have any particular theory. I think they're just confused because it's exotic.' Among the other possibilities, the banker's son lists 'an organisation that wanted to hurt the Church or a faction within the Church'. His own view is that 'the whole thing was set into motion by someone who wanted to damage the Vatican and my father' – perhaps the Soviet Union, because of the Pope's involvement in the Polish crisis. Clara Calvi, however, attributes the death of her husband to a power struggle within the Vatican.

An Italian politician who serves on the P2 commission lists several theories. He says:

'One possibility is the Mafia – some people say that the underworld tried to acquire the money and power Calvi had, others say that Calvi had done what in Mafia language is called a *sgarbo* – an offence in regard to the organisation – for which he had to be punished. Some people believe that Calvi was ready to reveal sensitive information about the Church's political activities in Poland and Latin America, and he met opposition within the Vatican. Others believe that enemies of the Church wanted to give a signal to the Vatican. This would connect the elimination of Calvi with the attempt to assassinate the Pope. Some believe that Calvi was eliminated in order to expose the relationship between Ambrosiano and its boss and the Vatican – in order to hurt the Vatican. That hypothesis is connected to the previous one.'

Some of the evidence – much of which is obviously highly speculative – for these and for the various other theories can be summarised as follows.

The Mafia. This theory assumes that the Mafia was acting on its own, and not on behalf of anyone else, and is based largely on the underworld connections of some of the people close to Calvi. One possible motive was to prevent Calvi from revealing what he knew about the criminal underworld.

Enemies of the Church. The enemy most frequently cited is the Soviet bloc, which has also been implicated in the 1981 attempt on the life of Pope John Paul II. In support of this theory Carlo Calvi cites the tremendous damage the Church has suffered – financially and to its image – in the wake of his father's death. Sindona, although not always the most reliable witness, has said he lends support to this theory. He blames Calvi's death on elements of 'the left', which he says were enemies of both Calvi and himself because of the bankers' anti-Communist activities.

A Faction within the Church. This is obviously the most controversial theory, but it is one the banker's widow has often put forward. When Calvi spoke of his enemies in the months before his death, he mentioned 'the priests' more often than anyone else. Two possible motives cited in support of this hypothesis are to block the Opus Dei deal, which he said

182

would have given that organisation greater clout within the Church, or to prevent Calvi from revealing what he knew about the secrets of the Vatican.

The P2 Lodge. Calvi may have died as the result of a fight over a 'P2 treasure' – money from Ambrosiano stashed in Swiss bank accounts. Another motive for killing Calvi would be to prevent him from telling the magistrates about the P2 Lodge – as a bargaining tactic during his appeals trial. In support of the notion that 'the P2 did it', some people cite the alleged 'masonic symbols' connected with Calvi's death. *L'Espresso* magazine has noted that the rocks in Calvi's pockets could represent the brick of the mason; the arches of the bridge in a semi-circle could signify the compass; while death by hanging is the penalty prescribed in some masonic initiation oaths for those who are known to have betrayed 'the secrets of the lodge'.

Politicians. Calvi distributed money to nearly every major political party, including the Socialists, the Christian Democrats and even the Communists. He was thus in a position to damage political leaders by revealing these illegal payments to the Italian magistracy. In fact, during his trial Calvi told magistrates about his payments to the Socialist Party, and, according to his family, this provoked threats from the Socialists. Before his death, Calvi said that if his political 'protectors' did not provide him with any assistance in his appeals trial, he would 'name names' once again.

The presence of so many shadowy characters in the Calvi and P2 stories has prompted some conspiracy theorists to concoct 'master plots' in an attempt to explain everything. Perhaps the most bizarre theory was put forward in July 1982 by the Progressive Labor Party, a left-wing political cult run by an American fanatic named Lyndon La Rouche Jr. According to La Rouche, the Calvi and P2 scandals are part of a massive international criminal conspiracy run by the British royal family!

As outlandish as that theory is, the temptation to find a 'master plot' linking everybody is understandable. Such a theory would make life infinitely simpler. It would be reminiscent of the solution to Agatha Christie's mystery *Murder on the Orient Express.* Detective Hercule Poirot found that every passenger had a motive for killing the victim and discovered, in the end, that *they all did it.* As tempting as it would be to find a 'grand design' to explain the P2 and Calvi scandals, there are limits to which life imitates art.

But if there is no master plot, that does not mean that the multiple relationships of people like Calvi's 'fixers' are purely coincidental.

Rather, there appear to be a number of overlapping interests that prompt certain organisations and individuals to form ad hoc working relationships.

One way of understanding these relationships is to examine how some of the 'underworlds' mentioned in the P2 and Calvi scandals have worked together in Italy since World War II, and how this pattern has been duplicated in other parts of the world.

When Mussolini seized power in 1922 he suppressed – among others – the Mafia. When the Allies decided to begin the invasion of Italy with a landing in Sicily, the American intelligence agency, the Office of Strategic Services (the predecessor of the CIA) recruited Italian-American Mafiosi for assistance. For example, a deal was struck with Lucky Luciano, a New York Mafia leader later to be commemorated in movies. After the July 1943 landing in Sicily, American forces worked closely with local Mafia leaders and even installed some of them as mayors of Sicilian towns.

During the occupation, Michele Sindona apparently had contacts in both the Mafia and the occupying American forces. He purchased a Dodge truck from the Americans and used it to transport lemons to the cities. Journalist Umberto Venturini of *Il Mondo,* who has followed Sindona's career for many years, says: 'Sindona got produce from the local farmers and sold it to the American soldiers, who paid him in weapons. He then sold the weapons to the *Independentisti'* – Sicilian separatists who were fighting, often alongside Mafiosi, to break away from Italy. Venturini adds that there is evidence that many of the people involved with Sindona and Gelli in the 1960s and 1970s met during this period. For example John McCaffrey, a British intelligence officer in Europe, was the Italian representative of Hambros Bank in the 1960s and worked closely with Sindona. When Sindona was fighting extradition from the United States, McCaffrey filed an affidavit in support of Sindona's claims that he was the victim of a 'Communist plot' in Italy. Says Venturini: 'The theory is that the old boys' network originated then.'

Lucky Luciano, the New York Mafioso, was rewarded for his efforts by being released from prison and deported to Italy. His application for executive clemency from New York Governor Thomas E. Dewey was backed by intelligence agents who said he had 'cooperated with high military authorities [and was] rendering a definite service to the war effort'. A representative of the US Office of Naval Intelligence said that Luciano had 'helped shorten the war in Sicily and Italy'. Thanks to the help of the American spies, the Mafia quickly regained the power it had previously wielded in Sicily, penetrating the political structure and profiting from construction activity in the building boom that followed the war.

After the war, US intelligence was active again in Italy. This time their partners were the Christian Democratic Party and the Vatican. The goal was to prevent the Communist and Socialist parties from winning the April 1948 election. During the war the left-wing parties had been the most active components of the Italian Resistance, and thus came out of the war regarded by many voters as heroes. Conversely, the Vatican was tainted by charges that it had done little or nothing to fight Mussolini and Hitler.

The Christian Democratic Party (the 'DC') became the focal point for the efforts of the Church and the Americans to keep the Communists out of government. The DC and the Church portrayed the election as a choice between 'Christ or the Devil'. Parish priests instructed their parishioners to vote for the DC Party. The successor to the OSS, the CIA, became the tool for US intervention in the election. This activity was the harbinger of many of the CIA 'covert operations' that were to follow, according to Thomas Powers in his book on former CIA director Richard Helms, *The Man Who Kept the Secrets*. The CIA, writes Powers, formed a 'Special Procedures Group' at the end of 1947, which provided funds to centrist political parties and mounted a 'disinformation' campaign – for example, forging documents purporting to come from the Communist Party. For years after that, the CIA continued to provide financial assistance to the Christian Democrats.

Another partner in these anti-Communist efforts was the Mafia. The Christian Democrats were anxious to capture parliamentary seats in Sicily. This pact led to what has been described as 'the most tragic episode in Sicilian postwar history': a massacre of ordinary Sicilian citizens who had voted for leftist candidates. During May Day celebrations in 1947, Mafia-hired gunmen opened fire with machine guns on people in the town of Portella della Ginestra, killing eleven and wounding fifty-five. In subsequent elections Christian Democratic candidates increased their share of the votes. The Catholic Church itself has also been linked with Mafiosi, particularly in Sicily. As one writer has neatly summed it up: 'A Sicilian Mafioso with three sons tries to place one in the Church, one in the medical profession, and one in the law. The result is that churchmen in Sicily acquiesce to a great extent in the doings of the Mafia while the *capofamiglia* of a district may even be the local priest.'

It would be wrong to suggest that the Christian Democrats' electoral success was only because of backing from the Church, the Americans and the Mafia. At the time, the Italian Communist Party was very closely identified with the Soviet Union, and there were widespread fears that its entry into the government would lead to a Soviet takeover. Another reason why the DC did well was its mastery of the art of *clientelismo* – 'clientelism' – dispensing favours in exchange for votes and financial support.

In the early 1960s, though, support for the DC waned, and it was forced to take the Socialist Party into the governing coalition, in the so-called 'opening to the left'. In 1968 Italy, like France and some other countries, went through a period of massive left-wing demonstrations by students and workers, and the governing coalitions took on more of a left-wing flavour – although they were still led by Christian Democratic prime ministers.

This drift to the left helped spawn the emergence of another underworld: coup-plotters. In the 1960s and early 1970s a number of right-wing plots to overthrow the Italian government were devised, generally involving military and intelligence officers. These schemes included the following.

In 1964 there was a plot in which the involvement of a very senior politician was rumoured. It was conceived by General Giovanni De Lorenzo, commander of the *Carabinieri* (the paramilitary police) and later Army chief of staff.

In 1970 Prince Junio Valerio Borghese planned a coup code-named 'Tora Tora'. It was to begin on the night of 8 December, but was abruptly called off.

In 1974, writes Paul Wilkinson in his book *The New Fascists,* there was a series of coup scares and arrests. The most dramatic arrest, in October, was that of General Vito Miceli, who had been chief of military intelligence. Miceli was implicated in both the 'Tora Tora' plot and in a plan to poison Rome's water supply with radioactive material. Wilkinson writes: 'The plotter evidently believed this would stimulate a left-wing backlash, which would in turn force the military to intervene. The coup leaders planned to seize power jointly with the military, offering themselves as "saviours" of the nation.'

This tactic of using terrorism in the hope of bringing forth calls for a right-wing government has been labelled 'the strategy of tension'. It is, Wilkinson explains, 'designed to provoke maximum disruption of democratic institutions and to polarise the political situation with the aim of staging a coup to "save the country" from communist dictatorship'. In fact, a number of acts of terrorism have been attributed to the 'strategy of tension', and thus to coup-plotters. One of the first major examples of right-wing or 'black' terrorism occurred on 12

December 1969, when a bomb exploded at Piazza della Fontana in Milan, killing 14 and wounding 80.

During the 1970s 'red terrorism' – that is, from the left – tended to overshadow 'black terrorism', with the growth of organisations like the Red Brigades. But later the black terrorists seemed to stage a comeback. For example, fascists have been blamed for the 1980 bombing in Bologna railway station.

Yet another underworld involved in all this is the Mafia. In the early 1970s investigating magistrates made public their concerns about evidence of ties between neo-fascists and Mafiosi. These connections involved the drug trade, kidnapping and – most importantly – arms-trafficking.

One man who appears to have been at the centre of this nexus of coup-plotters, spies and right-wing terrorists is Licio Gelli. Among his closest contacts were officials of Italy's intelligence agencies, which may explain how secret service dossiers were discovered in Gelli's archives. He was, for example, a close friend of General Miceli, the coup-plotter arrested in 1974. They reportedly met in 1968, when Miceli was head of military intelligence. When Gelli's files were searched and the presumed membership list of P2 was found, the names included General Giuseppe Santovito, head of SISMI (military intelligence) and General Giulio Grassini, head of SISDE (civilian intelligence).

Gelli's links with the secret services have been explored in detail at hearings of the parliamentary commission on the P2 Lodge. In June 1982 General Miceli testified that Gelli had been a counter-espionage agent of SID (army intelligence). Antonio Viezzer, another former SID official, characterised Gelli as a sort of informant: 'He was a person who could be useful, at a high level. He had his hooks everywhere – even the US Embassy in Rome.' In October General Grassini told the P2 commission that Gelli had been asked to carry out an 'international operation'. A few days later, the nature of this 'operation' was revealed: in 1979 Gelli was asked by the agency to put it in touch with Argentine intelligence agencies for help in tracking down left-wing Italian terrorists hiding in Latin America.

There were also reports in 1982 that the P2 leader was directly involved in right-wing terrorist attacks. To quote one instance it was even alleged that Gelli had planned the 1980 bombing of Bologna railway station at a meeting of a 'super lodge' he had established in Monte Carlo.

The coup plots and fascist terrorism of the early 1970s did not prevent the Italian Communist Party (PCI) from gaining support. It remained the second largest party in Italy and the largest Communist party in the West. The PCI profited from voters' disenchantment with corruption in the Christian Democratic party. The Communists also projected a more moderate image than in the past. For example, the PCI condemned the 1968 invasion of Czechoslovakia by the Soviets and claimed that it was in favour of Italy remaining in NATO. It began to sound little different from social democratic parties in other parts of Europe. It started to look as if the party could – in partnership with the Socialists – form a left-wing coalition government.

Fears of growing Communist strength once again prompted intervention in Italian politics by the US. Roger Morris, a former official of the US National Security Council, writes that Graham Martin, the US Ambassador to Italy, 'covertly spent $10 million to swing the 1972 elections to the Christian Democratic party'. Part of that money went to General Miceli, the coup-plotter. Nonetheless, the Communist Party garnered 27.2 per cent of the votes, compared with the 38.8 per cent achieved by the Christian Democrats.

Although the Communists now seemed closer to power than ever, they soon changed their strategy. In 1973 the coalition government of Marxist President Salvador Allende of Chile was overthrown in a military coup, believed to have been backed by the United States. The lesson the Italian Communists took from this was that it could be foolhardy to form a left-wing coalition government and run the risk of provoking a backlash from the right. The PCI decided it would be better to work directly with the Christian Democrats, through what it called an 'historic compromise'.

In spite of the increasingly moderate policies of the Italian Communists, the United States remained highly opposed to Communist entry in the government. The late Aldo Moro, a leading Christian Democrat who was among the most open to PCI participation, visited the United States in 1974 and, according to his family, received veiled but disturbing threats from US officials. When Moro was kidnapped by the Red Brigades in March 1978, his Christian Democratic colleagues refused to bargain with the terrorists and some of them were later accused of letting him die because they feared that if he survived he would bring the Communists into the government.

One man who was evidently involved in the anti-Communist schemes of this period – working with the Christian Democrats, the Vatican and the United States – was Michele Sindona. Sindona was the main financial partner of the Vatican – which continued to give strong backing to the Christian Democrats – and a major contributor to the Christian Democrats in his own right. One of his American connections was Ambassador Martin. In the early 1970s a US congressional committee was investigating CIA 'front' operations. Martin – it has been alleged – feared that Congress would discover that the CIA secretly owned an English-language newspaper in Rome, the *Daily American*. In 1971, Sindona bought the newspaper so that the CIA link could be concealed. (Martin has denied this.)

Another American contact of Sindona's – also involved in the war against Communism in Italy – was John Connally, former Governor of Texas who served as Treasury Secretary under Nixon. In 1976 Connally helped form a 'Committee for the Defense of the Mediterranean' aimed at arousing public opinion about the Communist threat. Seminars were held with such speakers as Clare Booth Luce, a US Ambassador to Italy during the 1950s, and William Colby, a former director of the CIA. Connally and his friends also concocted a scheme reminiscent of the sort of tactics that the CIA had used in the 1948 election. Italian-Americans were urged to write to their relatives in the old country and threaten to stop sending them money if they let the Communists win. A more ambitious scheme – which never came off – was to charter jumbo jets and fly expatriate Italians back to Italy to vote against the Communists.

Sindona was an avid supporter of Connally's efforts, as were several other people in right-wing/intelligence/P2 circles on both sides of the Atlantic. One friend of both Sindona and Gelli who was involved with Connally's efforts was Phil Guarino, an official of the Republican National Committee. Guarino raised money for the Republicans from Italian-Americans and also served as a contact man when Italian politicians visited Washington.

In the 1976 elections the Communists increased their share of the vote from 27.2 per cent to 34.4 per cent – their highest level ever. The DC vote was about stagnant: 38.7 per cent. They still did not join the cabinet but agreed to vote with the coalition and were granted leadership positions in Parliament. The 'historic compromise' seemed closer than ever.

This proved to be a boon to Gelli's recruiting efforts, and he began portraying his lodge as an anti-Communist league. Says Gustavo Minervini, a left-wing Member of Parliament: 'The PCI was entering the area of power with various formulas in 1976 to 1979. The P2 existed before that – but after 1976 started to assume a form of resistance to the Communists. That explains why there were generals, heads of the secret services, and so on in the lodge.'

In fact, it appears that Gelli may have become bored with watching his friends plot coups d'état and decided to devise a plan of his own. His idea was that Italy's party-dominated parliamentary system should be replaced by a de Gaulle-style 'presidential republic'. Plans for this so-called 'civil coup' were found in the possession of his daughter. On 4 July 1981 Maria Grazia Gelli was detained at Rome's Fiumicino Airport and an envelope containing two reports was found in a false-bottomed suitcase. The reports contained details of a plot for a bloodless seizure of power, hence the appellation 'civil coup'.

One of the more disturbing questions is whether Gelli and previous coup-plotters had the approval of senior politicians. In 1970, at a time when Gelli was associating with General Miceli, the P2 leader entertained as a guest at his villa in Arezzo Giuseppe Saragat, then President of the Republic. Under the Italian system, the presidency is a largely ceremonial post, given to an elder statesman. But Saragat reportedly endorsed the idea of a 'presidential republic', although he vociferously denied it. As for Gelli's own plan, there have been rumours that it was shown to Saragat's successor, Giovanni Leone. In late 1982 both former heads of state were called to testify to the P2 commission about their contacts with Gelli, and denied any involvement in Gelli's plans.

Roberto Calvi, of course, was introduced by Sindona to many of his friends in both Italy and the US. John Connally, for example, soon became one of Calvi's closest contacts, according to the Calvi family. Calvi and his wife visited Connally at his Texas ranch and, according to a US-based Ambrosiano official, Calvi never failed to get in touch with the politician on visits to the United States. Carlo Calvi says that he and his father also visited Phil Guarino in Washington, and that, on one of those visits, Guarino was with General Miceli.

Another American involved in Italian affairs was an academic named Michael Ledeen, associated with a think tank at Georgetown University called the Center for Strategic and International Studies, which was the setting for Connally's seminars on Communism in Italy. In the 1970s Ledeen spent some time in Italy as a journalist, and had a surprising number of high-level contacts. 'He had access to everybody,' says an Italian journalist. 'He was on a first-name basis with half the Christian Democrats.' In fact Federico D'Amato, a former intelligence official, has told the P2 commission that Ledeen was a US intelligence agent – although Ledeen insists this is false.

A close associate of Ledeen was Alexander Haig, who served as chief of staff in the Nixon Administration and later became commander of NATO forces in Europe. It is interesting that Haig's tenure in those posts coincided with US efforts against Eurocommunism and Gelli's recruitment of intelligence and military chiefs into his lodge. After Ronald Reagan was elected President in 1980 Haig was appointed

Secretary of State, and Ledeen was brought into the State Department as one of Haig's advisers.

It is worthwhile going into Ledeen's background because he provides a link with yet another character in the Calvi saga: Francesco Pazienza. Pazienza has repeatedly dropped Ledeen's name. For example, Pazienza has claimed that he arranged – through Ledeen – for a leading Christian Democrat to meet Haig during a visit to Washington. Ledeen says he had nothing to do with the visit.

A more fascinating episode was recounted by D'Amato, the former intelligence officer, during his testimony to the P2 commission. According to D'Amato, Pazienza and Ledeen publicised the 'Billygate' affair. When Ronald Reagan was running against Jimmy Carter, the President's wayward brother was invited to visit Libya where he met strongman Muammar Qaddafi. This quickly became an issue in the election campaign, and the US press predictably dubbed the affair 'Billygate'. Shortly before the November 1980 election, Ledeen wrote a number of articles reporting that Billy Carter had met Palestinian terrorists Yassir Arafat and George Habash during his Libyan trip – a disclosure that seriously damaged President Carter. (The articles appeared in the *New Republic* in the US and two European magazines owned by Sir James Goldsmith, the short-lived *NOW!* in Britain and France's *L'Express*.) D'Amato told the P2 commission that Pazienza had helped Ledeen collect the damaging information. Ledeen declines to say whether or not Pazienza played a role in his research.

Carboni's connections with both intelligence agencies and the criminal underworld have not been too surprising to Italian investigators, who point out that spies – of both the West and the Soviet bloc – have often worked with gangsters. Criminal organisations often have just the sort of skills and contacts needed by intelligence agencies. A member of the parliamentary P2 commission says: 'The secret services are connected to the *malavita* [criminal underworld] – it's part of their job. They need people in different countries they can use to acquire information, to blackmail people, and so on.' As mentioned earlier, American intelligence agents used the Mafia in the invasion of Sicily, and the Italian intelligence officials have worked with right-wing coup-plotters and terrorists who were, in turn, linked with the Mafia.

Another example occurred in the early 1960s. The CIA worked on a number of plans – evidently with the approval of the Kennedy administration – to assassinate Cuban leader Fidel Castro. This was a perfect opportunity for CIA/Mafia collaboration. The US government wanted to rid the western hemisphere of Communist influence; the mob wanted to regain control of the hotels and casinos they had lost when Castro seized power. In 1960 a Mafioso named John Rosselli was approached by the CIA to carry out the assassination. Rosselli enlisted the help of two other gangsters, Sam Giancana and Santos Trafficante, who, in turn, began recruiting Cubans for the job. In February 1961 a CIA official personally delivered botulinum toxin pills to Rosselli in Miami. It is worth noting that Sindona has allegedly helped to launder drug money from some of the same Mafiosi.

In fact, Latin America is one part of the world where many of the relationships mentioned so far – the floating alliances involving the Church, right-wing politicians, spies and gangsters – have been duplicated, often involving the same people. The two main 'respectable' institutions actively involved in this region are the US government and the Vatican. It has been US policy for years to fight the rise of left-wing governments in Latin America, as shown by its involvement in right-wing coups or efforts to prop up such governments after they have obtained power. Just a few of many examples are Guatemala (1954), Brazil (1964), the Dominican Republic (1965), Chile (1973), and more recently, El Salvador and Nicaragua.

The Church has been more divided. Many priests and bishops in Latin America are active opponents of right-wing regimes, sometimes espousing Marxist philosophies or even taking up arms with left-wing guerillas. The upper echelons of the Vatican, however, have generally been much more comfortable with right-wing regimes – whether Mussolini, Franco or their Latin American counterparts. The Church's experiences in Cuba help to explain this attitude. In the early sixties, Peter Nichols writes in his book *The Pope's Divisions*, Castro expelled hundreds of priests and more than 2,000 nuns from Cuba, nationalised Catholic schools and took other steps against Catholics. Before Castro took over in 1958 more than 90 per cent of the population were practising Catholics; now there are no more than 40 per cent.

As a result of their anti-Communist policies the US Government and the Vatican have often served as props to some of the most bloodthirsty regimes in the world. In such countries as Argentina, Bolivia, Chile, El Salvador, Guatemala and Paraguay, officially sanctioned 'death squads' have been used to make opponents 'disappear' – sometimes after the victims have been worked over by professional torturers. The leaders of some of these regimes – Bolivia, for example – have also been actively involved in drug-trafficking and international terrorism, which puts them into alliance with some of the Italians who have been mentioned above.

Perhaps the most extreme example of a person who has been involved in many of these worlds is Klaus Barbie. During World War II

Barbie was a Gestapo official in the French city of Lyon. His role in torturing and murdering Jews and Resistance leaders won him the title 'the butcher of Lyon'. Altogether 4,000 deaths have been attributed to him. At the end of World War II many US officials were so concerned about the Soviet threat that they were willing to work with Nazi war criminals whom they felt could be of assistance. Between 1947 and 1951 Barbie was a paid informant of US Army intelligence, which helped him to elude capture.

With American help, Barbie settled in Latin America and started a new life in Bolivia under the name of Klaus Altman. He was involved with both drug-trading and death squads, in association with the former military leaders of Bolivia. This circle was, in turn, connected to Italian terrorists. Two of the men linked to the 1980 Bologna massacre – Stefano delle Chiaie and Pierluigi Pagliai – were believed to have been given refuge in Bolivia.

Here, the story points back to the P2 Lodge, for Gelli was in the same Italian and Bolivian circles. A veteran foreign correspondent in Latin America says that 'Gelli was linked with the military in Bolivia and the army there is in the drug business. And into the drug business were pulled – or stepped – people like Barbie and the hit squads.'

Gelli's connections in Latin America, of course, extended beyond Bolivia. At one time or another he has had friends among the leaders of Argentina, Brazil, Nicaragua (under Somoza), Peru and Uruguay. His closest associates in Argentina included men accused of organising that country's death squads, such as José López Rega.

The involvement of Banco Ambrosiano – and perhaps even the Vatican bank – with Latin American regimes has been the subject of intense speculation. One theory is that Calvi and Gelli used Ambrosiano's network of banks and ghost companies to funnel money to right-wing regimes. After Calvi's death Michele Sindona put forward this view on several occasions. 'Calvi', he said, 'was directly financing all the anti-communists of South America. He wanted to defend the world from communists – about which he had become paranoid like me.' This scheme, he said, was conceived with Gelli and Ortolani. Sindona told a reporter for ABC Television that the ghost companies bought newspapers, real estate and companies in Argentina, Peru, Uruguay and Paraguay. The purchases, he said, were made at inflated prices and the excess money was paid to right-wing political parties and military leaders.

Was the Vatican also involved? According to Sindona, the answer is yes. Sindona says that right-wing factions within the Vatican approved of the Latin American operations 'because to fight communism automatically means supporting Catholicism'. An American banker with long experience in Central America takes this theory one step further. He believes strongly that elements in the Vatican were working in association with the CIA to funnel money to right-wing forces in Latin America.

The belief that these elements work closely with US intelligence officials is not new, and there seems to be considerable support for it. For example, Archbishop Marcinkus is a staunch anti-Communist in the 1950s' mould, who frequently uses expressions like 'the Iron Curtain countries'. He has long been the most senior American citizen in the Vatican, and, according to a US diplomat, is therefore the main point of contact between the State Department and the Vatican. For instance, before papal tours US officials would arrange through Marcinkus to brief the Pope on the countries he was visiting. The Pope also reportedly received CIA briefings on events in Poland.

One Latin America venture that seems to pull together many of these interests is a project to develop oil in Guatemala. In 1977 the concession was awarded by that country's military rulers to Basic Resources International SA (BRISA), a Luxembourg company one of whose board members has been Antonio Tonello, chairman of Calvi's Credito Varesino and a director of various other Ambrosiano subsidiaries. In May 1981 General Vernon Walters, a retired CIA official, visited Guatemala as a 'goodwill ambassador' of the Reagan Administration. At the same time, though, he was representing BRISA, which was seeking permission to export more oil. The Guatemalan military granted the request.

During his long career in American foreign policy and intelligence circles General Walters has worked with the Christian Democrats in Italy and Latin American juntas. He was deputy director of the CIA from 1972 to 1976, a period that included the overthrow of Allende in Chile.

Like many retired CIA men, General Walters appears to have used on behalf of private enterprise the contacts he acquired during his government service. It is a long tradition, perhaps best exemplified by Kermit Roosevelt (a grandson of Theodore Roosevelt), who helped to return the Shah of Iran to power in the 1950s, and then sold him arms in the 1970s. Walters has been a consultant to a US company which was reportedly involved in selling arms to Morocco.

At this stage it should be emphasised that it is not only *western* intelligence agents who consort with nefarious characters. There is a parallel network, connected to the Soviet bloc, which involves left-wing terrorists, drug dealers and arms traffickers.

In her pioneering study, *The Terror Network,* Claire Sterling provides overwhelming evidence to back up her thesis that the Soviets have been training, arming, financing and sheltering terrorists in Europe, the Middle East and Latin America for more than a decade. In August 1982 she revealed the strong East European connections of Mehmet Ali Agca, the Turkish terrorist who tried to murder Pope John Paul II in May 1981. Sterling argued that the KGB was probably behind the attempt.

At first, there was widespread scepticism that the Soviets would be involved in such a bold scheme. However in December 1982 Italy's Defence Minister, Lelio Lagorio, made a startling speech in which he produced evidence of KGB involvement in the attempt on the Pope, and went on to describe eastern bloc links with Italian terrorists. For example, he revealed that when US General James Dozier, a NATO official, was kidnapped by the Red Brigades in December 1981, he was interrogated by Bulgarian secret service agents. At the same time Italian officials described a massive arms and drug smuggling trade centred in Bulgaria, involving terrorist groups and the Mafia.

When these disclosures emerged, they provided still more material for conspiracy theorists – including those who link the KGB to the death of Calvi. The Soviets, for their part, responded by accusing the CIA of sponsoring terrorism, the P2 Lodge of trying to murder the Pope, and Lech Walesa of having a secret account at the Vatican bank. It seemed that the whole story had come full circle.

It would be a futile exercise to try to find a single concept to explain the complicated web of intrigue surrounding the Calvi and P2 scandals. Life just isn't like an Agatha Christie thriller. But a few observations can be made:

1. There are incredibly extensive links among a vast array of 'underworlds', including intelligence agencies, organised crime, terrorists and drug traffickers.

2. Ostensibly 'respectable' individuals, such as government officials, churchmen and business leaders, use these networks. The US government and the Vatican, for example, have, in their war against Communism, allied themselves with some of the most loathsome people imaginable, including gangsters, drug pushers and terrorists. This raises disturbing questions about whether the ends justify the means.

3. A parallel network, involving the Soviet Union, is concerned with destabilising the West.

4. Some individuals and organisations appear to have worked for both sides. Sicilian Mafiosi, for example, have been involved with both

right-wing terrorists and the Bulgarian-based arms and drug ring. There is strong evidence linking Licio Gelli to both the East and the West. This raises the question: who is using whom?

5. Finally, if the P2 and Calvi scandals produced a positive side effect it was this: they helped to reveal how the world works. Unfortunately, Roberto Calvi's world view may have been far more accurate than anyone realised.

30

From Master to Servant

Banco Ambrosiano had been in existence for half a century when Roberto Calvi became an employee. When he reached the executive suite the bank was seventy-five years old. But Calvi did so much to transform it that he regarded himself – and was regarded by many others – almost as if he were the founder. He had inherited a provincial, Catholic bank but had turned it into an international financial empire. As one Italian banker puts it: 'Banco Ambrosiano *was* Calvi.'

The shareholders and depositors clearly identified Ambrosiano with its chairman. When Calvi was arrested, the share price fell. When he was defended by political leaders, the price rose again. When he vanished from Italy, there was panic. Roberto Rosone reflected this view when, after Calvi's disappearance, he insisted that 'the destiny of an institution like the Ambrosiano group must remain separate from that of its leaders'.

Rosone was wrong. The fate of the man and the bank were inextricably woven. When Calvi died, his empire crumbled.

Roberto Calvi is but one of countless casualties in the Calvi affair. Other lives have been lost, while many careers, fortunes and reputations have been destroyed. Nearly 40,000 investors have seen their shares in Ambrosiano become worthless. Public officials who provided political 'protection' have been discredited. Board members of Ambrosiano have been sued, some of the executives have been imprisoned. The image of the Vatican has been tainted.

Perhaps the biggest victim of all has been the Italian people, whose already fragile confidence in their leaders and institutions has been further eroded. For the Calvi scandal could never have occurred if there had not been collusion with and protection from politicians and civil servants. Stefano Rodotà, a left-wing Member of Parliament, has stated this case eloquently:

'Too many politicians, too many respected men defended him until the end. Is it possible that they didn't suspect anything? Is it possible that they knew nothing of the network of protections, extortions and favours which the banker enjoyed? . . . The system of government was not blind: it did not want to see. It was not defeated, because many of its troops were on the side of the victor.'

Many, but not all. If there is one reassuring aspect of the Calvi affair it is this: a large number of people behaved courageously, often at great personal cost to themselves. At the Bank of Italy, Paolo Baffi and Mario Sarcinelli fearlessly carried out their duties. Several magistrates performed honourably even though it sometimes meant risking their lives. Probably the most moving example is that of Giorgio Ambrosoli, whose pursuit of Sindona cost him his life.

There have been other glimmers of hope in Italy. In 1982 and 1983 crackdowns on terrorism and organised crime have led to hundreds of arrests and convictions. And this has been achieved without destroying democratic freedoms.

A small instance of the fact that people have not given up hope occurred in September 1982. Tina Anselmi, chairman of the parliamentary commission investigating the P2 Lodge, was at a public gathering when the arrest of Licio Gelli was announced. Hundreds of young people clustered around and asked her to autograph tee-shirts – as if she were a sports star. 'Come on, Tina, Come on, Tina,' they shouted, 'clean things up, get rid of the P2!'

One man who would have every reason to feel cynical is Mario Sarcinelli. In 1979 he was arrested, imprisoned, and forced out of his job at the Bank of Italy. His only apparent 'crime' was that he had investigated corrupt bankers. He was later fully exonerated and, in 1981, was given the most senior post in Italy's civil service: Director General of the Treasury Ministry. Sarcinelli freely admits that he was tempted to give up hope in his country after that bitter experience. He even thought of emigrating. Eventually, he says,

'I decided to remain in this country and raise my family here. Italy's problem is a question of growth. In a certain sense, we have to become mature. And when we do, this kind of unlawful manifestation of power will subside. I still have faith in this country. I'm confident that there are good people – competent, honest – who just want to work and discharge their duties according to the laws of the country.'

Encouraging as these sentiments are, the size of the task ahead should not be underestimated. For example, the 'Mafia mentality' has developed in Sicily over the course of centuries. Concepts like 'state' and 'public service' are comparatively remote and abstract. And when

198

the state shows that it does not deserve the people's trust, the old ways of thinking prevail.

Since the exposure of the P2 Lodge, the term 'P2' has become a new synonym for this mentality. As one Italian businessman puts it: 'The P2 still exists, whatever you want to call it. In this country, everything depends on "the good friends": my "good friend" is sure that you will get that job you want, so you can go ahead and apply for it. This is our way of doing things. This is our mentality.' In other words the Sindona, P2 and Calvi scandals are products of a mentality and a system. As a government official puts it: 'Unless we change the rules of the game, another Calvi can be born.'

Of the countless mysteries in this story, one of the most fascinating is the mind and character of Roberto Calvi. He was a man who craved and sought 'protection', and yet the schemes he devised to secure protection contained the seeds of their own destruction. He tried to seize control of his bank, and yet the plan ultimately destroyed the bank, since it involved a reckless gamble on foreign exchange rates and interest rates. He joined the P2 Lodge to obtain political protection, and yet this only made his problems worse. It may well be that Calvi felt he did not really deserve the power he had obtained, and thus subconsciously undermined himself.

Valerio Mazzola, a lawyer who represented Calvi during his trial in 1981, suggested that Calvi's fatal flaw was that he had a dual character or, as Mazzola put it, 'two brains'. 'How can you defend a client with two brains?' Mazzola asked at the time of the trial. 'Brain number one is good. It's the brain that has built Banco Ambrosiano into a big, solid, prosperous, well-run bank. Brain number two thinks the world is run by conspiracies.'

Calvi's dual nature was reflected in the financial empire he created. 'It was two banks,' says an American banker in Milan. 'One was a normal Milanese bank, heavy in deposits. And then there was this other institution [the foreign network] that nobody understood.'

Finally, Calvi's personality was expressed in the way he built his career and tried to protect himself and his bank. He felt it was not enough to run a successful, profitable bank; he also had to ally himself with 'hidden powers.' This need for what he called *potere occulto* is reminiscent of nothing so much as the Faust legend. Of that story, one scholar has written: 'It presents the career of a . . . man of humble origin who has acquired great learning. His arrogance will cause him to overreach and ruin himself. We are to witness a tragedy of presumption.' In the Christopher Marlowe version of the tale, Faust even travels to the Vatican and makes a fool of the Pope – a parallel with the Calvi story which is too close for comfort.

Calvi's need for hidden powers can be blamed in part on the 'P2 mentality' mentioned earlier, which made it possible for men like Sindona and Gelli to survive and prosper for years. But it was also a product of Calvi's personal isolation and insecurity. His banking skills were unsurpassed, but he was ill-prepared to judge and deal with other people, and thus vulnerable to the blandishments of 'fixers' who offered him help.

Like Faust, Roberto Calvi made a pact to extend his power and influence. And in the end he paid a much higher price than he had ever anticipated. He became the tool, then the puppet, and then the victim of Licio Gelli. In the last months of his life Calvi was more isolated and desperate than ever before, which drove him into the arms of new 'fixers' and 'protectors', and he appears to have become their victim as well. Mario Sarcinelli puts it this way: 'Perhaps he began as a servant, then became a master, only to become the servant of other masters later on.'

Calvi's remains were flown to Italy in October 1982. A new autopsy was conducted, and the body was then transported to the village of Drezzo where the Calvi family had their country house. It was an appropriate resting place, for when he was alive Calvi probably only felt safe with his family.

The funeral was held on 13 November 1982. It was attended by his family, a few servants and bodyguards, and two or three employees of Ambrosiano. Not one of the political leaders, industrialists, financiers and publishers who had courted him and received money and favours from Calvi attended the service. The priest was forbidden by his bishop from saying a simple sermon over the body of the man who had been known as 'God's Banker'.

In death, Roberto Calvi was as he had been in life. Alone.

Epilogue

Detective Chief Superintendent Barry Tarbun of the City of London Police took charge of the Calvi case in the summer of 1982. Early the following year he said: 'In every police officer's life you have a job that will never leave you. This is one of them.' Indeed, the Calvi story never seems to end, it just pauses and then continues in a new direction. For example, these words are being written shortly after yet another important development in the case: on the morning of 10 August 1983 Licio Gelli disappeared from his cell in a Swiss prison, just days before the Swiss government was expected to rule favourably on Italy's request to extradite him.

Although it is not possible – it will probably never be possible – to tie up the story in a neat package, a great many of the mysteries surrounding Calvi's life and death have now been clarified. We know, for example, that although Calvi appeared to be the absolute ruler of Banco Ambrosiano, he was in reality being secretly manipulated by others. We know the fate of much of the 'missing money' from the ghost company scheme. We also know that the Vatican Bank was intimately involved in that scheme.

The murder-versus-suicide puzzle had not been solved at the time this book was being completed, and Carboni's version of events was adding to the speculation. Emilio Pellicani, a close associate of Carboni's who was involved in Calvi's trip, began giving new details of the trip to investigating magistrates in late 1982. In many ways he contradicted the versions of Carboni and Vittor. For example, Pellicani said that Vittor had taken Calvi's famous black briefcase – containing confidential papers – shortly before the banker left Italy. Carboni and Vittor had claimed to know nothing about the black bag.

On 12 January 1983 the Calvi family was granted leave to challenge the suicide verdict of the coroner's inquest. On 28 and 29 March the appeal was heard by the High Court. George Carman, a barrister representing the Calvi family, argued that the inquest was a 'miscarriage of justice'. He cited among other things the great length of time the jurors had sat, questionable comments made by the coroner in his summing up, and the failure of the coroner to warn the jury that the written statements from Carboni and Vittor may not have been credible. On 29 March the three judges, led by Lord Lane, the Lord Chief Justice, voted unanimously to quash the suicide verdict and order a new inquest.

The Ambrosiano group is now a shadow of its former self. Calvi's foreign subsidiaries – with the exception of Banca del Gottardo in Switzerland – are nearly all defunct. Typical is the case of Banco Ambrosiano Overseas, the Bahamas bank Calvi established in 1971. In September 1982 it went into voluntary liquidation. The impressive building – Ambrosiano House – that had been officially opened in April 1981 was soon occupied by liquidators and a handful of employees kept on to deal with lawsuits from creditors.

In Via Clerici in Milan, offices in the fourth-floor executive suite were divided between executives of Nuovo Banco Ambrosiano and liquidators of the 'old' Ambrosiano. Much of their time has been spent in litigation. The new bank sued directors and executives of the old bank. Creditors of the Luxembourg holding company have named Nuovo Ambrosiano in legal action. In March 1983 it was reported that nearly eighty of the eighty-eight creditors of the holding company were seeking damages of between $300 million and $400 million from Nuovo Ambrosiano.

Legal actions from the old bank's shareholders were also pending, although executives of Nuovo Ambrosiano have devised a scheme to give partial compensation to small shareholders.

In November 1982 the Vatican appointed a four-man panel of lay financial experts to examine Vatican finances. It consisted of the 'three wise men', plus a German banker, Hermann Abs, former chief executive of Deutsche Bank. Even this effort at reform provoked a mini-scandal, as a Jewish organisation pointed out that Abs had been a prominent financial leader during the Nazi era. At the same time the six-man Italy-Vatican commission discussed a financial settlement. By the summer of 1983 there were reports that the Vatican would be willing to pay some $300 million as partial settlement of the ghost companies' debts.

The impact of the Ambrosiano crisis on the international banking system prompted central bankers to draft a new code for international banking supervision, to supplant the now discredited Basle Concordat.

In March 1983 one newspaper noted: 'The new code...is largely in response to the collapse last year of Banco Ambrosiano's Luxembourg offshoot...' In Italy, efforts to tighten accounting and auditing standards were underway.

Michele Sindona has been in prison in the United States since 1980 because of his role in the collapse of Franklin National. In July 1981 he was charged – but has not yet been tried – with ordering the assassination of Giorgio Ambrosoli, the liquidator of Sindona's Banca Privata. In June 1982 one of the men accused of carrying out that killing, an American Mafioso named William Aricò, was arrested by the FBI. Sindona, a 'guest' at the Federal Medium Security Prison at Otisville, New York, spends much of his time reading books on finance and economics, and granting interviews to reporters about the Calvi affair.

Before his disappearance from a Swiss prison in August 1983, Licio Gelli was said to have completed his memoirs – a project that many Italians interpreted as another of the P2 leader's efforts at blackmail. He reportedly turned down a $1 million advance from an American publisher.

Several of Calvi's subordinates have been sacked. His former deputy, Roberto Rosone, is also haunted by the thought of an attempt on his life. Rosone has confided to friends that he is 'afraid that someone will kill me'. Regarding himself as a victim, he has said: 'I did what I could to save the bank. I loved it the way one can love a woman. Now I'm paying for that love with my skin.'

Roberto Calvi's family no longer lives in Italy. His widow is in the Bahamas, his daughter and son are in America.

The Second Inquest

On Monday 13 June 1983 the new coroner's inquest into Calvi's death began. The setting was the same as the previous one, Milton Court in the City of London, but many of the characters were different. A new coroner, Dr Arthur Gordon Davies, was 'imported' from the borough of Southwark in south London. The two legal teams had also been reshuffled. Sir David Napley did not appear in court for the Calvis; instead, his firm acted as instructing solicitors to George Carman, the barrister who had argued the appeal before the High Court judges. Carboni's lawyer from the previous inquest, John Blofeld, was now a judge. His place was taken by barrister Richard Du Cann. Both Carman and Du Cann were Queen's Counsel, members of the elite 10 per cent of Britain's 4,000 barristers.

A new jury, of course, had been installed, and they proved to be extremely conscientious. On the first evening of the inquest they asked to visit Blackfriars Bridge. The following day some of them went for a second visit after midnight – to see what conditions would have been like around the time of Calvi's death, when the tide was low. (A reasonable comparison could be made since this was almost a year to the day since the body had been found there.)

The previous inquest had been squeezed into one day; there was little risk that this one could be regarded as too rushed. It lasted two weeks, during which nearly forty witnesses were examined. Most of those who had testified in 1982 appeared this time, but there were several important new witnesses too. Clara, Carlo and Anna Calvi appeared, as did three of the people who were with Roberto Calvi in London: Silvano Vittor and the Kleinszig sisters.

Once again, Professor Simpson was a key witness. This time, though, Carman succeeded in raising some doubts about the pathologist's conclusion that Calvi had committed suicide. Carman described the 'acrobatic' manoeuvres Calvi would have to have made to hang himself, and Professor Simpson agreed that it would have been difficult for Calvi to kill himself. When Carman suggested that it would have been easier for men on a boat to have hanged Calvi, Simpson agreed. Carman then mentioned several possible ways in which Calvi could have been immobilised without leaving evidence in the corpse. He suggested that such drugs as ethyl chloride or 'a curare-like substance' would not necessarily have left traces. Simpson accepted the possibility, though he regarded it as remote.

The Calvi family testified that the banker was in fear of his life. Clara Calvi listed among his many enemies politicians, elements within the Vatican and others. She said that her husband was prepared – if necessary – to 'name names' of political and Vatican figures at his appeals trial. She also revealed that in May 1982, a month before his death, her husband had told her that a senior official of IOR was trying to get hold of his records of his business dealings with the Vatican bank.

The Vatican was also mentioned in the testimony of Robert Clarke, the London solicitor who had helped arrange Calvi's accommodation at the Chelsea Cloisters on behalf of Hans Kunz, Carboni's Swiss friend. According to Clarke, Kunz told him after Calvi's death that Carboni had been acting 'on behalf of Vatican interests' and that if the arrangements for the trip to London had not been made 'the government [of Italy] might have fallen'.

Carman did not say 'who did it' and the coroner's rules did not permit him to make a speech outlining a theory of how the murder was

204

committed. However, in the course of examining witnesses he made a few remarks that showed what his hypothesis was. 'We say beyond question that Roberto Calvi met his death at the hand of others...we are quite unable to say who those others are may be.' But he said that 'the overwhelming inference is that they were professional criminals recruited for that purpose. As for the role of Carboni and/or Vittor, we say it is shrouded with suspicion...we call into question their conduct and their truthfulness.'

Indeed, much of his case involved attacking the credibility of Carboni and his entourage. Carman brought out evidence of Carboni's Mafia connections. He mentioned the payments Carboni had made into Swiss bank accounts belonging to his mistresses, Manuela Kleinszig and Laura Scanu-Concas, both of whom testified on Carboni's behalf at the new inquest.

When he examined Manuela Kleinszig, Carman asked if she had overheard any of the thirty telephone calls Carboni had made from a Zurich hotel room a few days before Calvi died. No, she said, she was out with her sister shopping, buying shoes. Later, when she said she was shopping also on 17 June, he struck a quizzical pose and inquired: 'Shoes?' At another point she claimed that when she spoke to Carboni for the first time after Calvi died, they did not discuss the death.

Michaela Kleinszig, Vittor's girlfriend (and the mother of his daughter), was subjected to similar treatment. Carman asked her: 'Was this a usual week for you – as the mother of a young child – to go to Switzerland, Amsterdam and London in three days?'

When Vittor said his occupation was 'businessman', Carman described Vittor's activities before and after Calvi's death as 'fourteen days in the life of a businessman'.

Richard Du Cann, representing Carboni, based his case on several points. He stressed the evidence for suicide in his questioning of Professor Simpson and the police detectives. He pointed out Calvi's suicide attempt during his trial. Du Cann also noted that, just hours before Calvi died, his powers as chairman had been withdrawn and his secretary had plunged to her death. If the jury delivered a verdict of suicide, Du Cann said, the Calvi family would forfeit a life insurance policy worth about $3 million.

The suspicious behaviour of Carboni – going into hiding, for example – was obviously a problem for Carboni's lawyer. Du Cann dealt with it this way: his questions implied that if Carboni had committed the crime of helping Calvi jump bail, it would be perfectly normal for Carboni to go into hiding.

On Monday 27 June 1983, at about 11 a.m., Dr Davies, the coroner, began his summing-up. It was quite different from that of the previous coroner. For example, he said that the jurors needed strong evidence of suicide to deliver a suicide verdict and strong evidence of murder for a murder verdict. If they were not firmly convinced either way, he said, then it is 'perfectly right and proper that you should reach an open verdict'.

After three and a half hours of deliberation, the jurors said they had decided. Just before 3 p.m. the doors of the coroner's court were opened and the lawyers, the Calvi family, and perhaps three dozen journalists came in and took their seats. The jurors entered, followed by the coroner. He then addressed the jury foreman:

Coroner: Members of the jury, do you have your verdict?
Foreman: Open verdict, sir.
Coroner: Is that the verdict of you all?
Foreman: Yes, sir.
Coroner: I am obliged. I will then record that Roberto Calvi of Via Frua 9, Milan, Italy, has died of asphyxia due to hanging. At 7.30 hours on the 18th of June 1982 at Blackfriars Bridge, he was founding hanging from the scaffold, and the jury returned an open verdict.

Reconstruction of the 'Ghost Company' Network

Owes Banco Andino $157,420,146 guaranteed by Banco Ambrosiano shares in the names of Finkurs, Sansinvest, Finprogram, La Fidele

MANIC HOLDING SA
Luxembourg equity capital: $45 million

SANSINVEST
Liechtenstein

At 7 July 1982 possessed 154,321 shares of Banco Ambrosiano

FINKURS AG
Liechtenstein

At 7 July 1982 possessed 158,642 shares of Banco Ambrosiano

The Banco Ambrosiano shares had been acquired on 2 December 1975 on the orders of Banca del Gottardo

LA FIDELE
financial company Panama

At 7 July 1982 possessed 340,000 shares of Banco Ambrosiano

FINPROGRAM
financial company Panama

At 7 July 1982 possessed 440,000 shares of Banco Ambrosiano

The shares had been acquired on 24 February 1975 on the orders of Banca del Gottardo at 21,000 lire each

LARAMIE CO. INC.
Panama equity capital: $10,000

Owes Managua $27,875.512 guaranteed by 2 million shares of Vianini which however were not materially consigned

ASTOLFINE
Panama equity capital: $10,000

Owes Banco Andino $486,639,517 guaranteed by the Banco Ambrosiano shares possessed by its subsidiaries Cascadilla, Lantana, Orfeo and Marbella – altogether 1,367,717 shares equal to 2.735% of the capital of Banco Ambrosiano

WORLD WIDE TRADING
Panama equity capital:

Owes Banco Ambrosi Managua $49,998 guaranteed by 52% shares of TV Sorrisi e possessed by World W managed on a fiducia by Rothschild Bank o

FINANCIERA ESTEBINA

At 7 July 1982 possessed 111,112 shares of Banco Ambrosiano of Milan

ORFEO

At 7 July 1982 possessed 308,642 shares of Banco Ambrosiano of Milan

MARBELLA

At 7 July 1982 possessed 133,149 shares of Banco Ambrosiano of Milan

LANTANA

At 7 July 1982 possessed 462,963 shares of Banco Ambrosiano of Milan

CASCADIL

At 7 July 198 possessed 462,963 shares Banco Ambrosi of Milan

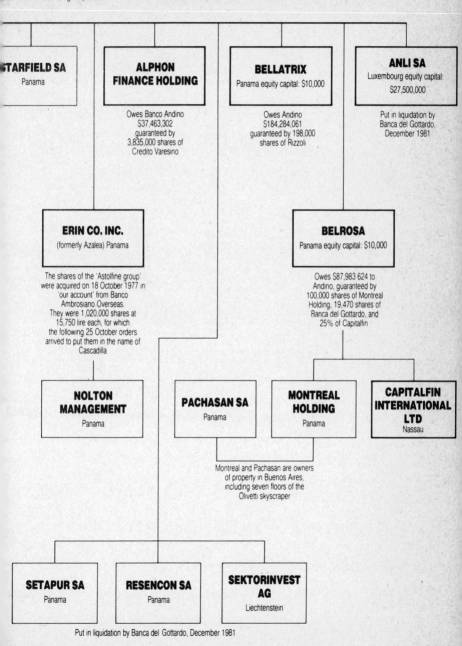

is the 'super holding' that was the beneficiary, directly or through corporations it
...lled, of most of the loans (now unrecoverable) granted by Banco Ambrosiano
...o and by Ambrosiano Group Banco Commercial of Nicaragua. Manic, Astolfine,
...Bellatrix, Belrosa, Starfield, Laramie and World Wide were supported by IOR with
...etters of 1 September 1981. The other 'super holding' involved in the collapse of
...osiano is United Trading Corporation.

STARFIELD SA
Panama

ALPHON FINANCE HOLDING

Owes Banco Andino
$37,463,302
guaranteed by
3,835,000 shares of
Credito Varesino

BELLATRIX
Panama equity capital: $10,000

Owes Andino
$184,284,061
guaranteed by 198,000
shares of Rizzoli

ANLI SA
Luxembourg equity capital:
$27,500,000

Put in liquidation by
Banca del Gottardo,
December 1981

ERIN CO. INC.
(formerly Azalea) Panama

The shares of the 'Astolfine group'
were acquired on 18 October 1977 in
'our account' from Banco
Ambrosiano Overseas.
They were 1,020,000 shares at
15,750 lire each, for which
the following 25 October orders
arrived to put them in the name of
Cascadilla

BELROSA
Panama equity capital: $10,000

Owes $87,983 624 to
Andino, guaranteed by
100,000 shares of Montreal
Holding, 19,470 shares of
Banca del Gottardo, and
25% of Capitalfin

NOLTON MANAGEMENT
Panama

PACHASAN SA
Panama

MONTREAL HOLDING
Panama

CAPITALFIN INTERNATIONAL LTD
Nassau

Montreal and Pachasan are owners
of property in Buenos Aires,
including seven floors of the
Olivetti skyscraper

SETAPUR SA
Panama

RESENCON SA
Panama

SEKTORINVEST AG
Liechtenstein

Put in liquidation by Banca del Gottardo, December 1981

Source: Il Mondo, 20 June 1983

Bibliography and Notes

Several types of sources were used in the preparation of this book, including interviews, articles in the press, books and documents. Interviews are indicated by the name of the interviewee followed by the words 'to author'. For articles, title of publication (sometimes abbreviated) and date are given. Books are identified by surname of author and page number. Where a book has more than one author, only the first is mentioned. Where the bibliography contains more than one work by the same author an abbreviated form of the title is included. Documents and other sources are either identified fully or abbreviated.

The notes give a somewhat misleading impression of the sources used in this book, since most of those interviewed by the author insisted on anonymity. As a result, an article or book is often cited as the only source for a fact when that is not really the case; the information in books and articles has often been confirmed in interviews.

BARBERI, Andrea, BUONGIORNO, Pino, DE LUCA, Maurizio, PAGANI, Nazareno, PANSA, Giampaolo, SCALFARI, Eugenio, and TURANI, Giuseppe, *L'Italia della P2*, Milan, Arnoldo Mondadori Editore, 1981.

BOWEN, Muriel, CARROLL, Nicholas, DE ZULUETA, Tana, HEBBLETHWAITE, Peter, and WHALE, John (ed.), *The Pope from Poland, An Assessment*, London, Collins, 1980.

BRANCOLI, Rodolfo, *Spettatori Interessati*, Milan, Aldo Garzanti Editore, 1980.

BROWN, Anthony Cave (ed.), *The Secret War Report of the OSS*, New York, Berkley Medallion, 1976.

CARLI, Guido, preface to CANTONI, Renato, *1973/1974 Il Terremoto Monetario*, Milan, Etas Libri.

CASSELS, Alan, *Fascist Italy*, London, Routledge & Kegan Paul, 1969.

DIFONZO, Luigi, *St Peter's Banker*, New York, Franklin Watts, 1983.

HAMMER, Richard, *The Vatican Connection*, New York, Holt, Rinehart & Winston, 1982.

KRÜGER, Henrik, *The Great Heroin Coup: Drugs, Intelligence and International Fascism*, Boston, South End Press, 1980.

JOHNSON, Paul, *Pope John Paul II and the Catholic Restoration*, London, Weidenfeld and Nicolson, 1982.

211

JUMP, John D., preface to MARLOWE, Christopher, *Doctor Faustus,* London, Methuen, 1981 edition.

LO BELLO, Nino, *The Vatican Empire,* New York, Trident Press, 1968.

——, *The Vatican Papers,* London, New English Library, 1982.

'LOMBARD', *Soldi Truccati: I Segreti del Sistema Sindona,* Milan, Giangiacomo Feltrinelli Editore, 1980.

MACADAM, Alta (ed.), *Blue Guide Rome and Environs,* London, Ernest Benn, 1979.

MACHIAVELLI, Niccolò, *The Prince,* trans. Detmold, Christian E., New York, Airmont, 1965.

MACKENZIE, Norman (ed.), *Secret Societies,* London, Aldus Books, 1967.

MARTIN, Malachy, *The Decline and Fall of the Roman Church,* New York, Bantam edition, 1983.

MORRIS, Roger, *Uncertain Greatness, Henry Kissinger and American Foreign Policy,* London, Quartet Books, 1977.

MORTON, H. V., *A Traveller in Italy,* London, Methuen, 1964.

NICHOLS, Peter, *Italia, Italia,* London, Macmillan, 1973.

——, *The Pope's Divisions,* London, Penguin edition, 1982.

PIAZZESI, Gianfranco, *Gelli, La Carriera di un Eroe di Questa Italia,* Milan, Garzanti Editore, 1983.

POWERS, Thomas, *The Man Who Kept the Secrets, Richard Helms and the CIA,* New York, Pocket Books edition, 1981.

REID, Margaret, *The Secondary Banking Crisis, 1973–75,* London, Macmillan, 1982.

SAMPSON, Anthony, *The Arms Bazaar,* New York, Viking, 1977.

SERVADIO, Gaia, *Mafioso,* London, Secker & Warburg, 1976.

SIMPSON, Keith, *Forty Years of Murder,* London, Granada edition, 1980.

SISTI, Leo and MODOLO, Gianfranco, *Il Banco Paga, Roberto Calvi e l'Avventura dell'Ambrosiano,* Milan, Arnoldo Mondadori Editore, 1982.

SPERO, Joan Edelman, *The Failure of the Franklin National Bank,* New York, Columbia University Press, 1980.

STERLING, Claire, *The Terror Network,* London, Weidenfeld and Nicolson, 1981.

TEODORI, Massimo, *La Banda Sindona,* Milan, Gammalibri, 1982.

THOMAS, Gordon and MORGAN-WITTS, Max, *Pontiff,* London, Granada, 1983.

WEST, Morris, *The Salamander,* London, Coronet edition, 1981.

WILKINSON, Paul, *The New Fascists,* London, Grant McIntyre, 1981.

WISKEMANN, Elizabeth, *Fascism in Italy: its Development and Influence,* London, Macmillan, 1969.

Abbreviations Used in the Notes

| Anna interrog. | Interrogation of Anna Calvi on 22–23 Oct. 1982 by magistrates Bruno Siclari and Pierluigi Dell'Osso. Reprinted in *Panorama,* 10 Jan. 1983. |

BA	Banco Ambrosiano.
BA ann rep.	Banco Ambrosiano annual report.
Both inquests	Coroner's inquests of 23 July 1982 and 13–27 June 1983.
Carboni's tapes	Secret tape recordings of conversations made by Flavio Carboni in 1982. Portions reprinted in various magazines, cited in notes.
Corsera	*Corriere della Sera.*
FT	*Financial Times.*
Giornale	*Il Giornale Nuovo.*
IHT	*International Herald Tribune.*
Inquest 1	Coroner's inquest of 23 July 1982.
Inquest 2	Coroner's inquest of 13–27 June 1983.
NYT	*New York Times.*
Padalino	Report of 1978 inspection of Banco Ambrosiano by Bank of Italy. Team of inspectors led by Giulio Padalino.
Paxman	Television report broadcast on BBC-1 *Panorama* programme, 20 Dec. 1982, entitled 'Called to Account – How Roberto Calvi Died'. Reporter: Jeremy Paxman.
Repub.	*La Repubblica.*
R.C.	Roberto Calvi.
Sindona commission report	Final report by Parliamentary commission of inquiry into the Sindona case, submitted 24 March 1982. References in notes distinguish between majority report and the minority reports.
Sindona warrant	Warrant for the arrest of Michele Sindona for death threats and related offences. According to the warrant, those threatened included Giorgio Ambrosoli, Roberto Calvi and Enrico Cuccia. Issued 22 Oct. 1982 by magistrate Giuliano Turone.
Sole	*Il Sole-24 Ore.*
Times	*The Times* of London.

213

Vittor statement   Interrogation of Silvano Vittor, 24 June 1982, by magistrate Domenico Sica. Portions of it were read to jurors at both inquests.

Writ   Writ served by creditors of Banco Ambrosiano Holding on Nuovo Banco Ambrosiano, March 1983.

WSJ   *Wall Street Journal.*

vii Machiavelli quote: Machiavelli, 35.
xv Discovery of body: Huntley and police witnesses, both inquests.
xv Contents of suit: police, both inquests.
xvi More than a dozen: BA prospectus issued in early 1982 showed BA-controlled companies in ten foreign countries. Through Inter Alpha group, it was in another three.
xvii Spaventa quote: Spaventa to author.

Chapter 1

1 Turbulence in Italy, Cassels quotes: Cassels, 23.
1 Seizure of Milan City Hall: Cassels, 37.
1 Courtship of Vatican: Wiskemann, 27.
1–2 Concordat: Macadam, 261–2.
2–4 R.C.'s early life: Leone, Clara and Carlo Calvi to author.
3 Sisti and Modolo quotes: Sisti, 40.
3 Italy joins war: Cassels, 98.
3 War with Russia: Cassels, 101.
3 R.C. reports to duty: call-up notice, supplied by Calvi family.
3 Russian campaign: Wiskemann, 79.
3 How R.C. kept warm: *L'Espresso*, 22 Aug. 1982.
4 R.C. mentioned in history of cavalry: Sisti, 40.

Chapter 2

5 St Ambrose: Morton, 22.
5 Quote from early executive: quoted in *Rinascita,* 25 June 1982.
6 'Divine Providence': each annual report of Ambrosiano closed with a statement like the following (taken from the 1976 report): 'In closing this report we address ourselves with a grateful spirit to Providence, invoking its continued help in our work and in the future of the Bank.' This practice continued throughout Calvi's chairmanship.
6 'Backward personnel': Barberi, 134.
6 'Work machine': Giuseppe Prisco, former BA board member, in *Giornale,* 3 Oct. 1982.

6 Meets Clara: Clara Calvi to author.
7 Canesi 'very bossy': Carlo Calvi to author.
7 Sisti and Modolo on Canesi: *L'Espresso,* 20 June 1982.
7 R.C.'s travels: Clara Calvi to author.
7 Interitalia: Barberi, 135.
7–8 Date of Gottardo deal: *Mondo Econ.,* 15 Sept. 1982.
8 Purchase of Drezzo house: the amount is converted at the rate then prevailing – 625 lire to the dollar. (All other amounts are converted at about 1,000 to the dollar.)
9 Sindona on 'discovering' R.C.: ABC-TV, quoted in *La Stampa,* 25 July 1982.

Chapter 3

10 'Vital' lemon business: *New York* magazine, 24 Sept. 1979.
10 DiFonzo quote: DiFonzo, 25.
11 IOR as funnel for flight capital: countless sources, including B. of Italy officials.
11 Venturini on IOR: Venturini to author.
12 Sindona meets Spada: *Repub.,* 23 July 1982.
12 Sindona raises funds for Montini: DiFonzo, 35.
12 IOR buys shares in Sindona banks: DiFonzo, 11.
12 Relations with Hambros, Continental, Paribas: Spero, 53.
13 Vatican's controversial investments: *Newsweek* magazine, 25 Sept. 1978; various other sources.
13 Loss of tax exemption: *New York* magazine, 24 Sept. 1979.
13 Pope Paul chose Sindona: Lo Bello, *Papers,* 222–3; DiFonzo, 11.
13 D'Alema quote: D'Alema to author.
13 Marcinkus's origins: several sources, including *NYT,* 1 Oct. 1979.
13 Marcinkus's Vatican career: *Il Sabato,* 23–29 Oct. 1982.
14 Manila trip: *NYT,* 1 Oct. 1979; Vatican press office.
14 *Salamander* quote: West, 178.
14 Hail Marys': Lo Bello, *Papers,* 223; *FT,* 17 Nov. 1982.
14 'Never altogether clear': Lo Bello, *Papers,* 227.
14 Laundering Mafia money: DiFonzo, 83, 147.
14 Sindona/English banker: *Sunday Times,* 27 Jan. 1980.
15 Garibaldi as masonic leader: MacKenzie, 172.
15 *Critica Sociale:* quoted in *Mondo Econ.,* 15 Sept. 1982.
15 Marcinkus 'blessed' the pact: Sisti, 46.

Chapter 4

16 St Moritz trip: Clara Calvi to author.
16 Marzollo scandal: *Mondo Econ.,* 15 Sept. 1982.

17 Marcinkus on BAO board: BAO ann. rep.

17 Sindona claims about BAO: *La Stampa*, 3 Oct. 1982.

18 Modolo on 'illegality': Modolo to author.

18 Carli on La Centrale deal: Carli to author.

18 D'Alema on Carli's behaviour: D'Alema to author.

18 *L'Europeo* on Sindona: quoted in Carli preface.

18 Hambros' attitude to Sindona: Carlo Calvi to author.

18 Sindona wanted 'biggest group': *La Stampa*, 3 Oct. 1982.

18 Sindona's plans: Carli preface.

18 'Exorbitant': Carli preface.

18 Carli blocked Bastogi deal: DiFonzo, 113.

19 Leemans on R.C.'s dealmaking: Leemans to author.

19 R.C. on Banca Cattolica deal: Carboni tape, *Panorama,* 16 Aug. 1982.

19–20 Clara Calvi on Toro deal: Clara Calvi to author.

20 R.C.'s capital exports: findings of court in 'Calvi trial', July 1981.

20 Merzagora complaints: *Panorama,* 23 Aug. 1982.

20–21 Catholic depositors' complaints: *La Stampa,* 15 Oct. 1982.

21 Luciani's complaints: *Panorama,* 5 July 1982.

Chapter 5

22–3 Franklin deal: mainly Spero, DiFonzo, and *New York* magazine, 24 Sept. 1979. Specific sources follow.

22 Sindona on Americans' attitude: DiFonzo, 59.

22 Size of Franklin National: its relative size fluctuated over the years, and there are different ways of ranking banks (assets, deposits, equity, etc.). It is often described as the twentieth largest bank in the US. However, a chart published in *The Banker,* June 1972 (reprinted in Spero, 33–7) shows it as twenty-third largest US bank (in terms of assets), with total assets of $3.460 billion at end 1971, shortly before Sindona's takeover.

22 Union Commerce deal: *Il Mondo,* 7 June 1982, and Leemans to author.

23–4 Sindona's US lobbying: DiFonzo, Ch. 21; *New York* magazine, 24 Sept. 1979.

24 Payment to Nixon campaign: widely reported (e.g. *New York* magazine, 18 Nov. 1974); what has been disputed is whether the payment was accepted.

24 Sindona payment to Christian Democrats: Sindona commission majority report, 199.

24 Sindona says loan wasn't repaid: Sindona's testimony to P2 commission, *Giornale,* 12 Dec. 1982.

24 Lobbying by Andreotti: Sindona commission report.

24 Sindona on Gelli's help: *La Stampa,* 3 Oct. 1982.

24 Quote on Gelli's role: Sindona commission, minority report by D'Alema et al., 378–9.

24 Officials on P2 list: *L'Espresso,* 31 May 1981.

25 NatWest denial: Reid, 124.

25 No extradition from Taiwan: *Il Mondo,* 5 July 1981.

25 IOR's losses: *NYT*, 28 July 1982, quotes estimate of $30 million. Other estimates have varied widely. Marcinkus has always claimed that he only made 'paper losses'. That is, earlier profits made from Sindona deals more than offset losses when Sindona's banks crashed.

25 IOR stake in BCV: *La Stampa*, 15 Oct. 1982.

25 De Strobel on board of BCV: *Times*, 12 July 1982.

25 IOR stake in Gottardo: *Il Mondo*, 16 Aug. 1982.

25–26 IOR stake in BAO: *Repub.*, 23 July 1982.

26 IOR's letter about Suprafin: quoted in *Panorama*, 15 June 1981.

26 'Il Signor Carlo': *Il Globo*, 27–28 June 1982.

26 Carlo Calvi on Mennini and Macchi: Carlo Calvi to author.

26 Sindona on using Marcinkus's name: *Time* magazine, 13 Sept. 1982.

26 *Il Mondo* quote: *Il Mondo*, 29 June 1982.

Chapter 6

28 Bombacci quote: Bombacci to author.

28 'Arrival in society', Cavaliere del Lavoro: *Repub.*, 13 June 1982.

28 Ambrosian Library: Leone Calvi to author.

28 R.C.'s height and weight: Inquest 1.

29 Chair anecdote: Leemans to author.

30 R.C.'s attitude to aristocrats: Sindona to *Time* magazine, 13 Sept. 1982.

30 Leemans quotes on insecurity: Leemans to author.

30 Dealing with politicians: Clara and Carlo Calvi to author.

31 Security devices: *Giornale*, 19 Oct. 1982.

31 Clash over use of chapel: *La Stampa*, 14 Nov. 1982.

31 'Bunkers': *Giornale*, 19 Oct. 1982.

31 Bodyguards: testimony by Calvi family at Inquest 2 and several other sources.

Chapter 7

33 Restricted market: Guido Rossi to author.

33 Shares in 'friendly' hands: Padalino.

34 Andrea Rizzoli's reputation: Sisti, 126–7.

34 Angelo Rizzoli on his father: *L' Espresso*, 23 May 1982.

34 'Financing Italian exports': creditor banks to author.

34 Telexes: writ.

35 'Board meetings were rituals': Orazio Bagnasco, *Panorama*, 16 Aug. 1982.

35 Lines of credit to political parties: Padalino report shows a direct loan to the Socialist Party. Roberto Rosone, in his P2 commission testimony, mentioned other lines of credit, *Giornale*, 24 Nov. 1982.

36 Leemans on R.C.'s gullibility: Leemans to author.

36 'World run by conspiracies': Valerio Mazzola, *Euromoney*, March 1982.

36 R.C.'s initiation into P2: Barberi, 52.

Chapter 8

37 Sindona's PR campaign: *New York* magazine, 24 Sept. 1979; DiFonzo, Ch. 21.

37 Lectures: DiFonzo, 291–2.

37 McCaffrey affidavit: McCaffrey submitted a 'Notice of Intention to offer Evidence' in which he said his affidavit would state, among other things, 'that defendant planned a coup d'état in Italy in 1972 designed to establish a pro-American, capitalist government...'

37–8 DiFonzo on Cavallo's activities: DiFonzo, 229–30.

38 Cavallo on Sindona's attitude to R.C.: Sindona warrant.

38 Feb. 1977 *Agenzia A:* Sindona commission minority report by Teodori, 580.

38 Gelli as mediator: Rodolfo Guzzi quoted in Sindona warrant.

38–9 July to Nov. 1977 *Agenzia A* and wall posters: Sindona warrant and Sisti, 21, 24–5 and 32.

39 Cavallo letter to Baffi: Sisti, 27–31.

39 Guzzi visit to R.C.: Sindona warrant.

39 Leemans on bodyguards: Leemans to author.

39 Clara Calvi on R.C.'s fear of Sindona: *Il Mondo,* 20 Dec. 1982.

Chapter 9

41 Italcasse arrests: *Il Mondo,* 4 April 1980.

41 Sarcinelli quote: Sarcinelli to author.

41–3 Padalino findings: Padalino.

43 Capital exports: *Il Mondo,* 1 June 1981.

43 Cavallo's attacks, Guzzi's calls: Sindona warrant.

43 Extradition request: DiFonzo, 233.

43 Circulation of rescue plan: Sindona warrant.

44 Pirelli on Cuccia: *Giornale,* 10 Nov. 1982.

44 Threats to Ambrosoli: Sindona warrant.

44 Franklin officials convicted: DiFonzo, 235.

44 Sindona indicted: DiFonzo, 237.

44 Indictment of Baffi and Sarcinelli: *WSJ,* 19 April 1979.

45 $6.5 million commission: this was the finding of Giorgio Ambrosoli, liquidator of Sindona's Banca Privata, quoted in *Repub.,* 23 July 1982. Modolo told author that Ambrosoli showed him the name of the 'American archbishop' shortly before his death. Marcinkus has always denied taking such a payment.

45 'I will pay a very dear price': *Euromoney,* March 1983, and other sources.

45 Ambrosoli death: *L'Europeo,* 8 Aug. 1981.

45–6 Sindona fake kidnapping: Sindona commission report; Sindona warrant; DiFonzo, Ch. 23.

45–6 Threats to Cuccia: Sindona warrant.

46 Casaroli overrules depositions: Lo Bello, *Papers*, 232.
46 Sindona convicted: *Newsweek*, 13 Sept. 1982.
46 Suicide attempt and sentencing: DiFonzo, 258.
46 Viola on Sindona: *Giornale*, 17 Nov. 1982.
46 Volcker, Miller: Brancoli, 29–30.
46 'Staff intimidated': Sarcinelli to author.
47 D'Alema on B. of Italy: D'Alema to author.

Chapter 10

48 Relative size of BA group: *Il Mondo*, 25 May 1979.
48 La Centrale board members: Sisti, 8.
48–9 'Holy alliance': unnamed Italian weekly quoted in *Il Mondo*, 5 Sept. 1981.
49 Gelli in Spain: Barberi, 25–6.
49 Gelli's early links with left and right: Barberi, 24–33. Piazzesi goes into great detail about Gelli's links with the left, e.g. business dealings with Romania.
49 Gelli in Rome: Barberi, 34.
50 Acquaintances became friends: *L'Europeo*, 15 June 1981.
50 Covered lodge for VIPs: according to one report *(Giornale*, 28 March 1983): 'P2 was born as a covered lodge in 1800 to recruit personages and personalities whose public or political role required absolute secrecy – it is the lodge of the powerful.'
50 Vatican nobleman: *L'Espresso*, 28 June 1981.
50 Saragat visit: Barberi, 43.
50 Gelli's office: Piazzesi, 217, quoting Gelli's secretary in *Domenica del Corriere*.
51 Biagi on 'pilgrimages': *Panorama*, 4 Oct. 1982.
51 Gelli's use of files: Barberi, 25–6.
51 Nisticò anecdote: *L'Espresso*, 6 July 1981.
51–2 Gelli's links with Guarino: Barberi, 108–9; Venturini to author.
52 Uruguay villa: *L'Europeo*, 6 July 1981; Sisti 151.
52 Met Peron in 1971: Barberi, 111.
52 'Reverential regard': *L'Europeo*, 27 Dec. 1982.
52 'Perón knelt': *Panorama*, 27 Sept. 1982.
52 López Rega's background: *L'Espresso*, 5 Dec. 1982.
53 Trilateral deal: *L'Espresso*, 14 June 1981.
53 Massera/Gelli arms deals: Barberi, 118.
53 1976 arms deal: Sisti, 150.
54 Andrea Rizzoli on Ortolani: *Giornale*, 21 Feb. 1983.
54 Tassan Din on 'losing control': *La Stampa*, 16 Feb. 1983.

Chapter 11

55 Leemans on BA foreign offices: Leemans to author.

55 Ambrosiano House: *L'Espresso*, 31 Oct. 1982.

55–6 R.C. attitude to Latin America: Clara Calvi to author and other sources.

56 5.5 per cent of Bafisud: BAO 1980 ann. rep.

56 Meetings with Somoza: Carlo Calvi to author.

57 R.C. attitude to Nicaragua: Carlo Calvi to author.

57 Nicaragua passports: Carlo Calvi to author.

57 Loans to Somoza: *Il Mondo* reported (9 May 1983) that Somoza's heirs (he was assassinated 9 Sept. 1980) say they are ready to repay loans he received from BA's Bahamas and Nicaragua subsidiaries.

57 1977 Peru visit and business deals: Sisti, 153–4.

57 1979 visit to Silva Ruete: *FT*, 7 July 1982.

57 Andino's loans: a former director of Andino to author.

57 'Into the Andes': *Il Mondo*, 23 Nov. 1979.

58 Nación got money to pay for shares: former Andino director to author.

58 Telexes from Europe: former Andino director; long quotation is from writ.

59 Voxson loan: Padalino lists it as 'irregular'; Rosone, quoted in *L'Espresso*, 4 July 1982.

59–60 Genghini loan: Padalino lists exposure to Genghini group as 'irregular'. Rosone, quoted in Sisti, 160–61. *Giornale;* 5 Sept. 1982.

60 Genghini crash: *Il Mondo*, 6 Aug. 1982.

60 Genghini arrest: *Corsera*, 11 Nov. 1982.

60–61 ENI loans to BA group: *L'Europeo*, 27 Dec. 1982. Total exposure was eventually 222.7 billion lire, according to Gianni De Michelis, Minister for State Holdings.

60 ENI/Petromin deal: *Mondo Econ.*, 29 Sept. 1982 and *WSJ*,31 Jan. 1983.

60–61 Mazzanti sees Gelli's file: Mazzanti interview in *L'Espresso*, 7 June 1981.

61 BNL as creditor: BNL officials to author. One source at BNL points out that since BNL is one of the shareholders to Nuovo Banco Ambrosiano and also a lender to the Luxembourg holding company 'We are in the awkward position of suing ourselves.' (In early 1983, creditors of BAH began suing Nuovo Ambrosiano.)

61 Mazzanti joins P2: *L'Europeo*, 1 June 1981.

61 Calvi payment to Socialists: when interrogated in prison in July 1981 (see Ch. 13), Calvi said he paid $15 million to the Socialist Party in late 1979/early 1980. He said the money was paid from his Bahamas bank to Ortolani's Uruguayan bank. The Socialists denied receiving the funds. In June 1983 Giacomo Botta, a former top official of Ambrosiano, confirmed Calvi's version to magistrates, as quoted in *L'Espresso*, 3 July 1983.

61 Siegenthaler's many hats: *Il Mondo*, 16 Aug. 1982.

Chapter 12

62 Bologna bombing: Sterling, 1.

62 Sterling on Alessandrini: Sterling, 293.

62–4 Investigation of Calvi: described in detail in Sisti; other sources include judicial officials to author and sources cited below.

63 Oct. 1979 interrogation: *L'Unità*, 5 June 1981.

63 Evidence of crimes: *Repub.*, 13 June 1982.

64 Magistrates cleared of wrongdoing: *Repub.*, 18 March 1983.

64 Feb. 1979 issue of *OP*: *L'Espresso*, 7 June 1981.

64 March 1979 issue of *OP*: *Panorama*, 24 Jan. 1983.

65–6 Interrogation of Miceli Crimi and discovery of Gelli's files: Barberi, 58–60.

66 43 MPs including three cabinet ministers: Wilkinson, 138–9.

65–6 Other P2 members: *L'Espresso*, 7 June 1981; *Il Mondo*, 5 June 1981; and various other sources.

66 Spaventa on P2: Spaventa to author.

66 Forlani locked up P2 lists: *L'Europeo*, 1 June 1981.

66 R.C.'s attitude to Gelli: Anna interrog.

67 Calvi documents in Gelli's files: Sindona warrant.

67 R.C. announces Rizzoli deal: Rosone to author; Leemans to author; *L'Espresso*, 4 July 1982.

67 'The drop that made the pot overflow': *Giornale*, 6 July 1982.

67 Indictments of financiers: eleven financiers from the Ambrosiano group (in the role as directors of La Centrale) and from the so-called 'Bonomi-Invest group' were charged with involvement in schemes to export 23.5 billion lire from Italy through complicated share transactions (outlined in Ch. 9). One of the accused, Carlo Canesi, Calvi's one-time patron, died during the trial, on 13 June 1981. *La Stampa*, 11 June 1981.

Chapter 13

68 Arrest of R.C.: *Panorama*, 1 June 1981; Sisti, 102; Clara Calvi to author.

68 'Unprecedented earhquake': *L'Europeo*, 1 June 1981.

69 'Moral emergency': *FT*, 29 June 1982.

69 R.C. asks family to lobby: Clara and Carlo Calvi to author.

69 'This trial named IOR': *Sunday Times*, 13 Feb. 1983.

70 Pazienza's fee: *Repub.*, 13 July 1982.

70 Lobbying in Rome: Clara Calvi to author. Ciarrapico has confirmed that he was with her, but denies that he told her to remind politicians of Calvi's payments to their parties *(Giornale*, 12 Jan. 1983).

70 Flew to Bahamas, called Marcinkus: Carlo Calvi to author.

70–71 Visit to Cheli: *Panorama*, 29 Nov. 1982.

71 R.C.'s reaction to prison: Leemans and Clara Calvi to author.

71–2 Interrogation by D'Ambrosio: *L'Unità*, 15 June 1981 and *Panorama*, 15 June 1981.

72 'Bankers not dangerous': Sisti, 107–8.

72 'The rich are different': *L'Unità*, 11 June 1981.

73 R.C. 'like a student': *Repub.*, 11 June 1981.

73 R.C.'s bad impression: Mazzola to Leemans; Leemans to author.

73 R.C.'s threats to name names: Anna interrog..

73–4 Anna approached by Rizzoli officials: Carlo Calvi to author.

74 R.C. interrogated 2 July: Sisti, 69 and 174–5; *L'Europeo*, 27 July 1981.

74 Stiff sentence sought: *Repub.*, 4 July 1981.

74 Threats from Socialists: Clara Calvi, *L'Espresso*, 21 Nov. 1982.

75 R.C. interrogated 5 July: *L'Espresso*, 21 July 1982; *L'Europeo*, 12 Oct. 1981.

75 'Not an excessive dose': *L'Unità*, 10 July 1981.

75 'Not in danger': Carlo Calvi to author.

75 Clara called it a 'suicide attempt': *La Stampa*, 28 Oct. 1982.

75 Family didn't ask R.C. about it: Carlo Calvi to author.

75 R.C. defended by Piccoli, Craxi and Longo: *L'Europeo*, 27 July 1981.

76 'Great person, Calvi!': *L'Europeo*, 27 July 1981.

76 Verdicts: *Corsera*, 21 June 1982.

76 Judges' comments: *Repub.*, 22 Sept. 1981.

Chapter 14

77 Trade union bulletin: dated 30 June 1981, and titled 'Analysis of the Recent Events Regarding the Banco Ambrosiano Group'.

77 Rosone's origins: *Corsera*, 28 April 1982; *Repub.*, 13 July 1982.

77–8 Rosone on 'press bombardment': *Giornale*, 5 Sept. 1982.

78 Campaign to remove R.C.: *Repub.*, 13 July 1982, and Rosone to author.

78 Ciampi and Dini met R.C.: Clara Calvi to author.

78 28 July board meeting: minutes of meeting.

78 'Rigours of justice': Barberi, 13.

78 R.C. took Rosone aside: Rosone to author.

79 Leemans on R.C.'s self-control: Leemans to author.

79 BA share price: BA April 1982 prospectus.

79 BA rights issue: BA 1981 brochure.

79 Number of shareholders: BA 1981 ann. rep.

79 Share price 'absurd': Modolo to author.

80 'Three umbrellas': Bombacci to author.

Chapter 15

82 Audit of BAO: *Sunday Times*, 27 March 1983.
82 'Basket of crabs': *WSJ*, 30 Aug. 1982.
82 Leoni, Costa and Botta resign: *Il Mondo*, 13 Dec. 1982.
82 Nassano meeting in Aug. 1982: *FT*, 21 July 1982.
83 Text of patronage letters: *Observer*, 23 Jan. 1983, and other sources.
83 Nassano received 'strong comfort letter': former director of Andino to author.
83 'No intention to pay': this can be deduced from (1) the fact that R.C. gave him the 'counter-letter'; (2) Marcinkus's repeated refusals to pay; (3) his claims to Italian authorities that IOR had no obligation to pay.
83 Hoeffner's comments: *Giornale*, 13 July 1982.

Chapter 16

84 Carboni and Pazienza meet in Rome: *L'Espresso*, 4 July 1982.
84 Had met in office of police official: Emilio Pellicani to magistrates, quoted in *Panorama*, 13 Dec. 1982.
85 'Appointment with Pazienza': *L'Espresso*, 1 Aug. 1982.
85 R.C. flew to Rome: Clara Calvi to author.
85 R.C. urges wife and daughter to leave: Anna interrog. and Clara Calvi to author.
85 R.C.'s attitude to Pazienza: Anna interrog.
85–6 R.C. lends to Carboni: *Panorama*, 11 Oct. 1982.
86 'Long conversations': Anna interrog.
86 R.C. felt persecuted: Carboni's version, quoted in *Panorama*, 11 Oct. 1982.
86 Carboni becomes lobbyist: *Panorama*, 11 Oct. 1982.
86 'People who make you afraid…': *Repub.*, 13 July 1982.
86 'Good-for-nothing': *Panorama*, 26 July 1982.

Chapter 17

87–91 This chapter is based mainly on De Benedetti's version, given in *Panorama*, 1 March 1982, supplemented by author's interviews with sources involved in the deal. Other sources are cited below.
87 'Two Italys': Piero Ottone to author.
87 De Benedetti's background: *FT*, 29 March 1982.
87 'Most powerful': *Il Mondo*, 21 Sept. 1979 and *Panorama*, 7 Dec. 1981.
88 Terms of the deal: *Sole*, 19 Nov. 1981.

89 Public reactions by Andreatta and B. of Italy source: *Sole*, 19 Nov. 1981.

89 Cuccia reaction: *FT*, 29 March 1982.

89 Carlo Calvi on his father's reaction: *L'Espresso*, 21 Nov. 1982.

89 'Get your ass out of here!': Roberto Rosone, quoted in *Repub.*, 13 July 1982.

89 R.C.'s comments on De Benedetti's interviews: Anna interrog.

90 Anonymous threats to De Benedetti: *L'Espresso*, 20 Dec. 1981.

90 Warning from Angelo Rizzoli: *L'Espresso*, 22 Aug. 1982.

91 'Marriage of bad faith': Bank chairman to author.

Chapter 18

92 Bagnasco's background: *Il Mondo*, 5 Feb. 1982.

92 Terms of the deal: *Il Mondo*, 5 Feb. 1982.

92 'Bank is not a tram': Anna interrog.

92–3 Bagnasco's attitude: *Il Mondo*, 5 Feb. 1982.

93 BA's 1981 results: BA 1981 ann. rep.

93 'Solidity of the group': *Mondo Econ.*, 10 March 1982.

93 'Ambrosiano doing fine': *FT*, 23 April 1982.

93 'Behind those loans is the Vatican': Rosone, quoted in *Giornale*, 5 Aug. 1982.

93–4 'Central bank of the Vatican': Rosone, quoted in *Giornale*, 5 Sept. 1982.

94 Nassano's trip to Milan: *FT*, 21 July 1982.

94 Letters marked 'confidential': Michel Leemans to author and *L'Espresso*, 4 July 1982.

94 'Treated like criminals': *WSJ*, 9 Aug. 1982, quoting Italian news agency reports.

94 R.C.'s dealings with CONSOB: Guido Rossi to author.

95 Sindona commission: Sindona commission report, 9–10.

95 P2 commission: began its work 8 Dec. 1981 according to *Giornale*, 11 Feb. 1983.

95 R.C.'s testimony on Sindona: Sisti, 20.

95 De Benedetti's disclosures: *Panorama*, 1 March 1982.

95 Questions by Spaventi and Minervini: Spaventa and Minervini to author.

95 B. of Italy's February letter: *Giornale*, 13 Aug. 1982.

95 Board meeting on 17 Feb. 1982: minutes of board meeting.

95–6 R.C. dominated annual meeting: Gianni Bombacci to author.

96 Shareholders' comments: *FT*, 23 April 1982.

96 Rosone's threats to resign: Rosone to author; other sources.

96 Shooting of Rosone: *Repub.*, 13 July 1982; *Giornale*, 30 July 1982.

96 'They want to intimidate us': *Repub.*, 13 July 1982.

96 'By striking at Rosone...': *Giornale*, 5 Sept. 1982.

Chapter 19

97 Self-control is remarkable': *FT*, 23 April 1982.

97 R.C. agitated: Anna interrog.

97 R.C. trembling: Clara Calvi, quoted in *Panorama*, 29 Nov. 1982.

97 R.C. new danger was around: Anna interrog.

97 'They're killing me': Clara Calvi, quoted in *Giornale*, 7 Dec. 1982.

97 'Fear of returning to prison': *Repub.*, 25–26 July 1982.

97 R.C.'s promise to Andino head: *FT*, 21 July 1982, quoting Giorgio Nassano.

97 Appeal set for 21 June: Inquest 2.

98 Lobbying of Pisanu: *Panorama*, 5 July 1982.

98 Pisanu's reply in Parliament: Gustavo Minervini to author; *Panorama*, 26 July 1982.

98 Charges against Vitalone: *Giornale*, 28 June 1982.

98 Meetings with Caracciolo: Emilio Pellicani to magistrates, quoted in *Panorama*, 13 Dec. 1982.

98 Meetings with Corona: Corona testimony to P2 commission, quoted in *Repub.*, 30 July 1982.

98 Carboni's reception: *Giornale*, 12 Sept. 1982.

98 Pazienza got assignment while Calvi was in prison: Pazienza, quoted in *Giornale*, 6 July 1982.

98 12 per cent: Pazienza, quoted in *L'Espresso*, 12 Dec. 1982.

99 Workings of restricted market: Guido Rossi to author.

99 BA share purchases: *Giornale*, 6 July 1982.

100 Coopers & Lybrand suggested deal: Peter de Savary, interviewed in *Il Mondo*, 12 July 1982.

100 St James's Club: *Il Mondo*, 12 July 1982.

100 Artoc deal: *Giornale*, 11 July 1982.

100 B. of Italy vetoes deal: letter from Milan branch of B. of Italy, 31 March 1982.

100 BAO's stake drops to 10 per cent: *Giornale*, 11 July 1982.

100 Pazienza's consortium: *L'Espresso*, 12Dec. 1982.

101 Carboni deal: *Panorama*, 13 Sept. 1983; other sources.

101 'Superholding': *Epoca*, 30 July 1982; *Il Mondo*, 18 Oct. 1982; *Newsweek*, 13 Sept. 1982.

101 Fiorini Plan: *Giornale*, 5 July, 1982; other sources.

102 Opus Dei deal: Anna, Clara and Carlo Calvi at Inquest 2.

102 Carboni approached D'Agostini: Carboni, quoted in *Panorama*, 11 Oct. 1982.

102 Hilary Franco: Emilio Pellicani to magistrates, *Panorama*, 13 Dec. 1982.

102 Nature of Opus Dei: *L'Espresso*, 7 Nov. 1982, and other sources.

Chapter 20

Chapter 21

109 BA share price: *Giornale*, 8 July 1982.

109 Pesenti share price: *La Stampa*, 18 June 1982.

109 Marcinkus resigns from BAO: *Sunday Times*, 27 March 1982.

109 Leemans and Rosone get patronage letters: *Il Mondo*, 29 June 1982.

109 Rosone 'immobilised': Leemans to author.

109 Marcinkus out of the office: *Il Mondo*, 29 June 1982.

109–11 Visit to IOR: Leemans and Rosone to author; *L'Espresso*, 8 Aug. 1982; *WSJ*, 23 Nov. 1982.

Chapter 22

111 Nino Sindona quote: DiFonzo, 245.

111 R.C.'s snack: *Giornale*, 6 July 1982.

111 Call to Carlo: *Panorama*, 26 July 1982.

111 Call to Carboni: Carboni's version, 11 Oct. 1982.

112 Vittor a smuggler: Vittor statement.

112 Girlfriend/mistress distinction: Vittor is divorced, Carboni still married (although separated from his wife) and supports two women much younger than himself, according to testimony at Inquest 2.

112 Vittor sought job: Vittor statement.

112 R.C. phones Vittor: Vittor statement.

112 R.C. goes to Rome airport: *Giornale*, 24 June 1982.

112 Trip from Rome to Trieste: *Giornale*, 24 June 1982.

112 Meeting at Trieste hotel: Vittor statement.

112 Pilot of Carboni's plane: *La Stampa*, 30 Dec. 1982.

112 Passengers on plane: *L'Espresso*, 14 Nov. 1982.

112 Diotallevi's background: *La Stampa*, 11 June 1982.

112 Cost of passport: *La Stampa*, 30 Dec. 1982.

112 Vittor's version of R.C.'s trip to Austria: Vittor, Inquest 2.

112 Pellicani's version: *La Stampa*, 5 Jan. 1983 and *Sunday Times*, 13 Feb. 1983.

113 'Good German': *L'Espresso*, 22 Aug. 1982.

113 R.C. asks to wait: Michaela, Inquest 2.

113 Offered to find hotel: *L'Espresso*, 22 Aug. 1982.

113 R.C. calls Anna: Anna interrog.

113 R.C. naps and eats: *Giornale*, 8 July 1982.

113 R.C. angered by Pazienza's call: Anna interrog.

113 Carboni and Manuela arrive: Michaela, Inquest 2.

113 R.C.'s comments at dinner: *L'Espresso*, 22 Aug 1982.

113 Vittor's arrival: Vittor, Inquest 2.

114 R.C. calls Anna and Clara: Anna interrog.; Clara, Inquest 2.

114 R.C. refuses to enter restaurant: Manuela, Inquest 2.

114 R.C. and Vittor trip to Innsbruck: Vittor statement and Vittor quoted in *L'Espresso*, 22 Aug. 1982.

114 R.C.'s calls to Clara: Clara, Inquest 2.

114 Carboni and sisters fly to Zurich: Michaela, Inquest 2.

114 Kunz a 'fixer': Robert Clarke, Inquest 2.

114 Kunz background: *Corsera*, 5 Dec. 1982.

114 How Kunz met Carboni: *Corsera*, 2 Sept. 1982, quoting *Tribune le Matin* of Lausanne, Switzerland.

114 Carboni's phone calls: George Carman, Inquest 2, quoting police findings.

114–15 Stay in Bregenz: Vittor statement.

114 R.C. calls Anna: Anna interrog.

115 Leaves message for Carboni: Vittor, Inquest 2.

115 Carboni and Kunz arrive at 10 p.m.: Vittor, Inquest 2.

115 Clarke receives call: Clarke, both inquests.

115 'The little apartment': *Giornale*, 8 July 1982.

115 'Mr Vittor plus one': Reginald Mulligan, Inquest 2.

115 Trip to Innsbruck airport: Vittor statement.

115 Amstel Hotel: Inquest 2.

115 Two-hour flight: Reginald Mulligan, Inquest 2.

115 R.C. chats on plane: Vittor, *L'Espresso*, 22 Aug. 1982.

115 Arrival in London: Vittor, Inquest 2.

115 'G.R. Calvini': Inquest 2.

115 Vittor pays driver: Vittor statement.

115 Size of Chelsea Cloisters: Margaret Lilley (Manager of Chelsea Cloisters), Inquest 2.

115 Used for students: Paxman.

116 R.C. had been expecting a house: Vittor, *L'Espresso*, 22 Aug. 1982.

116 'Horrible place': Vittor, Inquest 2.

116 Size of room: Margaret Lilley, Inquest 2.

116 'Squalid environment': Vittor, *L'Espresso*, 22 Aug. 1982.

116 R.C. phones Kunz: Vittor, Inquest 2.

116 Vittor watched TV: Vittor, *L'Espresso*, 22 Aug. 1982.

116 Vittor gives lease to manager: Margaret Lilley, Inquest 2.

116 Brasserie: Vittor, Inquest 2.

116 Pink newspaper: Vittor, *L'Espresso*, 22 Aug. 1982.

116 Vittor must phone often: Vittor statement.

116 'Enough television': *L'Espresso*, 22 Aug. 1982.

116 Register in Michaela's name: statement from hotel clerk, both inquests.

116–17 Meeting near Hyde Park: Vittor, Inquest 2 and *L'Espresso*, 1 Aug. 1982.

117 Morrises agree to meet Carboni: William Morris, Inquest 2.

117 'Join your mother': *Panorama*, 5 July 1982.
117 'You will be protected': Clara Calvi statement to magistrates, quoted at Inquest 2.
117 R.C.'s 16 June conversation with Clara: Inquest 2; *La Stampa*, 7 Oct. 1982; *La Stampa*, 29 Oct. 1982; and *Panorama*, 29 Nov. 1982.

Chapter 23

118–20 Details of board meeting are based mostly on the minutes of the meeting, as published in *Il Mondo*, 12 July 1982. Other sources follow.
118 B. of Italy letter in press: *Sole*, 17 June 1982.
119 'You knew everything...': *Giornale*, 11 July 1982.
119 'What do I know?': *Giornale*, 11 July 1982.
119–21 Leemans meeting with Marcinkus: *WSJ*, 23 Nov. 1982.
120 'Dirty political manoeuvre...': *Giornale*, 11 July 1982.
120 Andreatta, Ciampi, Rossi meeting: *Giornale*, 11 July 1982.
120 BA share price: *La Stampa*, 18 June 1982.
120 Rosone interview with *L'Espresso*: *L'Espresso*, 27 June 1982.
121 Corrocher background: *Giornale*, 11 July 1982.
122 Corrocher's note: *Giornale*, 11 July 1982 and *La Stampa Sera*, 21 June 1982.

Chapter 24

122 Discovery of body: Huntley testimony at both inquests.
122 Removal of body, contents of suit: police testimony at both inquests.
123 Anna's activities in Zurich interrog. and Inquest 2.
124 'BA financially sound': *FT*, 19 June 1982.
124 'A possible hole': *Repub.*, 18 June 1982.
124 City Police activities: John White, Inquest 2.
124 Simpson's findings: both inquests.
124 'Spice of life': Simpson, 17.
125 Hanging seldom murder: Simpson, 138.
125 Rosone meeting with Marra: Rosone to author; *La Stampa*, 21 June 1982; and *Repub.*, 13 July 1982.
126 Anna arrives in Washington: Inquest 2.
126 Clara's reaction to R.C.'s death: *La Stampa*, 29 Oct. 1982 and *La Stampa*, 15 July 1982.
126 Family moves to Watergate complex: Anna interrog. and Inquest 2.
126 White meets Italian officials: White, Inquest 2.
126 Fingerprints: White, Inquest 2.
127 Murders in Britain: Simpson, 25.
127 Murders in USA: *Observer*, 8 May 1983.
127–8 Robert Clarke's activities: both inquests.

127 Press conference: *Times*, 21 June 1982.
127 Acrobatic manoeuvres: *Giornale*, 22 June 1982.
127 *La Stampa* headline: *La Stampa*, 21 June 1982.
128 Clarke calls police, White goes to Chelsea Cloisters: Inquest 2.
128 *Giornale* column: *Giornale*, 22 June 1982.
128 Run on the bank: *Il Mondo*, 2 Aug. 1982.
128 Three commissioners: *La Stampa Sera*, 21 June 1982.
129 Reaction story: *La Stampa*, 22 June 1982.
129 Bankers' Association: *Giornale*, 23 June 1982 and *FT*, 23 June 1982.
129 Patronage letters: *La Stampa*, 21 and 23 June 1982.
129 P2 commission: *Corsera*, 23 June 1982.
129 Rosone meets the press: *Repub.*, 23 June 1982.
129 Rosone blurts out: *L'Unità*, 23 June 1982.
129 Pellicani interrogated: *L'Espresso*, 4 July 1982 and *Giornale*, 27 June 1982.
130 Questions in parliament: *Corsera*, 24 June 1982.
130 'Calvi overthrown…': *L'Unità*, 23 June 1982.
130 'The second Sindona…': *Sole*, 18 June 1982.
130 Letter from shareholder: *Sole*, 24 June 1982.
130 Identification of body: both inquests.
130 R.C.'s relatives believe it was murder: *Corsera*, 24 June 1982.
130 Lawyers believe it was murder: *Repub.*, 24 July 1982.
130 Searching for Carboni: *La Stampa*, 22 June 1982.
130 'I'm coming…': *Giornale*, 24 June 1982.
131 Vittor interrogated: Inquest 2.
131 Fiorini suspended: *FT*, 26 June 1982.
131 R.C.'s wife and children say it was murder: *Repub.*, 26–27 June 1982.
131 Vitalone arrested: *Giornale*, 28 June 1982 and *L'Unità*, 28 June 1982.
131 Midland-led loan: sources among creditor banks.
131 Stock market 'under that bridge': *La Stampa*, 29 June 1982.
131 Stock market losses in June: *Giornale*, 11 July 1982.
132 Commissioners thrown out: *Time* magazine, 26 July 1982.
132 Andreatta background: *Giornale*, 12 Oct. 1982.
132 'War with Switzerland': *L'Espresso*, 24 Oct. 1982.
132 'Abnormal transactions'': writ.
132 *'De facto* partner': *Repub.*, 23 July 1982.
133 Giunchiglia testimony: *La Stampa*, 7 July 1982.
133 Link to Bologna bombing: *Repub.*, 7 July 1982.
133 Rognoni quote: *Repub.*, 16 July 1982, quoting Tina Anselmi.
133 Thatcher denies: *Observer*, 11 July 1982.
133 Money to Solidarity: *Giornale*, 11 July 1982.
133 Rescue pool formed: *FT*, 12 July 1982.
133 Midland group declares default: *FT*, 16 July 1982.
133 NatWest group declares default: *FT*, 16 July 1982.
133–4 Confidence in Luxembourg: *The Economist*, 16 Oct. 1982.
134 Vatican appoints 'wise men': *Giornale*, 14 July 1983.

Chapter 25

Chapter 26

151–2 Employee/shareholders: *Corsera,* 8 Aug. 1982.

152 IBI/CARIPLO deal: takeover talks first reported in late July in, e.g., *Sole,* 30 July 1982. The deal took place a few months later.

152 Andino suspended: *FT,* 21 July 1982.

152 BAO suspended; 'all the nerve centres': *Sole,* 21 July 1982.

153 Reid on Herstatt failure: Reid, 115.

153 Basle Declaration and Basle Concordat: *Bank of England Quarterly Bulletin,* June 1981.

154 German banker's reaction: *WSJ,* 1 Sept. 1982.

154 AGEFI survey: quoted in *La Stampa,* 2 Sept. 1982.

154 Central bankers' reactions: *Times,* 20 July 1982 and *IHT,* 26 July 1982.

154 Federal Reserve reaction (Dale quote): *Business Week,* 16 Aug. 1982.

154 Andreatta interview: *WSJ,* 1 Sept. 1982.

155–6 Creditors' meetings: interviews with bankers who attended BAH meeting; *Il Mondo,* 9 Aug. 1982; and 30 July 1982 issues of *FT, WSJ* and *Sole.*

156 Lost 700 billion lire in deposits: *Economist,* 14 Aug. 1982.

156 Liabilities exceeded assets: this was as of 6 Aug. 1982, according to *FT,* 27 Aug. 1982.

157 Andreatta comments on BA crash: *IHT,* 7 Aug. 1982 and *Corsera,* 8 Aug. 1982.

157 Bigger than stock market issues: *La Stampa,* 14 Oct. 1982.

157–59 Bazoli's comments: Bazoli to author.

158 'My father was a founder...': *Repub.,* 10 Aug. 1982.

158 Ad. placed by Nuovo Ambrosiano: in several national newspapers, e.g.*Corsera,* 1 Oct. 1982.

159 Fall in deposits: *Corsera,* 17 Aug. 1982.

Chapter 27

161 Papers in cornfield: *Observer,* 4 July 1982.

161 Carboni's tapes: *L'Espresso,* 22 Aug. 1982.

161 Carboni a 'dangerous person': *La Stampa,* 27 Aug. 1982.

162 Carboni's statements: including telephone interview he gave to *Il Messaggero,* 22 July 1982, and letter read at first inquest.

162 'Jacket buttoned wrong': *L'Espresso,* 1 Aug. 1982.

162 Telephone records: *Corsera,* 14 Sept. 1982.

162 'Life of luxury': described by George Carman at Inquest 2, based on information he received from Swiss authorities.

162 Arrest of Carboni: *Corsera,* 1 and 2 Aug. 1982.

162 Documents in Carboni's car: *Il Mondo,* 16 Aug. 1982 and *Panorama,* 27 Sept. 1982.

163 $20 million mentioned on tape: Carboni's tapes, quoted in *Panorama,* 13 Sept. 1982.

163 Calvi went to get documents: Pellicani to magistrates, *L'Espresso*, 30 Jan. 1983.

163 'Something very important will happen': Anna interrog.

163 Leemans' theory: Leemans to author.

163–4 Evidence Carboni knew Gelli: *La Stampa*, 16 Sept. 1982.

164 Plastic surgery: *Panorama*, 1 March 1982.

164 Gelli eludes Italian agents in France: *La Stampa*, 15 Sept. 1982 and *Panorama*, 27 Sept. 1982.

164 Anselmi's request to Swiss: *Panorama*, 27 Sept. 1982.

164 Carboni's bank records: *Corsera*, 14 Sept. 1982.

164 Sindona on 'P2 treasure': ABC-TV, quoted in *Panorama*, 27 Sept. 1982.

165 Bernasconi froze accounts: *Giornale*, 15 Sept. 1982 and *Panorama*, 27 Sept. 1982.

165 Arrest of Gelli: 14 and 15 Sept. 1982 editions of *Giornale* and *Corsera; Panorama*, 27 Sept. 1982.

165 'First official charge': *WSJ*, 20 Sept. 1982.

Chapter 28

167 700 million Catholics: Nichols, *Pope*, 18.

169 'Media lies': *L'Osservatore Romano*, quoted in *Observer*, 15 Aug. 1982.

169 'Never done anything fraudulent': *Corsera*, 8 July 1982.

169 *FT* on seven ghost companies: *FT*, 22 July 1982.

169 Vatican denial: *Sole*, 28 July 1982.

169 Reports of investigation *La Stampa*, 28 July 1982.

169 Judicial communications sent: *Corsera*, 29 July 1982.

169 Returned unopened: *FT*, 30 July 1982.

169 Spadolini meets Darida and Ciampi: *Giornale*, 4 Aug. 1982.

169–70 Andreatta meets Casaroli: *Newsweek* magazine, 30 Aug. 1982.

170 Casaroli will resist paying: *L'Espresso*, 22 Aug. 1982.

170 CONSOB investigation: *La Stampa*, 3 Oct. 1982, quoting forthcoming issue of *Il Mondo* (dated 11 Oct. 1982).

170 Version labelled as IOR's: *La Stampa*, 17 Oct. 1982 and *Corsera*, 17 Oct. 1982.

170–1 Wise men's report: various sources, including *WSJ*, 29 Nov. 1982 and *FT*, 27 Nov. 1982.

171 Vatican began negotiating: *La Stampa*, 5 Dec. 1982.

171 Italy-Vatican commission: *La Stampa* and *Corsera*, 27 Dec. 1982.

171 Vianini connection: *L'Espresso*, 24 Oct. 1982.

171 Nov. 1981 letter from IOR: *WSJ*, 23 Oct. 1982.

171 Leoni and Rosone testimony: *Corsera*, 24 Nov. 1982.

171–2 Carlo Calvi's findings: Carlo Calvi to author; *Panorama*, 29 Nov. 1982; *Il Mondo*, 27 Dec. 1982.

172 'Pumped money from Ambrosiano': *Panorama*, 29 Nov. 1982.

172 IOR's instructions to Gottardo: *Sunday Times*, 13 Feb. 1983.

172 Coopers & Lybrand audit: *Sunday Times*, 27 March 1983.

173 Cippico scandal: *La Stampa*, 4 Oct. 1983.

173 IOR customers contribute to the Church: *Giornale*, 20 Aug. 1982.

173 *Newsweek* quote: *Newsweek* magazine, 13 Sept. 1982.

173–4 SEC charges: *Times*, 4 June 1975 and Lo Bello, *Papers*.

174 Forged securities: *WSJ*, 6 Aug. 1982; Hammer.

174 Security National: *NYT*, 13 April 1976 and *Il Mondo*, 12 July 1982.

175 Lo Bello on Marcinkus's survival: Lo Bello, *Papers*, 222–3.

175 Dates popes served: Macadam, 31.

175 Felici and Benelli meetings: Thomas, 246–8.

175 Number of Poles in Chicago: Bowen, 218.

175 Channels funds to Poland: Thomas, 73 and other sources.

175 Felici and Benelli meetings with John Paul II: Thomas, 370.

175 Mexico plans: Thomas, 370.

175 Fifteen trips: *NYT*, in *IHT*, 20 Oct. 1982.

175 Pope distracted: *WSJ*, 29 July 1982 and other sources.

176 Marcinkus delivers letter: first reported on NBC-TV News, quoted in *IHT*, 20 Oct. 1982.

176 Marcinkus's role: Thomas, 429–30.

176 Marcinkus as adviser on Polish crisis: Thomas, 465–6.

176 Marcinkus not on Spain trip: *WSJ*, 23 Sept. 1982.

176 Marcinkus not made a cardinal: *Guardian*, 6 Jan. 1983.

176 'A widow's money': *La Stampa*, 27 Nov. 1982.

177 IOR negotiations with American Express: *WSJ*, 21 Jan. 1983.

177 Reports of loan negotiations: *L'Espresso*, 12 Dec. 1982.

177 Pope Leo X: Martin, 167.

177 Rothschild loan: Lo Bello, *Empire*, 53.

177 Holy Year: *La Stampa*, 27 Nov. 1982.

177 Normally every 25 years: Macadam.

177 Vatican art treasures: *Panorama*, 29 Nov. 1982 and 11 April 1983; *Giornale*, 20 April 1983.

177 'For twenty years': *Corsera*, 28 Nov. 1982.

177 Meaning of 'personal prelature': Johnson, 183–4.

177 New status announced: *Corsera*, 28 Nov. 1982.

177–8 Martin quote: Paxman.

178 Clara Calvi quote: *Sunday Times*, 5 Dec. 1982.

Chapter 29

179 Teodori quote: stenographic summary of 8 Oct. 1982 session of Chamber of Deputies.

179 Spadolini on 'new Mafia': *Corsera*, 14 Sept. 1982.

179–80 D'Alema on P2: *L'Espresso*, 6 Dec. 1981.

180 Balducci's connection to that clan: *Giornale*, 11 July 1982.

180 Carboni's banking transactions: George Carman and Dr Davies at Inquest 2, quoting Swiss investigating magistrates.

180 Carboni extradition: *Corsera*, 31 Oct. 1982.

180 Feb. 1983 charges against Carboni: *Corsera*, 6 Feb. 1983.

180 April 1983 charge against Carboni: *Gionale*, 10 June 1983.

180 Pazienza admits links with SISMI: Pazienza testimony to P2 commission, *Giornale*, 10 Dec. 1982.

181 'Known Ortolani since 1955': Carboni tapes, quoted in *Panorama*, 15 Aug. 1982.

181 Letter from Gelli: *La Stampa*, 16 Sept. 1982.

181 Carboni links Pazienza to P2 leaders: Carboni interrogation by Swiss police, in *Panorama*, 18 Oct. 1982.

181 Knights of Malta: *L'Espresso*, 28 June 1981.

181 Gelli not the head of P2: Tina Anselmi, quoted in *Corsera*, 15 Sept. 1982.

182 Calvi family's theories: Carlo Calvi to author.

182 Sindona says 'the left' did it: Sindona's testimony to P2 commission, *Giornale*, 12 Dec. 1982.

183 *L'Espresso* on 'masonic symbols': *L'Espresso*, 4 July 1982.

184 Progressive Labour Party: characterised as 'left-wing cult' in *Observer*, 3 Oct. 1982.

184 LaRouche's theory: *Executive Intelligence Review*, 27 July 1982.

184 OSS deal with Luciano: Brown, 190–91.

184 Mafiosi installed as mayors: *WSJ*, 4 Jan. 1983.

184 Sindona's links with allies and *Independentisti*: Venturini to author; other sources.

184 'Old boys' network': Venturini to author.

184 Luciano deported: Brown, 190–91.

185 Mafia profits from construction: *WSJ*, 4 Jan. 1983.

185 CIA intervention in 1948 election: Powers, 35–6.

185 CIA support to Christian Democrats: Powers, 97–8.

185 Massacre at Portella della Ginestra: MacKenzie, 256–7.

186 Church/Mafia quote: MacKenzie, 261.

186 1964 coup plot: Wilkinson,131.

186 'Tora Tora' coup plot: Servadio, 258 and Wilkinson,131.

186–7 1974 scares: Wilkinson, 131.

186 Miceli head of military intelligence: Barberi, 45.
186 Poisoning water supply: Wilkinson, 131.
186 'Strategy of tension': Wilkinson, 116.
187 Piazza della Fontana: Wilkinson, 67.
187 Red terrorism predominated: Sterling, 1–2.
187 Mafia/fascist links: Servadio, 259 and 263–4.
187 Gelli met Miceli: Barberi, 45.
187 Miceli's testimony: *La Stampa*, 30 June 1982.
187 Viezzer testimony: *La Stampa*, 15 Sept. 1982.
187 Grassini testimony: *Corsera*, 22 Oct. 1982.
187 1979 'mission': *Corsera*, 29 Oct. 1982.
187–8 'Super lodge' ordered Bologna bombing: *Panorama*, 23 Aug. 1982.
188 $10 million payment to DC: Morris, 277, also DiFonzo, 102, quoting report by Pike Committee (US Congressional committee).
188 Funds to Miceli: $800,000 went to Miceli, according to Pike Committee, quoted in DiFonzo, 277 and Wilkinson, 131–2.
188 US threats to Moro: *Panorama*, 11 Oct. 1982 and Brancoli, Ch. 7.
189 Sindona/*Daily American*: Umberto Venturini to author.
189 Luce and Colby as speakers: press release from committee, dated 2 April 1976.
189 Letter-writing, jumbo jets: Venturini to author.
189–90 Minervini on P2's anti-Communist role: Gustavo Minervini to author.
190 Gelli's daughter detained: *L'Espresso*, 26 July 1981.
190 'Civil coup': *Repub.*, 14 July 1982.
190 Gelli entertained Saragat: Barberi, 43.
190 Saragat's denial: Nichols, *Italy*, 104–5.
190 Plan shown to Leone: *Repub.*, 14 July 1982.
190 Calvi's friendship with Connally: Calvi family to author.
190 Visit to Guarino and Miceli: Carlo Calvi to author.
191 D'Amato's P2 testimony: *Panorama*, 6 Dec. 1982.
191 Ledeen denial: *Il Mondo*, 12 July 1982.
191–2 Ledeen's role in exposing 'Billygate': *Panorama*, 6 Dec. 1982; Ledeen to author.
192 Mafia role in CIA plots on Castro's life: Powers, 186–7.
192 Treatment of Church by Castro: Nichols, *Pope*, 24–5.
193 French charges against Barbie: *IHT*, 28 Jan. 1983.
193 Barbie was US informant: *IHT*, 17 Aug. 1983.
193 Barbie and Italian terrorists in Bolivia: *Sunday Times*, 6 Feb. 1983 and other sources.
193 'Calvi financing anti-Communists': ABC-TV, quoted in *La Stampa*, 25 July 1982.
193 Gelli and Ortolani involved: *WSJ*, 23 Nov. 1982.
193–4 Ghost companies' purchases: ABC-TV, quoted in *NYT*, 9 Sept. 1982.
194 CIA briefings to Pope: Thomas, 386, 392; US officials to author.
194–5 BRISA deal: *Il Mondo*, 12 July 1982.

195 Walters's role in BRISA deal: *Il Mondo*, 12 July 1982, quoting *New Statesman* and *Covert Action Information Bulletin*.
195 Kermit Roosevelt's background: Sampson, 195–6, 246–70.
195 Walters's consulting work: *FT*, 30 July 1982.
195 Sterling article on Ali Agca: quoted in *Times*, 19 Aug. 1982.
195 Lagorio's speech: *Economist*, 25 Dec. 1982 and other sources.
196 Soviets'accusations: CIA sponsors terrorism, *Washington Post* quoting Tass, in *IHT*, 30 Dec. 1982. P2 Lodge in pope plot, *Isveztia* quoted in *Giornale*, 27 Dec. 1982. Accusation against Walesa, in smear sheet distributed in Poland, presumably with official backing, quoted in *Sunday Times*, 17 April, 1983.

Chapter 30

197 Rosone on destiny of BA: *La Stampa*, 14 June 1982.
197–8 Rodotà on how politicians defended Calvi: column in *Panorama*, 5 July 1982.
198 Anselmi giving autographs: *Corsera*, 15 Sept. 1982.
198 Sarcinelli has not lost hope: Sarcinelli to author.
199 Mazzola on R.C.'s 'two brains': *Euromoney*, March 1982.
199 Quote on Faust story: Jump, 44.
200 'Began as a servant...': Sarcinelli to author.
200 Funeral: *Giornale* and *La Stampa*, 14 Nov. 1982.

Epilogue

201 Tarbun quote: *Times*, 16 Jan. 1983.
201 Pellicani's statements: *Corsera*, 3 Dec. 1982; *La Stampa*, 30 Dec. 1982; *L'Espresso*, 30 Jan. 1983.
202 Feb. 1983 warrant for Carboni: *Corsera*, 6 Feb. 1983.
202 April 1983 warrant for Carboni: *Giornale*, 16 April 1983. The charges were restored in June 1983,
202 Granted leave to challenge verdict: *Times*, 13 Jan. 1983.
202 28–29 March 1983 appeal: author's notes from attending appeal.
202 BAO in liquidation: notice published by BAO in *WSJ*, 17 Sept. 1982.
202 Law suits by BAH's creditors: *FT*, 19 March 1983.
202 Protest about Abs: *Times*, 8 Jan. 1983. Protest was from Simon Wiesenthal Center for Holocaust Studies, Los Angeles.
203 Sindona charged in Ambrosoli death: Sindona warrant and *L'Unità*, 23 June 1982. As this book was going to press, Sindona has not yet been extradited to stand trial on any of the charges against him in Italy.
203 Arrest of Aricò: *L'Unità*, 23 June 1982.
203 Rosone's reaction: *Giornale*, 5 Sept. 1982.
203–6 Second inquest: authort's notes taken at inquest.

Index

240

245

248